HUMAN MOTIVATION

HUMAN MOTIVATION

M. D. VERNON

M.A., SC.D.

Emeritus Professor of Psychology
University of Reading

CAMBRIDGE UNIVERSITY PRESS

Published by the Syndics of the Cambridge University Press

Bentley House, 200 Euston Road, London NW1 2DB

American Branch: 32 East 57th Street, New York, N.Y.10022

Library of Congress Catalogue Card Number: 69-14396

ISBNS:

0 521 07419 3 hard covers

0 521 09580 8 paperback

First published 1969

Reprinted 1971 1972 1973

Printed in Great Britain

at the University Printing House, Cambridge

(Brooke Crutchley, University Printer)

CONTENTS

Foreword   *page* vii

1   The nature of motivation   1
    1   *Introduction*   1
    2   *Instinct in man*   3
    3   *Ethological studies of instinctive behaviour in animals*   6
    4   *The concept of drive*   8

2   Emergence and development of motivation in children   14
    1   *Reflex actions*   14
    2   *Development of more complex behaviour patterns*   15
    3   *Fear, anger and aggression*   17
    4   *Curiosity, exploration and play*   20
    5   *Social relations with adults*   25
    6   *The effects of upbringing on motivated behaviour*   28
    7   *Social relations with other children*   31
    8   *Development of self-awareness*   34

3   The satisfaction of the biological needs   36
    1   *Homeostatic motivation*   36
    2   *Sexual behaviour*   40
    3   *Maternal behaviour*   46

4   Motivated behaviour in the emergency reactions   49
    1   *Fear and avoidance*   49
    2   *Fight*   56
    3   *Other forms of aggression*   62

5   The emotions   71
    1   *The functions of the emotions*   71
    2   *Emotional expression*   75
    3   *Physiological processes in emotion*   77
    4   *Complex emotions*   81

6　Activation, arousal, exploration and competence　　*page* 85
　1　*Activation*　85
　2　*Arousal*　88
　3　*Play and variety*　90
　4　*Exploration and competence*　91

7　Social motivation　94
　1　*Membership of social groups*　94
　2　*The effects on motivated behaviour of different types*
　　　of social group　96
　3　*The study of socially-motivated behaviour*　99
　4　*Affiliation and social conformity*　102
　5　*Power and dominance*　106

8　Goal-directed behaviour　108
　1　*Interests*　108
　2　*Sentiments*　112
　3　*The self-regarding sentiment and self-actualization*　115
　4　*Level of aspiration*　117
　5　*Achievement motivation*　121
　6　*Work*　128

9　Frustration and conflict　134
　1　*The consequences of failure*　134
　2　*Lewin's theory as to the nature and consequences of*
　　　motivational conflict　137
　3　*Anxiety*　144
　4　*The mechanisms of defence*　147
　5　*The causes of variation in frustration behaviour*　154

10　Individual differences in motivated behaviour　157

　Appendix: Assessment of motivation　163

　Notes and references　166

　Index of Authors　187

　Index of Subjects　188

FOREWORD

It seems desirable to provide a preliminary explanation as to why this book was written, especially since it covers a field which the author has not previously entered.

During the past forty years, psychologists have shown by the increasing expertise of their experimental design and techniques that they can effectively apply scientific method to the psychological investigation of the cognitive processes—perceiving, learning, thinking, etc.—and obtain valid findings of great significance to our understanding of these processes. In their enquiries psychologists have used mainly the technique of laboratory experiment, which provides a better means of controlling adequately the conditions of study than do investigations carried out in the field. However, it is sometimes overlooked that even in the laboratory each person brings with him an extensive endowment of knowledge, ideas and capacities for action which may exert as much influence on his behaviour as the experimental conditions themselves. This is even more true of experiments on the motivational and emotional processes. Moreover, inferences as to the nature of the motivation on which behaviour is based are difficult to make; and indeed in the laboratory situation this behaviour may be somewhat artifactual. The information which the individual himself can provide as to the nature of his motives for action is not very reliable; he may not be fully aware of these, and he may even in some cases deliberately conceal them. For these and other reasons, the investigation of human motivation has lagged far behind that of cognition.

However, the difficulty of the problems involved in motivational studies does not absolve psychologists from their obligation as scientists to pursue the discovery of truth; nor their social obligation to seek some understanding of processes which are of fundamental importance to human existence. Rather they should endeavour to develop methods, perhaps in field studies, which may advance their knowledge. Moreover, as this book may show, even laboratory studies of some types of motivation, such as aggression and achievement, have produced information which may lead to some understanding of human motivation and the behaviour which is based on it.

Yet the literature on human motivation is extremely limited, by comparison with what has been written on animal behaviour, instincts and drives. No doubt animal behaviour is itself an interesting and important subject for study; and it is more amenable to laboratory investigation than is human behaviour. Yet as regards the latter, the findings of animal studies are no more than suggestive, except perhaps in the case of the sub-human primates, the monkeys and apes; and even with these, field studies of behaviour in natural conditions are on the whole the most significant. Furthermore, though Kipling may have under-rated the abilities of the 'Bandar-log'—'Now we're going to—never mind; Brother, thy tail hangs down behind!'—it is true that the study of these animals can tell us little of the long-term purposive goal-directed behaviour which is such an important feature of human activity.

The paucity of comprehensive books on human motivation is particularly unfortunate for students who are beginning courses in psychology, whether for degree or diploma. Many of them are especially anxious to learn something about this puzzling and enthralling subject. At present it would seem that 'the hungry sheep look up and are not fed'. It is hoped that to some extent this book may supply their wants, though it cannot do so fully. It omits large areas of importance, such as much of the data in the literature on personality; and it may well show a lack of understanding, and even some error, in its coverage of others. Little is said as to the relation between human learning and motivation. However, this topic is extensively explored by Hebron.* Also there is little discussion of motivational theories, partly because these are to a considerable extent irrelevant to human motivation; but mainly because theory is difficult for the beginner to understand and assess until he has gained some acquaintance with the relevant data. It is hoped that he may find some of these data in this book, and that they may suggest to him an approach to aspects of human motivation which have hitherto been somewhat neglected. Still better, the book might stimulate some other author, with more knowledge and expertise in this subject, to write a more satisfactory book in order to remedy the shortcomings of the present author!

* M. E. Hebron, *Motivated Learning*. London: Methuen. 1966.

1

THE NATURE OF MOTIVATION

I. INTRODUCTION

We are all familiar with the experience of being urged or driven to behave in certain ways, and of desiring to act in a particular manner in order to achieve certain ends or objects. We usually attribute these impulses and desires to motivation, and believe that we are motivated to seek, for instance, food, sex, wealth, social relations, and so on. We regard motives such as these as the basic causes and determinants of all behaviour that is not haphazard, trivial or purely habitual. Motivation is thought of as some kind of internal force which arouses, regulates and sustains all our more important actions. However, it is clear that motivation is an internal experience which cannot be studied directly. We infer its existence and nature from observation and experience of behaviour. We attribute a motivational basis particularly to types of behaviour which are recurrent and persistent, and involve the employment of considerable energy; and which may also be accompanied by feelings of impulsion and desire. But since, especially in man, this behaviour is bewildering in its variety and exceedingly difficult to classify satisfactorily, the underlying motives are correspondingly difficult to define, delimit and classify with any exactitude.

We may regard the varieties of motivated behaviour as extending along a continuum between two poles. The first pole is constituted by behaviour in which the individual feels himself to be forced, perhaps almost against his will, to act in certain particular ways; for instance, to seek for food or sexual satisfaction. Behaviour is impulsive, possibly irrational, without intention or clear foresight of any particular goal. In fact, as St Paul said in the *Epistle to the Romans:* 'What I would, that do I not; what I hate that do I.' Behaviour may appear as a sudden outburst of activity stimulated by the perception of certain events, for instance, flight from a potential danger; and it may disappear as soon as the situation alters, especially if the sudden urge or impulse has been relieved or satisfied.

At the opposite pole is behaviour in which the individual is clearly conscious of a definite end or goal towards the attainment of which his actions are consistently, persistently and forcefully directed. The direction is determined, controlled and guided at least in part by deliberation and thought, though it may not be completely under conscious direction. Thus in some cases people may misapprehend the basic cause even of this type of behaviour. Its origin may lie in the unconscious mind, and they may suppose themselves to be motivated to achieve conscious goals of quite a different nature, which may in fact be substitutes for the underlying aim.

The first type of motivated behaviour would seem to occur frequently in the child and the unintelligent or immature adult, while the second does not appear until a certain degree of maturity has developed. However, there is a whole range of intermediate behaviour in which the more impulsive has been modified by learning until it approximates to the intentional. For instance, gourmets regard the attainment of good food as a persistent aim, not merely for the satisfaction of hunger. Again, in all adults impulsive behaviour may arise in situations of stress or excessive deprivation; and it may interrupt and conflict with consciously goal-directed behaviour and even inhibit it altogether. Or the conflict may be indefinitely prolonged.

Other types of motivated behaviour would appear to lie within the intermediate range, though again beginning impulsively in infancy and becoming increasingly modified and deliberate in adults. Social behaviour is an example. Even the infant seems to be impelled to make some kind of social contact with those around him; and such behaviour appears to be universal, and to persist throughout life. Nevertheless, social behaviour is sustained and developed along very various lines, in part through deliberate intention, and is often adapted and guided towards consciously realized goals. Another example of a similar kind is behaviour associated with curiosity and exploration.

In animals other than man, behaviour is primarily impulsive, though often modified by learning to assume forms differing from its initial pattern. But deliberately thought-out behaviour directed towards a consciously envisaged goal occurs only in man, and can be observed only in studies of human behaviour. But by virtue of its nature and complexity, it is difficult to investigate fully and systematically in laboratory experiments. Consequently, as we shall see in the subsequent discussion, our knowledge of it is partial and incomplete, and depends to a considerable extent on unsystematic observation and experience in everyday life. The impulsive type of motivated behaviour is easier to manipulate and control by means of suitable external stimulation which can be applied in laboratory experiments. Nevertheless, we shall find that even this is affected by experiences and motivation which have occurred previously in everyday life, and are thus not subject to experimental control. Therefore, in order to study simpler and more adequately controlled motivated behaviour, many American and British psychologists have preferred to investigate the behaviour of animals other than man. The principal type of behaviour studied experimentally has been that of animals learning to press bars, choose between shapes and run through mazes in order to obtain food or drink, or escape from electric shocks. There have been other methods of investigating motivated behaviour, but these learning studies predominate. Based on observations of behaviour in these rather limited and artificial situations, various theories have been developed as to the nature of the motivation producing learning. Furthermore, these theories have been applied to human motivated learning and other forms of behaviour without adequate consideration of the great differences between these and the behaviour of other animals. In particular, as we have noted, human behaviour is affected by a very complex body of acquired experience, and stimulated by motivation which, it will be clear from subsequent discussion, is seldom of the simple type occurring spontaneously even in children. Not only is the motivated behaviour of human adults very different from that of other animals; but in all probability the former possess forms of motivation, especially of the goal-directed type, which do not occur in the latter. We shall outline in section 3 some typical forms of animal motivated behaviour, in order that they may be contrasted with the human motivated behaviour described later; and in section 4 there will be a brief discussion of some of the concepts and theories related to motivated learning in animals.

2. INSTINCT IN MAN

Before proceeding to consider typical animal behaviour patterns, we must first examine the historical development of theories as to the nature and origin of motivation, much of which preceded any exact or detailed study of human behaviour. These theories were related to the somewhat sporadic and unsystematic observations and experiences of their authors of motivated behaviour in themselves and of other people in everyday life.

Until the early years of the present century, the most popular theory was that termed 'psychological hedonism' (pleasure seeking). It was supposed that action and desire were determined by attempts to achieve and maximize pleasure and to avoid or eliminate displeasure or pain. In general, people adopted courses of action likely to produce pleasurable states, and refrained from those which might lead to unpleasant states. As a rule, though not invariably, they were consciously aware of the pleasant or unpleasant consequences of their actions, and therefore deliberately adopted the appropriate form of behaviour. However, it was supposed that human beings could, or ought to be able to, act in such a way as to maximize the pleasure and minimize the pain of others, and not merely their own personal pleasure or pain. In this, they were guided by reason and by moral conscience; though sometimes an error of judgment or a failure of conscience led to actions which in fact had unpleasant or even harmful consequences for themselves or for others.

It was acknowledged that certain types of human behaviour were not hedonistically determined, for instance, automatic reflex responses outside conscious control; and habitual actions which might have been appropriate in the first instance, but had now ceased to be so. Moreover, animal behaviour fell into an entirely different category. It was determined by innate instincts, which gave rise automatically to rigid and stereotyped patterns of action by means of which the animal was able to preserve its existence and propagate its species. However, animals could seldom modify their behaviour in order to adapt to new or unusual circumstances, and hence might perish by continuing to perform totally inappropriate forms of action.

The Darwinian theory, which postulated a biological continuity from the sub-human species to man, suggested that there might also be some continuity in behaviour and in the springs of action. Moreover, it became apparent that human behaviour was often impulsive and ill-considered; and that people frequently seemed unable to direct their actions rationally in order to achieve pleasure and avoid displeasure. Indeed, the aim of achieving pleasure might be absent from even their more deliberate and willed actions. Nevertheless, the theory of psychological hedonism has by no means disappeared. It was revived by Troland,[1] and subsequently by Young,[2] though in a somewhat modified form. Thus Young supposed that some behaviour, though not all, was motivated by the attempt to select and obtain pleasurable experiences.

It would seem that the first person who disclaimed the hedonistic theory finally and entirely was William McDougall, who postulated in its place a 'hormic theory' based on the motivation of human beings by instincts similar in nature to those of other animals (*horme* is the Greek term used for animal instinct). McDougall considered that all life processes are fundamentally purposive, and that the behaviour of men and of other animals is characterized by striving in the pursuit of ends or goals. This goal-seeking behaviour shows persistence until the goal is achieved, through behaviour stimulated by certain particular stimuli in responses appropriate to these stimuli. In his earliest book on motivation, *An Introduction to Social Psychology*,[3] McDougall stressed the origin of this behaviour in innate and unlearnt instincts, which exist in all human beings, though there may be individual differences in their strengths. However, in man instinctive behaviour is less rigid and stereotyped than in many other animals; both the arousing stimuli and the detailed motor patterns of behaviour can be modified by learning. In these respects instincts differ from reflexes, which are less variable, less adaptable and also more persistent. Moreover, reflexes are aroused by simple sensory stimuli, whereas instincts depend on complex environmental and internal factors.

The following are the principal types of human instinct, and many of them are accompanied by appropriate emotions: flight and fear; repulsion and disgust; curiosity and wonder; pugnacity and anger; self-abasement and subjection; self-assertion and elation; parental instinct and tenderness; reproduction and sexual desire. With certain other instincts the emotional accompaniment is less clear; for instance, food and water seeking; gregariousness; acquisition; construction. McDougall also postulated the existence of certain complex emotional states and of sentiments, such as love and hate, which involve a variety of instinctive behaviour and emotion.

In a later book, *The Energies of Men*,[4] McDougall recognized that instinctive behaviour in man differed so radically from the stereotyped behaviour patterns of many animals that he ceased to attribute it to instinct, and instead stated that human behaviour is due to a number of innate 'propensities'. These are recognizable from the general nature of the goals towards which behaviour is impelled, and from the attainment of which satisfaction is obtained. Nevertheless, there is evolutionary continuity between human propensities and animal instincts. In fact, the propensities are given the same names as the instincts he previously proposed, with the addition of: appeal (crying for help); laughter; comfort; rest; wandering. Emotions such as those previously suggested occur in conjunction with the operation of some of these propensities; but in other cases, only when action is blocked.

The concept of instinct in relation to human behaviour has not received much attention in recent years, except in connection with the Freudian theory. However, the Freudian concepts differ so radically from those of other psychologists that they are not apposite here; and they will be considered in Chapter 3, in association with sexual behaviour. Fletcher suggests that the term 'instinct' can be used in human behaviour to cover internal dispositions to perceive and react to specific objects in the environment, leading to specific patterns of behaviour common to all members of the species.[5] Certain inherited cravings and recurrent and persistent impulses prompt behaviour aimed towards the attainment of specific and appropriate ends. Some of these, notably those connected with the maintenance of internal physiological equilibrium (homeostasis), are based on physiological conditions, including hormonal processes and internal sensory stimuli. But instinctive behaviour is plastic, and undergoes extensive modification through learning. Indeed, learning based on instinctive motivation is often necessary to secure the satisfactory operation of instincts. Not all instincts appear at birth, but may emerge at successive stages in maturation. Emotional processes form an important part of instinctive behaviour in man; indeed, in fear, for instance, emotion is the predominant element, associated with a multiplicity of behavioural responses. These we shall consider in Chapter 4.

In fact, Fletcher's concept of instinct in man is similar in many ways to the concept of 'drive' which we shall discuss in section 4. Both allow for the emergence of new forms of motivation and motivated behaviour independently of innate motivational tendencies. But in recent years the term 'instinct' has been used mainly for animal behaviour, and especially for the patterns of behaviour studied by the ethologists. These would appear to differ greatly from human motivated behaviour. Therefore they will be described briefly, in order that the contrast may become clear.

3. ETHOLOGICAL STUDIES OF INSTINCTIVE BEHAVIOUR IN ANIMALS

The extraordinarily complex instinctive behaviour of insects has been observed and studied over many years. But it is to the comparatively recent ethological studies and experiments of Lorenz and Tinbergen that we owe extensive and detailed information as to the instinctive patterns of behaviour, especially in fish and birds; and also theoretical formulations as to the nature of instinct.[6]

Ethologists emphasize the importance of 'fixed action patterns' in animals, which are distinct from chains of reflexes, and which are characteristic of particular species, appearing even in isolated animals which have had no opportunity of acquiring previous experience or of learning from other animals. The appearance of fixed action patterns may be preceded, if there is some blockage to the consummatory activity, by 'appetitive behaviour' which is random and exploratory. It is liable to occur in inexperienced animals, and may be adapted according to circumstances. It may either be directly terminated by the consummatory acts of fixed action patterns; or may lead to stimulus situations which initiate new fixed action patterns. These are not modifiable in accordance with particular situations, and indeed they may persist when biologically inappropriate. However, more recent research work has suggested that the distinction between appetitive and consummatory behaviour is not as rigid as Lorenz supposed, and that they may be flexibly intermingled with each other.

All these activities result from the operation of 'action-specific energy', that is to say, energy related to specific physiological needs which have been unsatisfied over a certain period of time, or have arisen through hormone secretion, for instance, in sexual behaviour. When the animal perceives certain appropriate environmental stimuli, called 'sign stimuli', 'innate releasing mechanisms' in the nervous system come into operation to allow the utilization of this energy in the relevant fixed action patterns. In some cases, if there is prolonged absence of appropriate sign stimuli, such behaviour may appear spontaneously, as 'vacuum activity', which occurs in courtship, hunting and escape.

One of the most interesting discoveries of the ethologists was the highly specific nature of the sign stimuli, the perception of which released appropriate fixed action patterns. These sign stimuli were studied experimentally by Tinbergen. Thus he found, using models he constructed, that the male stickleback would attack the crudest of models provided that its underside was red; if not, no attack was made. Again, the herring gull chick pecked towards a red patch on a model of the parent's bill, but was unaffected by the colour of the head or bill. But some sign stimuli are far more elaborate than these, for instance, the display appearing in the courtship of birds and the warning signals of bird song.

Fixed action patterns occur in food seeking, hiding and avoidance of danger, defence of territory against predators (animals of prey), courtship and sexual behaviour, nesting and the care of the young. According to Thorpe, there are six independent instincts, nutrition, fighting, reproduction, social relations, sleep and the care of the body surface. It is not clear, however, if all these involve fixed action patterns. Some of the latter are very elaborate, and there may be an interplay of actions between the two sexes, the action of one being the sign stimulus for that of the other. Many examples are given by Lorenz and Tinbergen. We may instance the mating behaviour of the stickleback. In the mating season, the male selects a suitable territory and digs a nest. He then approaches a female with a swollen belly, and performs the 'zig-zag' dance of alternate approach and retreat. She swims towards him and he leads her to the nest, pointing his head towards it, and she enters. He then thrusts at her rump with quick rhythmic movements which stimulate her to spawn, and he fertilizes the eggs as they are released. Thereafter he ventilates the eggs by fanning them until they hatch.

There are situations in which action patterns are not released in the normal fashion. Discharge of energy cannot then flow into the usual channel, and a different form of behaviour may appear, called 'displacement activity'. For instance, with certain birds, if courtship is interrupted, perhaps because the female does not provide the necessary sign stimuli for consummatory activity in copulation, the male may discontinue courtship and instead wipe its bill, or preen and shake its feathers. Displacement activity may also occur when there is a conflict between two types of motivation arising simultaneously. Thus whereas an animal usually attacks another at the centre of its territory and flees from attack when outside it, these two tendencies may occur simultaneously on the margin of the territory. Male sticklebacks may then dig as if making nests.

7

Birds may feed or drink, pluck nesting material or even go to sleep. But displacement activities may be detached from their original connotations and be modified through 'ritualization' to become part of an instinctive activity. Some elements of the original movement pattern may be exaggerated, others disappear altogether; and the whole pattern may be repeated in a stereotyped form. Such ritualization appears in the courtship displays of birds, as a component of sexual behaviour. An elaborate example is shown in the behaviour of the bower bird which selects a variety of objects and constructs from them a 'bower' near which it displays to its mate.

This is only a very brief and simplified outline of some of the more important aspects of ethological studies. It would be inappropriate to discuss them in detail here. But both Lorenz and Tinbergen have attempted to apply their findings to human behaviour; and the argument of Lorenz as regards the nature of aggression in man and other animals is discussed in Chapter 4. Tinbergen supposed that innate releasing mechanisms might exist in a man which stimulated by sign stimuli. For instance, he cites Lorenz as suggesting that the typical appearance and behaviour of the human infant act as sign stimuli for the release of parental behaviour. Again, displacement activities may take place in human conflict situations; and we shall consider in Chapter 9 the occurrence of substitute and other frustration activities which may be analogous to displacement activity in animals.

Nevertheless, it will be seen in the following discussion of human motivated behaviour that, although appetitive behaviour may be observed, there is no evidence of the highly specific sign stimuli and the rigid and stereotyped fixed action patterns described by the ethologists. Indeed, Thorpe considers that even in some animal behaviour, and still more in human behaviour, the concept of 'drive', which we shall discuss in the next section, may be more appropriate than that of instinct, since it does not postulate the extreme specificity characteristic of instinctive behaviour.

4. THE CONCEPT OF DRIVE

Before studying the concept of drive as a source of motivation in behaviour, we must first consider some of the earlier psychological theory and experiment which preceded this. McDougall's hormic theory and his hypotheses as to the importance of instinct in human behaviour gained little popularity in the United States, although for many years it was well regarded in Britain. It was quickly superseded in the United States by the theory of J. B. Watson termed 'behaviorism'.[7] Watson was mainly concerned to eliminate all arm-chair theorizing and introspective psychology, and to substitute the study of observable behaviour, together with accompanying physiological processes. And since it is easier to observe and assess accurately the behaviour of animals in captivity than that of human beings, much of his theorizing was derived from studies of animals; although he included some observations of children's behaviour. He considered that behaviour was based upon chains of stimuli and responses to these, some of which were covert kinaesthetic processes, such as implicit speech in thinking.

Later, Watson adopted from Pavlov the concept of the 'conditioned reflex'; and since then the processes of 'reinforcement' in conditioned learning have been regarded as important types of motivational process. In his prototype experiment, Pavlov employed the reflex response of salivation which occurs in a hungry dog on eating a piece of meat.[8] He found that if an auditory stimulus, the sound of a bell, repeatedly accompanied the presentation of the meat, eventually the dog would salivate when the bell was sounded without the meat; and this response associating salivation with the auditory stimulus was termed a 'conditioned reflex'. However, if the bell was sounded continually without the meat, after a time the dog ceased to salivate, and it was said that the conditioned reflex had been 'extinguished' through lack of 'reinforcement'. But if the meat was once more presented, the conditioned reflex was reinforced, and reappeared. Thus clearly the reinforcement of meat acted as a form of motivation in producing and maintaining the conditioned reflex.

Another form of conditioned reflex, withdrawal from pain, could be established when some neutral stimulus was presented with an electric shock. Watson employed a similar situation to demonstrate the establishment of conditioned fear in children.[9] A boy, Albert, was shown a white rat, while at the same time a loud noise sounded just behind him. Whereas he had begun to reach out and touch the rat, when he heard the noise he started and withdrew. After several repetitions of the experience, he showed signs of fear at the mere sight of the rat, and even of other furry animals. Therefore the conditioned reflex may generalize as a response to similar stimuli other than that to which it was originally attached. Albert was not studied for long enough to show whether his fear response became extinguished if it was not reinforced.

Thus to the innate equipment of reflexes was added a whole gamut of conditioned reflexes, in which reactions are elicited in response to new stimuli which have been repeatedly associated with the normal stimuli of the reflexes. At first it was considered that the conditioned response was in every way equivalent to the true reflex response; but the former is now regarded as a preparatory or substitute response which may differ in some ways from the latter. However, it must of course be reinforced from time to time to prevent extinction. This usually happens; for instance, the sight and smell of food are followed by its consumption.

9

It should be noted that Watson and many other psychologists who adopted his outlook were more concerned with the nature of learning than with that of motivation. But others, notably Thorndike and Clark Hull, gave more prominence to motivational factors, on which they considered learning depended. Thorndike, in his Law of Effect, postulated that learning took place in so far as it produced a 'satisfying effect' or enabled the avoidance of discomfort.[10] Hull, who constructed and formulated a very detailed and elaborate scheme of postulates as to the nature and causes of learning, included as basic factors 'drives' which energized and activated behaviour aimed at satisfying biological needs.[11] Learning was dependent on the reduction of drive strength produced by satisfaction of the need.

'Drive' has been defined by Thorpe as the complex of internal and external states and stimuli leading to a given behaviour, which is always of survival value.[12] Though the concept is thus very general in nature, it is in fact mainly applicable to the type of behaviour aimed at supplying fundamental biological needs, and for keeping the body in a state of physiological equilibrium or homeostasis. The principal homeostatic needs in mammals are for air, water, food and temperature control. When the supply of these is inadequate to maintain homeostasis, the organism is stimulated or 'driven' *via* certain specific centres situated in the hypothalamus of the brain to behave in such a way as to remedy the deficit. Extensive studies have been made of the causes and the effects of the hunger and thirst drives in animals; and it has been suggested that the strength of these may be assessed from the number of hours of food or water deprivation. However, it would seem that it is the extent of need rather than the strength of drive which is being measured. Undoubtedly these drives are of necessity innate in all animals, including man. But in the latter, the activities undertaken in accordance with drives vary far more than in other animals, and do not show the stereotyped patterns of animal instincts. They are extensively modified by learning from infancy upwards.

Other forms of behaviour have been attributed to innate drives, notably sex, mainly because they are due at least in part to internal physiological stimulation by hormone secretion. However, as we shall see, no state of deprivation is involved in sexual behaviour, and the need is for maintenance of the species and not of the individual. The same is true of maternal behaviour. The avoidance of pain, injury and danger by withdrawal or flight would seem also to be innate; and it is essential for the preservation of life. But no physiological deficit is involved. The same is true of defence by fighting. Whether or not these should be termed 'primary', as is homeostatic motivation, is mainly a matter of verbal argument.

All these forms of behaviour, in so far as they satisfy the basic needs of existence, reduce the strength of the accompanying drive. In other forms of human motivated behaviour, need reduction may not take place, though often they are directed towards obtaining some kind of satisfaction or reward; or away from some source of unpleasantness. It is not certain whether or to what extent these are innate; nor can their strength be objectively measured. Such are activities aimed at exploring and obtaining mastery of the physical environment; at initiating and maintaining social contacts and relationships; and at following and achieving success in a variety of occupations and activities. These may involve the prolonged expenditure of great energy and intellectual effort. They are clearly purposive, aimed towards certain general ends or goals. They are closely directed by these aims, but they do not lead to specific consummatory acts, such as eating and drinking, which reduce drive and terminate activity. Although the behaviour is often associated with specific reward, it is also frequently satisfying in itself; and the individual may continue to perform it for long periods, even for a life time.

Thus it would seem that human motivated behaviour cannot be regarded as of one single type; nor can it be attributed solely to modifications of homeostatic drives. No very satisfactory classification is feasible at present, though there may be a continuum of motivated behaviour such as was outlined at the beginning of this chapter. However, some form of internal driving force appears to be involved in every case; and it would be difficult to conceive of this behaviour without postulating the existence of motivational forces. But we must admit that we can say little as to the nature of these forces. Thus it seems best to consider the various types of human behaviour commonly regarded as motivated, and the circumstances in which they arise. When more is known of these, it may be possible to classify them adequately and to seek for their underlying physiological and psychological causes.

One topic which has been discussed at length, though mainly in relation to animal drives, is the following: Is drive to be regarded as a general force energizing all forms of motivated behaviour, or is there a number of different drives which direct behaviour and the utilization of energy along specific lines? Many writers, notably Woodworth, Hebb and Brown, have favoured the former hypothesis.[13] The general energizing function of drive may then be regarded as innate, whereas the particular directions in which it is employed are acquired by learning to respond to certain environmental 'cues' which lead to a reduction in the utilization of energy. We shall see in Chapter 6 that the energizing force may in fact arise from the arousal and activation functions of the reticular formation of the brain. But mere arousal produces only a general excitement, and in motivated behaviour it is specifically directed along certain lines and towards certain ends. Observations of infant behaviour (see Chapter 2) suggest that almost from birth such specific direction occurs, and in forms of behaviour which the infant can hardly be supposed to have learnt. Thus it would seem more in accordance with these observations to suppose that there are innate motivational tendencies which direct and regulate specific types of behaviour, as well as energizing them. But these do not take the form of elaborate and rigidly stereotyped patterns of activity; and they are undoubtedly controlled and modified by learning. Moreover, there are other forms of motivated behaviour in which energy is utilized which are learnt *ab initio*. But since this behaviour and its causes are so diverse, it would seem desirable not to attribute it to specific drives or motives, but rather to employ the terms 'motivation' and 'motivated behaviour'.

Motivated behaviour also involves awareness of and prompt reaction to particular features of the environment. In withdrawal and flight, for instance, some aspect of the environment is perceived as threatening danger, injury or pain. In cases such as these the particular type of motivated behaviour does not occur unless and until the environmental stimulus appears. In other cases, such as those of hunger, thirst and sex, the stimulation is internal, though the individual's attention may be very readily aroused to external stimuli which may lead to motivational satisfaction. Indeed, it has sometimes been claimed that people tend to perceive food objects more clearly when they are hungry; and to avoid perceiving unpleasant and painful stimuli. There is also a tendency to think unintentionally about relevant objects, for instance, about food when one is hungry. But in many important types of motivation it would seem that there exists a permanent psychological disposition, for instance, to make certain particular forms of social contact. Thus the individual deliberately and by choice sets himself to observe and react to particular features of his environment in certain particular ways, rather than remaining passive until they impinge upon him. Moreover, he may be conscious not only of the aims towards which his behaviour is directed, but also of a strong feeling of desire to act in such a way as to achieve them. He feels personally involved in and enthusiastic about what he is doing, and that his competence and self-esteem are to be assessed from his success in it.

In the following chapters we shall consider the types of motivated behaviour, innate in origin and impulsive in nature, which are essential for supplying the basic needs and maintaining life in the individual and the species. These include homeostatic motivation, which operates to preserve internal physiological equilibrium; and sex. Another motivational tendency which has sometimes been included in this category is maternal behaviour. Flight and fight also help to maintain life, though they are not caused by internal physiological stimulation; and with them are closely associated the emotions of fear and anger. We shall therefore consider these and other emotions, and their functions in relation to motivation. An important component of all motivated behaviour would appear to be the arousal and activation of energy discharge, which seems to provide the force which energizes them. Arousal will also be discussed especially in relation to the behaviour of exploration, play and the mastery of the physical environment.

Motivation arising in connection with social relationships plays a paramount part in the determination of much behaviour from childhood up, and it will therefore be discussed in some detail. But also, as we noted at the beginning of this chapter, there seems to operate in human beings, as distinct from other animals, a variety of types of deliberate and intentional goal-directed behaviour characterized by a marked degree of self-involvement, and closely associated with the expression and enhancement of the self. It is therefore particularly important to take into account this type of behaviour in considering human motivation. Finally, it is necessary to study the frequently occurring situations in which motivation is frustrated in its operation, both through encountering external obstacles and also through conflict with some other incompatible type of motivation. We shall see that a great variety of more or less adaptive behaviour may occur in consequence.

Before proceeding to discuss these various types of motivation in adults and the behaviour to which they lead, we shall set the stage by outlining motivation in children, how it arises and how it develops as age increases.

2

EMERGENCE AND DEVELOPMENT OF MOTIVATION IN CHILDREN

I. REFLEX ACTIONS

Although it would be inappropriate to attribute motivation of the kind possessed by adults to the new-born infant, he undoubtedly has a fairly extensive repertory of behaviour which is directed towards the maintenance of life. This behaviour in the main takes the form of the specific patterns of activity in response to specific stimulation which we have already described—termed the reflexes. These are involved in breathing, digestion and movement, and also in certain other responses to external visual, auditory and tactile stimulation.

While the human foetus is still in the uterus, much of its activity is undifferentiated and uncoordinated, a kind of slow wriggling and squirming.[1] Nevertheless, studies of foetuses removed before full-term by Caesarian section have shown that movement becomes increasingly precise as the foetus ages. Spontaneous heart beats, breathing movements and even weak crying movements appear. The capacity for reflex response to stimulation is well developed before normal birth. Thus touching the tongue produces sucking movements. Touching the hand lightly may result in grasping; and a stronger touch may produce withdrawal, and sometimes general bodily movement. In prematurely born infants of 32 weeks and upwards, responses to light, sound and even taste may occur.

It is usually supposed that at birth the first action to appear is the reflex gasp for air, followed by crying.[2] Sucking may be weak at first, but soon becomes adequate, and is accompanied by the normal succession of digestive reflexes. Moreover, some differentiation of taste is shown, in that the infant sucks sweet substances but attempts to spit out bitter substances. Responses to touch are well coordinated, and grasp is so strong that the infant can hang from his hands, as the infant monkey can cling and hang on to its mother's hair. However, the human infant can do this for only a few seconds; and unlike the monkey he does not normally cling to his mother when she carries him about.[3] There are also general postural adjustments to changes in spatial position. Painful stimulation causes reflex withdrawal, often accompanied by crying and general bodily movement. Infants are sensitive to heat and cold. A moderately warm stimulation of the skin may lead to movement towards the stimulus, whereas cold produces withdrawal. Atmospheric cold gives rise to shivering and general bodily movement; changes in respiration and circulation of the blood and other physiological processes are regulated automatically by the autonomic nervous system.

Visual stimulation by bright light produces reflex blinking and contraction of the pupil; and the eyes follow a moving light, though in a somewhat uncoordinated fashion. Some psychologists have stated that auditory sensitivity is poor in young infants, but it varies in different infants.[2] In one case, a new-born infant, at the sound of a series of clicks, opened his eyes and looked in the direction of the sound.[4] Responses to loud noises mainly take the form of the patterns of general activity which seem to be the forerunners of the expression of fear.[2] These are, firstly, the so-called 'Moro reflex', a general extension of the spine and limbs; and, secondly, the 'startle' response, which replaces it after 4–6 months. This is more rapid, and consists of flexion and withdrawal of the limbs, accompanied by blinking and closing the eyes, by changes in respiration and heart beat and sometimes by crying. A similar type of response persists throughout life as the sudden start at a potentially dangerous stimulus. Infants are mainly startled by sudden loud noises and changes in loudness of sound, or by other sudden sensory stimuli. It should be noted, however, that different infants show marked differences in reactivity to this stimulation.

Genital reflexes also appear early in life. Erection in male infants may occur in response to handling the penis by an adult. However, it has little significance at this age, and indeed it may be aroused by pressure in the bladder. Orgasm may also occur before the age of a year.

2. DEVELOPMENT OF MORE COMPLEX BEHAVIOUR PATTERNS

The initial innate reflexes become diversified in two ways. In the first place, through the process of conditioning they may be stimulated by events other than innate stimuli, which occur frequently in conjunction with these. The new or conditioned stimulus may then itself evoke the reflex response before the old innate stimulus appears. Thus the sucking of infants, which at first begins only when the lips touch the nipple, later arises when the cheek is touched; or even when the infant is taken up to be fed.[5] Experiments have demonstrated that infants as young as ten days may be conditioned to suck at the sound of a buzzer, if this is frequently presented just before the bottle is inserted in the mouth.[6] Reflex withdrawal from painful stimulation to the sole of the foot may also be conditioned to the sound of a buzzer, though this conditioned response is more difficult to obtain until the infant is older.[7] Conditioning of the eye blink has also been demonstrated in infants.

But in addition the simple reflex responses become replaced by or incorporated in the increasingly complex patterns of activity which constitute motivated behaviour. These include both activities leading to satisfaction of motivation, and also the consummatory behaviour of actual satisfaction. Considering first the satisfaction of the basic needs of hunger and thirst, it was found that by the age of about eight months an infant allowed to feed 'on demand', that is to say, whenever he wished, established a fairly regular routine schedule of five feedings at regular times of day.[2] In rather older children, the preliminary behaviour of crying is replaced by general restlessness, searching for something to eat or drink, and asking for it. After weaning, the consummatory behaviour is no longer sucking, but eating and drinking; and the particular forms of behaviour involved are learnt by the child from the actions and commands of his mother. Though digestive reflexes are conditioned to occur, for instance when food is seen or smelt, the actual pattern of physiological reflexes is relatively unmodified. But it may be affected by the palatability of various forms of food, as we shall describe in Chapter 3. Food preferences seem to be established largely by learning and imitation, from the parents and later from other children.

In the achievement of temperature control, the child learns from his parents as he grows up to seek shelter or put on more clothing in cold weather, though he may at first be reluctant to do this! But he retains unchanged the reflex responses of shivering when cold and sweating when hot.

Sexual behaviour also develops in the child, and may be firmly established before puberty. Young children masturbate frequently, having discovered that it produces pleasant sensations.[8] Sex play between children is common even in societies such as ours in which it is not socially approved. Coitus is frequent in societies in which it is not repressed, for instance in certain primitive societies.[9] Sexual curiosity, taking the form of questions related to sex, physical sex differences, etc., begins as early as two years in our society, and sexual display and exhibitionism are frequent in nursery school children.[10] Thus variable and complex patterns of sexually motivated behaviour develop during childhood; but in general adults, and especially the mother, seek to exercise some control over these, and therefore they are inhibited to a greater or less extent. In a survey in the United States relating to over 300 five-year-old children, 75 per cent of the mothers sought to prevent masturbation, and 80 per cent discouraged or prevented sex play between children.[11]

3. FEAR, ANGER AND AGGRESSION

There are two exceedingly important classes of motivated behaviour, avoidance of danger and its accompanying emotion of fear; and defensive or aggressive action, with the emotion of anger. Discussion of the interrelationship between motivation and emotion will be postponed to Chapter 5. But it seems desirable to consider here the development of both. It has already been mentioned that the Moro reflex, and still more the startle response, appear to be forerunners of actual fear.[8] Fear itself does not seem to occur in young infants even in apparently alarming situations, such as being dropped. In the early months infants appear to experience little beyond delight and distress. However, it is not really possible to know exactly what the infant feels. But at about the third month, open expression of fear may be seen, in shrinking, crying, screaming or in a kind of frozen immobility. As soon as the child is old enough, he may run away and try to escape; or seek the protection of parents. Thereafter, he endeavours to avoid such situations. But after a certain age this behaviour meets with social disapproval, and the child learns to control and to some extent inhibit it. We know, however, that even in adult life it may appear in panic in situations of great danger. The emotion of fear is undoubtedly strong in young children, and it is accompanied by internal physiological changes in heart rate, respiration, etc., and by blanching of the face. In older children and adults, the emotion may be stronger when overt escape behaviour is inhibited; whereas, when it is possible to escape immediately, the emotion may be less strong.

The causes of fear also change as the child grows older. In the first year, the most frequent causes are loud noises or other sudden events, and loss of support. These fears decline in importance during the second year, though suddenly appearing and rapidly moving animals, such as dogs, continue to be feared. It has sometimes been supposed that children possess an innate fear of snakes; however, it has been established that this fear does not occur under the age of three years.[12] At five months, the child begins to discriminate between familiar and strange people, and to show fear of the latter, especially when they approach him.[13] But such fears are less apparent in children who have had contacts with many different people than in those who have been somewhat isolated. There may also be fears of unfamiliar surroundings and situations. As the child becomes more familiar with his surroundings, these fears decline. But sometimes fear may be aroused by a combination of the strange and the familiar, a discrepancy between what was expected and what actually experienced. A phenomenon of this kind was observed by Hebb in four-month-old chimpanzees, who showed extreme fear at the sight of their keeper in strange clothes, a plaster cast of a chimpanzee head and a young chimpanzee anaesthetized.[14] Fears of the excessively novel and strange may persist in human beings into adult life, as we shall discuss in Chapter 6.

From the age of about two years, children are found to experience increasingly fears of darkness and solitude, and of more or less imaginary objects—robbers, imaginary animals, dreams and so forth.[15] But of course fear of real danger remains. Indeed, one study of free drawings produced by children when they were asked to draw 'what you feel are the most important events of your life' showed that even children of eleven years often reported fear of falling, from a horse or a bicycle; and fear of illness.[16]

Fears are often learnt, either through conditioning or through imitation. In Chapter 1 we discussed the conditioned fear established in Albert. As in his case, generalization of fear responses from one stimulus to other similar ones is not uncommon. Indeed, the association between stimuli may appear quite arbitrary. Thus it has been postulated that the 'phobias' of later life are caused by the association of irrelevant stimuli with fear-provoking events; and that the fear is thereafter re-aroused by the irrelevant stimulus. But it is probable that other factors are involved also.

There is little doubt that children are much affected by the fears of their parents. Infants may be unaffected by alarming events, such as air-raids in war-time, unless the mother displays fear. Moreover, studies have shown that the fears of children, particularly of dogs, insects and storms, may mirror those of the mother.[17] On the other hand, when the mother is calm and affectionate, and the child can maintain close contact with her, fear is less likely to arise, especially if the child has grown up in a secure and affectionate home atmosphere. But severity and the threat of punishment, still more of actual rejection, increase the tendency to fear.

Such a situation is illustrated clearly in the studies of Harlow and Zimmerman of the behaviour of infant monkeys.[18] In natural surroundings, an infant clings closely to the mother's hair, and she carries it with her everywhere. Harlow and Zimmerman brought up monkeys apart from their mothers; but they could make contact with one or other of two 'surrogate' mothers, upright wire frameworks one of which was covered with cloth. The monkeys clung predominantly to the 'cloth mother', even when the feeding bottle was attached to the 'wire mother'. When frightening objects were presented they clung particularly closely to the cloth mother; and after a time became sufficiently reassured to glance at the frightening object. But if only the wire mother was available, they crouched in the corner in paroxysms of terror.

Children show considerable individual differences in their tendencies to display fear. These may be due in part to differences in upbringing; but also they are associated with poor physical health and with temperamental differences. It is not clear, however, to what extent the tendency to feel fear is variable; or whether 'out-going' children express it more freely and openly, while 'in-going' children repress it. Again, it may be that children who have become familiar with a wide range of differing surroundings are less likely to be frightened by the strange and unfamiliar than are children whose experiences have been very restricted. In rather older children, acquired fears may develop in the form of anxiety, related to anticipation of social separation, deprivation, punishment or disapproval. The relationship of anxiety to fear will be discussed in Chapter 4.

We often tend to think of defensive, aggressive and hostile behaviour and anger as being opposed to fear and fearful behaviour. In some circumstances, however, they may be related and may alternate with each other in the same situation. Nevertheless, in infancy their overt expressions certainly differ. It is doubtful if defensive behaviour is reflex. But at quite an early age, interference with the infant's actions is followed by attempts on his part to push away the source of interference. General restraint of the body or limbs gives rise to stiffening or wriggling of the body, crying or screaming and flushing of the face.[2] Bridges considered that the accompanying emotion of anger develops at about three months.[19] Temper tantrums, in which the child throws himself about and yells, appear during the second year, usually reaching their peak at about 18 months, but re-appearing in conflicts with parents at about four years. However, angry behaviour becomes more specifically directed into aggressive action, and the child hits or kicks offending objects or persons. But also there may be obstinate and negative behaviour, or sullenness, peevishness and whining. In older children, blows may be replaced by angry words. Goodenough found that outbursts of anger in which actions were quite undirected (kicking and screaming, for instance) decreased from 89 per cent to 36 per cent of cases between the ages of 1 and 8 years; whereas outbursts with retaliatory actions, including hitting and calling names, increased from 1 per cent to 28 per cent.[20]

It would appear that defensive action and anger in general are caused not only by actual attack and interference, but also by thwarting of satisfaction of other needs. During the first year of life, infants may show angry behaviour if they are kept waiting for the bottle. Later, it may be caused by neglect of ordinary care and failure to pay attention to the child's wants and demands. The establishment of feeding and other habits and of toilet training is another cause. Increasingly, aggression and anger appear in social settings, for instance those of a nursery school, in which the child is opposed in his attempts to get what he wants, and in which his activities and plans are thwarted by other persons. But also even a temporary encouragement of aggression may cause it to appear more frequently.[21] Moreover, children tend to imitate the aggressive behaviour of adults and their specific acts of aggression, even when exhibited in films.[22] This happens particularly when the children are exposed to frustrating situations. They also imitate the example of aggression in other children, if this appears to produce successful results. However, irritability may be aggravated by poor health, and may be especially marked in those with naturally explosive and irritable temperaments.

4. CURIOSITY, EXPLORATION AND PLAY

There are certain important classes of behaviour in infants and young children which at first sight may not appear to be directly related to motivation, nor to lead to any satisfaction of need. Nevertheless, they play a very important part in survival and adjustment to the environment. Firstly, various forms of spontaneous activity have been observed in infants. Charlotte Bühler and her colleagues studied the behaviour of infants continuously throughout the twenty-four hours, and found short periods of spontaneous activity and experimental movement at birth. These increased to 11 per cent of the twenty-four hours at three months, 27 per cent at six months and 31 per cent at one year.[23] This activity is in part an exercise of the infant's limbs, leading to the development of muscle control; and it forms an important feature of later play activities. But it also includes the infant's early attempts to explore, firstly what he can do with his limbs, for instance in playing with his fingers; and secondly, the characteristics of objects which he puts in his mouth and later manipulates with his hands.

Another early development is that of visual exploration. Coordination of the eyes and fixation by the two eyes develop within 7–8 weeks. Though initially looking at and following the movements of a bright object may be reflex responses, they soon lead to attentive examination, accompanied by a decrease in other bodily activities. Numerous experiments by Fantz and others have shown that infants from the first week of life direct their gaze at certain types of object, preferring for instance to look at patterned rather than unpatterned ones.[24] It would seem that this attentive regard is the earliest form of visual exploration. By the age of 4–5 months, the infant examines visually objects which he reaches for, grasps and handles.[25] This combined visual and tactile exploration is a most important feature of his behaviour, enabling him to discover and understand during the first year of life the permanent nature of solid objects, their appearance, properties and uses.

This behaviour marks the beginning of a form of motivated activity which is of the greatest significance in human beings, differentiating them from most other animals except monkeys and apes. Recent writers have emphasized the importance of curiosity and exploration in attempts to understand, manipulate and adjust to the environment. It would appear that this form of behaviour occurs particularly in new and unfamiliar activities. Thus Stott noted how frequently his child, at the age of 4–18 months, liked to perform new activities.[26] As soon as he became familiar with them, he lost interest and abandoned them. So also children attend to unfamiliar rather than to familiar objects. Changes in visual and auditory stimulation produce, even in early infancy, an 'orienting response'—turning towards the changing stimulus, attending to it and ceasing other on-going activities. Infants from five months upwards were found to orient more persistently towards the picture of a face when this was presented to right or left unexpectedly and at random than when it was presented only in one position or alternated regularly.[27] Rather older children spent longer examining toys which were novel and complex than simple and relatively familiar toys.[28]

On the other hand, it would seem that this behaviour occurs only when the novel object or activity is not too strange—too 'dissonant' with the child's expectations. Too much uncertainty may give rise to withdrawal or even fear, as we noted above.* But whether orienting or fear responses appear depends a good deal on the child's earlier experiences. Some psychologists have adduced evidence that a rigid and restricted environment in early infancy may result in a decrease of orienting and exploration and a more ready onset of fear.[30] Thus upper-class children at a nursery school were more frightened than were lower-class children by going into a dark room or approaching a strangely dressed woman. The latter may have had more experience of unusual and startling events. On the other hand, children brought up in institutions often are subjected to an extremely restricted environment, which may account at least in part for their apathy and lack of cognitive development.[31]

Orienting, curiosity and exploration are also characteristic of the behaviour of young and older monkeys and apes. Attention is readily attracted by unexpected lights and sounds, but if these are repeated regularly, the monkeys become habituated to them and cease to attend. Infant monkeys reared by the mother readily pressed a bar which opened an aperture giving them a view of other monkeys; but those reared in isolation did not do so.[32] Adult monkeys confined in a closed box learnt to open a window which gave them a view of the surroundings, and they

---

* A recent study has distinguished between the behaviour of 'proximity seeking' (clinging or keeping close to an adult) which arises in novel situations causing anxiety; and 'attention seeking' (calling an adult's attention to novel and interesting events) when there is little or no anxiety.[29] In children of 3–5 years, the latter behaviour is frequent in a novel situation, but decreases with time as they become familiar with it. There is slight but persistent proximity seeking in the novel situation, which increases steadily if anxiety is repeatedly provoked.

continued to do this over long periods of time.[33] When monkeys were given a choice of objects to view, another monkey, a moving toy train or food, even hungry monkeys chose the other monkey or the toy train rather than the food.[34] Again, hungry monkeys persisted in manipulating puzzles over long periods of time without any reward of food for performing this activity.[35]

The most characteristic activity of children is play; and play would seem to include behaviour related to several types of motivation. We noted the importance to the child's development of the spontaneous activity involved in the exercise of the limbs and body, leading to the improvement of muscular control and of the capacity to explore the environment. Piaget observed that when the child has been making real efforts to understand and accommodate himself to his environment, he often repeats these actions 'for the fun of it', with smiles and laughter, and without any expectation of results.[36] Hutt made somewhat similar observations, which showed that play could be differentiated from exploration.[37] Children aged 3–5 years, presented with a novel toy among familiar ones, in most cases examined and explored it with concentrated attention until they found out what it would do. Thereafter, they ceased to attend to it unless its possibilities were sufficiently diverse; for instance, if it made noises as well as giving visual signals. In this case they continued playing with it, but in a more relaxed and nonchalant manner. Sometimes they made use of it in other types of play, such as climbing on it. Hutt therefore concluded that exploration occurred with something novel, to discover what it was; but with greater familiarity, exploration was replaced by play.

But skills may be acquired through play, for instance, in the use of babbling to develop speech and of manipulative play in producing fine control of the hands.[38] It has been pointed out that the playful execution by young children of activities which they find useful when older does not necessarily increase skill through practice. In play, sequences of actions are often informal and irregular, with exaggerated performance of some actions and unnecessary repetition of others; and also the introduction of quite irrelevant actions.

However, even if the term 'play' should properly be confined to the enjoyment of behaviour which is irrelevant to any specific purpose, it is frequently interwoven in young children with exploration and with the development of various abilities. Thus constructive play facilitates the development of reasoning, as the child works out for himself how objects are made, what makes mechanical toys 'go', and so on. Furthermore, Bühler has described the manner in which such activities enable the child to acquire the ability to work for himself, and to carry on goal-directed action.[23] At the age of about one and a half years he begins to make simple constructions, for instance, building piles of bricks. Increasingly, he plans his constructions, perseveres in his activities until he has achieved his aim, and experiences great satisfaction when he has done this. In early years, he does not name his construction and later he may name it regardless of what it resembles. But by five or six years he attempts to make realistic reproductions of definite objects, showing greater awareness of the nature of real objects. Bühler found that 80 per cent of children who failed in first grade work at school had not acquired this ability to work persistently for a goal. These included children from very poor homes who had lacked play material; but also those from well-to-do homes who had received too much help from adults in all they did.

A recent study was made of six-year-old children who were followed up in order to discover whether at eight years they were learning to read satisfactorily or had failed to do so.[39] It was noted that even at six years the former were able to organize their performance in a variety of perceptual and motor tests, channelling their energies towards efficient performance, working away independently and obviously experiencing delight when they succeeded. Among the latter were children whose behaviour was less mature. Some were boisterous, happy-go-lucky, lacking in control of behaviour and unable to mobilize energy in a goal-directed manner. They had not learnt how to carry out pre-conceived plans of action, but were concerned only with the immediate attainment of pleasure. Others, who were even more likely to fail to learn to read, were passive, dependent and infantile; their approach to the tests was bewildered and they were quite unable to organize their behaviour appropriately.

Thus it would appear that an important facet of maturation in the capacity for effective motivated behaviour is played by the child's attempts to master the physical environment and to obtain competence in so doing by means of his own efforts. This may in turn be associated with the development of 'achievement motivation' (see Chapter 8). At the age of 3–3½ years the child begins to experience pleasure in his *personal* competence to perform a specific task and regret and shame if he fails.[40] Moreover, he turns less frequently to adults for help and support, and the experience of competence becomes its own reward. At 4–5 years, some children, instead of trying to overcome failure by greater effort, may resort to avoidance of the situation, or denial or concealment of failure. Individual differences in achievement motivation begin to appear, at 5–6 years, in the degrees of difficulty of the tasks children seek to perform. For instance, those with a higher degree of achievement motivation choose a greater distance from which to toss rings over a stick than do those with less achievement motivation.[41] But as age increases further, failure is tolerated better, and greater attempts are made to overcome it; moreover, the children increasingly prefer to resume an unsolved than a solved problem. Individual differences are associated with parental behaviour and treatment of the children, and to their encouragement and reward of success, as we shall see in section 6.

Another function of play is the practising of adult roles in realistic activities often copied from the parents. Thus girls try out household skills such as cooking and cleaning. Sometimes the children perform these tasks themselves; sometimes they carry them out in doll play. These activities would appear to stem in part from the child's 'identification' with his parents, and hence his desire to imitate them; and partly from attempts to play the adult roles of those who are perceived as powerful figures, in the desire to exercise the same kind of power.[42] Moreover, imitative actions, if regarded by adults as desirable, may be directly rewarded.

But play may also perform the function of compensating or substituting for behaviour aimed at satisfying motivation when for some reason the latter is impossible or inhibited.[43] Frustration of overt action tends to produce aggression which the child may be unable or may fear to direct towards the cause of frustration, his parents. Or again this situation may arouse great anxiety. His aggressive impulses may find an outlet in rough, noisy and destructive activities such as beating, hammering or breaking objects in play. Or his play may provide a less obvious form of expression, in imaginative, 'make-believe' activities, which are the symbolic expression, similar to that of dreams, of conflicting motivation and emotions which the child cannot demonstrate openly or describe in words. Thus children play at 'cops' and robbers, Indians, wild animals, and so on. They may also draw, paint and model imaginative scenes, not only of human activities, but also of natural events of a catastrophic nature such as storms, fires and volcanic eruptions. These symbolize violence and aggression, as do also fighting play and imitation of wild animals. Fear may be symbolized in the flight of birds, in hiding in caves, in escape to desert islands. Difficulties in excretory control may be expressed by play with water and mud. These activities are of great importance to many children, especially to those who have difficulty in adjusting their behaviour and emotional expression to the social requirements of everyday life. Therefore they need every opportunity for this type of play, both in their homes and also in nursery and infant schools.

Finally, many games are played with other children, and this interaction facilitates the development of social contacts and social cooperation, as we shall consider in more detail in section 7.

5. SOCIAL RELATIONS WITH ADULTS

It has often been stated that one of the first actions in the infant which indicates a social response is the smile, and that this is an innate response to the human voice and face. However, recent studies have shown that infants under the age of about three months smiled at moving objects, which interested them and aroused them.[44] But from three months upwards, smiling is mainly a response to a human face, especially a smiling face, or to a human voice. The infant cries when he is left alone, but smiles, gestures and babbles when people play with him. Later in the first year, he smiles only to a familiar face, though before that he may smile at something which is partly strange and partly familiar. Infants who have been handled regularly smile sooner and more readily than those who have for the most part lain passively in their cots. But smiling is an innate response and is not imitative. It occurs in blind babies, in response to human voices, though it develops fully at a rather later age than in the normally sighted.[45] Vocalization is also affected by social stimulation. It was found that if, whenever a three-month infant vocalized, an adult smiled, clucked and touched him, his vocalizations increased considerably.[46] But if the adult subsequently looked him with an unsmiling face, the vocalization decreased rapidly to its previous level.

There can be no doubt that, whether or not social motives are innate, children from an early age display strong desires for affection and close personal contact with the mother; and later for other social relations in which they are accepted and approved, and can feel as if they 'belonged'. The importance to the child of his contact with his mother, from early infancy upwards, hardly requires emphasis. Indeed, the studies of Harlow and Zimmerman of infant monkeys (see p. 18) suggest that it is the actual bodily contact with the mother which is the most important factor at first. But also the human infant depends on his mother as the main source of nourishment, maintenance, security and affection. Indeed, it is sometimes supposed that her appearance, the sight of her face, the sound of her voice, the touch of her handling, combined with pleasurable sensations of sucking and warmth, together constitute the first set of complex sensory patterns which he recognizes as having their source in an object external to himself. Bodily contact with the mother reassures the infant in states of need and distress; and he clings to her and, later, follows her about. From six months upwards he develops close affectionate ties with her. Separation from her before that age may cause only moderate distress, and does not interfere with the child's future development.[30] But thereafter even a temporary separation may produce what Bowlby has called 'primary anxiety', which is sometimes reinforced by other fears.[47] Thus infants showed more fear and less adaptive behaviour when alone in rather frightening situations than did those accompanied by their mothers.[48] Children separated from their mothers for three weeks in a residential nursery were more aggressive, cried more and were more demanding of adults, than were children in a day nursery; and aggressive behaviour continued for about three weeks after their return home.[49] Other studies have shown the occurrence of intense distress in children of 1–2 years during short-term hospitalization.[50]

Infant monkeys show similar behaviour. When separated from their mothers for short periods at the age of 6–7 months, they screamed and protested violently at the separation, and subsequently became extremely depressed.[51, 52] Even if they were kept with other infant monkeys, they played little and showed no readiness to investigate their surroundings. After restoration to the mother, their attachment to her was closer than before, in some cases over a considerable period of time.

Long-term separation beginning between the ages of 6–18 months may, according to Bowlby, produce, first, protest; then depression and even despair; and finally immobilization or a defensive reaction of detachment or indifference.[53] Goldfarb found that children reared in institutions apart from their mothers may remain permanently maladjusted, showing anti-social behaviour and inability to develop normal social relations and affectionate feelings for others.[31] Of the infant monkeys observed by Harlow and Zimmerman (see p. 18), those brought up with wire mothers alone showed absence of affection and of sexual responsiveness in adult life, and exaggerated aggressiveness. Even those who had contact with cloth mothers were immature in their social relations, though not so markedly.

Another sign of the child's fierce attachment to his mother is the onset of jealousy, which may occur during the second year of life if he feels that she is giving more attention and affection to another child than to himself. It is particularly likely to emerge when a new baby is born, in the eldest child of a mother who has been excessively solicitous to him, making him highly dependent on her. Jealousy is an angry reaction to the child's fear of losing his mother's love.

However, even infants need not be exclusively dependent on the mother. But a single adult permanently in close contact with the child is more effective than a succession of different substitutes. An infant cared for in an institution by a single adult shows more social responsiveness both to this person and to others than does a child handled by a number of people.[54] But rather older children respond readily to familiar and friendly adults, especially when they have had frequent contact with them. Thus in the 'extended families' of primitive societies, children profit from their close contact with grandparents, uncles and aunts, and other relatives. Again, children brought up in the Israeli 'kibbutzin', in which contact with the parents is limited, appear to sustain no psychological impairment in consequence. However, their social surroundings are highly unusual, and they should not be compared with babies brought up in our own society.

But it must be realized that the mother is not only the source of satisfaction and affection for the child, but that she may also frustrate him; by failing to respond to his cries or to feed him as soon as he is hungry, and by trying to impose toilet training on him. As soon as he can crawl and walk, she restrains his movements; prevents him from going where he wishes to go, or from snatching, grabbing and handling objects he would like to obtain. As he increases in mobility and independence, he encounters these obstacles and controls increasingly often. It is true that he himself learns to some extent to accept modifications in his behaviour; to eat and drink rather than suck; to excrete at the right time and in the right place; to sleep throughout the night without instant demands for attention when he wakes. Nevertheless, control is seldom complete. Moreover, by the second to the third year the child wants to exercise his independence, to do things for himself and in his own way; and he may react angrily and aggressively to attempts on the part of disapproving adults to prevent him. Yet he is still completely dependent on them, and particularly on his mother, for care and affection; and he desires to retain these and fears to lose them as a retaliation to his disobedience and aggression. Thus he experiences considerable and frequent conflicts of motivation which tend to produce temper tantrums, obstinacy, or, in the case of more submissive children, anxiety and inhibition of activity.

The outcome of these conflicts depends largely on the manner in which the parents, and especially the mother, react to this difficult behaviour. Excessive control and punishment for naughtiness may aggravate the child's aggressive tendencies, especially if he is suddenly and forceably prevented from doing what he wants. But excessive indulgence leaves the conflict unresolved, and the child has difficulty in learning to adjust to later frustration. Over-protection and exaggerated displays of affection may make the child clinging and dependent, and prevent him from developing natural and desirable exploratory and independent action. Firm and reasonably permissive control will show him that certain behaviour is undesirable, but that not all independent action is prohibited; that some actions must be postponed until a later and more suitable occasion; and that a temporary withdrawal of approval need not result in a permanent loss of his mother's love. In time he learns to exercise natural control, to postpone immediate gratification of need; and he eventually develops a 'conscience' which warns him beforehand what will meet with social approval or disapproval. And conscience is strongly reinforced by positive desires to behave like his beloved parents. In this respect, the example and affection of the father are particularly important for boys; although they are customarily permitted more independent and even aggressive action than are girls. It seems possible also that boys to some extent identify themselves with the father's 'power'—his authority, his material and social effectiveness, etc.

In these ways the agonizing conflict between the child's desire for independence and his need for dependence, together with the fear of losing his parents' affection, is repressed and brought under control in later childhood. However, it is liable to reappear at adolescence, when the desire for independent action and the freedom to direct one's own life and actions becomes salient. At the same time, few adolescents are able to surrender entirely their dependence on their parents for material support, and for approval and affection; though nowadays they do in late adolescence acquire many independent interests of which their parents may not even be aware. But in early adolescence the conflict of desires often results in sullenness and rebellion against parents; or in anxiety and withdrawal into day-dreaming about the adult exploits in which they wish to participate.

6. THE EFFECTS OF UPBRINGING ON MOTIVATED BEHAVIOUR

At one time it was supposed, largely through the influence of Freudian theory, that certain methods of child-rearing, and especially of weaning and toilet training, might produce a profound effect on the child's personality development. Weaning from the breast, rigid schedules of feeding and strictly enforced toilet training at an early age, were supposed to inhibit the natural affection of the child for his mother, and stimulate aggression or anxiety. However, a number of careful and exact studies has been made of child-rearing practices, which suggest that they have little effect of this kind. Perhaps the best known of these investigations was carried out by Sears, Maccoby and Levin, who interviewed 379 middle and working class mothers living in New England, each with a child of about five years.[11] The mothers were extensively questioned as to their child-rearing practices and their children's reactions to these, their attitudes towards their children, and their methods of disciplining them, including the use of reward and punishment. The answers were subsequently rated on a number of dimensions, some of which we shall consider later.

From these and from other comparable studies, it appeared that the physical treatment of the child, apart from actual neglect, was much less important than the mother's attitude to her child, her affection and the manner in which she controlled him. Thus severity and rigidity, lack of warmth, and punishment by the mother in toilet training, might produce some tendency to maladjustment in the child as he grew older.

Numerous studies have been centred on the relation of aggression in children to parental treatment. These have demonstrated that indulgence of aggression increases aggressive tendencies. In some circumstances, excessive strictness may do so also, especially if accompanied by physical punishment. Such an aggravation of aggressive tendencies is particularly likely to occur if the parents punish aggression towards themselves, but encourage it when it is directed to people outside the home.[22] In other cases, children punished for aggression at home may be afraid to express it openly towards people, but may show it in doll play.[55]

The open expression of aggression by severely punished children was found to be firmly inhibited by twelve years. To some extent these children directed aggression into socially approved actions, such as enforcement of rules and condemnation of wrong-doers. But also any current stimulus to aggression tended to produce a high degree of anxiety, especially in girls; and strong feelings of guilt, particularly in boys with very strict and unaffectionate fathers. Control of aggression was most successful in children with moderately strict but affectionate parents, leading to the development of a firm conscience that then repressed their aggression. The employment of reasoning, in explaining to the child why he should desist from certain courses of action, was also valuable, though it was not effective unless combined with affection and a good example from the parents' behaviour.[56]

In earlier studies, the opposite tendency towards undesirable dependence on the mother was also found in some children who had been severely punished by her for aggression towards her. But also it tended to occur when she was over-protective or had shown the child much open affection, at the same time threatening to withdraw it for bad behaviour.[11] However, later studies gave a more complex picture, with effects varying considerably between boys and girls.[57] It seemed that in girls dependence was greatest when it had been permitted and encouraged by the parents, who regarded it as a socially desirable trait; whereas in boys, in whom it was considered less desirable and rather immature, it was related to neglect and frustration by parents. However, different forms of dependent behaviour had different origins, and it seems probable that in boys at least it is not a simple unitary form of motivated behaviour. An even more recent study suggests that the relation between parental upbringing and the child's dependence on his parents and his identification with them is excessively complex and impossible to trace clearly.[58] It should be noted that variation in the conclusions drawn as to the relations between different types of parental upbringing and characteristics of children are due in part to the difficulty in defining exactly both methods of upbringing and children's characteristics. Again, different methods of investigation have been used in different studies. Data on upbringing are frequently obtained by questioning the mothers as to the procedures they have employed; and it is likely that the mothers were not very clearly aware of those at the time, and did not remember them accurately afterwards.

It has been noted that children, especially after they had passed through the stage of severe conflict with the parents, often felt a positive desire to behave like beloved parents who were themselves affectionate and set a good example to the child. Thus they identified themselves with their parents and wanted to imitate them. Children of four years showed a strong tendency in a free play situation to imitate the actions of their parents.[59] Both dominance and warmth in the parents enhanced this imitation; though dominance in the father seemed to have more effect on the boys, and warmth in the mother on the girls.

But identification may also have a general effect on children's motivation, particularly on the development of independence and achievement. Initiative, independence and originality are more likely to occur when mothers are permissive rather than restrictive in their discipline.[60] Independence is further stimulated by the mother's encouragement, especially when she openly rewards it by kissing the child.[61] It is often related to achievement motivation.[62] But demands for these are not effective if made when the children are too young to accept them; indeed such demands may impose restrictiveness. Thus children from poor homes in which the mother enforces independence at an early age, for instance by making the child look after himself, tend to show low achievement motivation.[63] A recent study indicates that home discipline which is consistent, loving, firm but not authoritarian, and demanding a high standard of behaviour which is clearly explained to the child, is most likely to produce in four-year-old children behaviour which is independent and self-controlled, and also exploratory and competent.[64] It seems also that before six years, warmth and permissiveness are more important in producing achievement; whereas after that age parental firmness may be more influential. But indifference and laxity tend to result in apathy in the child.

In middle-class homes with parents who have themselves been successful in life, and who consistently set high standards of achievement, the children continue to be high in achievement motivation provided that the parents are closely involved in their children's success.[65] Maternal affectionate encouragement and rewards for achievement continue to be important in the intellectual achievement of older children, though in some cases achievement in girls is enhanced by the mother's critical comments. With boys the example of the father is perhaps more important.[62] But he should not try to dominate over his son; rather he should seek to encourage his independence. The effectiveness of parental encouragement has been demonstrated in studies of the achievement of

British school children also; it has appeared as one of the most important factors leading to success.[66]

The differences in attitude to and treatment of children is related in other respects to social class membership. It has been reported that American middle-class mothers are warmer, and make less use of punishment than do working-class mothers.[11] Working-class mothers are more severe in toilet training and in the control of sexual activity. In this country, Newson and Newson found that working-class mothers were slower to begin toilet training than were middle-class mothers, and were indeed fairly casual in enforcing it; but also, when they did so, the former tended to use more physical punishment.[67] Indeed, they were generally more punitive, and their children showed more temper tantrums. The middle-class mothers were more gentle and consistent in their methods of control, and on the whole the fathers showed more participation in bringing up the children. Himmelweit also found that middle-class homes were more child-related than were working-class homes; but there was more emphasis on values in the former.[68]

Middle-class parents, especially if well educated and upwardly mobile (going up in the world), are commonly more concerned than are working-class parents with the achievement and success of their children, particularly their sons, at school and in their careers subsequently. Naturally this affects the children's behaviour. Middle-class children have been found to be more industrious in school work; they show more responsibility and a higher degree of aspiration.[69] One study showed that their struggle for achievement was as great in a task for which there was no monetary reward as in one which was so rewarded; whereas working-class boys did not try hard to achieve in the former task.[70] The latter were also relatively less willing to work for a delayed than for an immediate reward. Working-class boys, especially those of comparatively poor intelligence, and with harsh and unrewarding parents, denied that they had failed in a task; whereas middle-class boys admitted it at the time, although they tended to forget it subsequently.[71]

7. SOCIAL RELATIONS WITH OTHER CHILDREN

From a fairly early age children are also affected by their relations with other children. From the fourth month an infant smiles at another child. From the ninth month he tries to make social contacts with other children, reaching out to them, touching and embracing them, and trying to play with them. But also from a year upwards he may try to take things from them, and he resists aggressively if they interfere with him. Attempts to make contact with other children increase in frequency with age, although contacts are commonly short-lived until three years and upwards. Moreover, the child may not be simultaneously aware of more than one or two other children. When at 3–4 years play groups are formed, these are not very stable and persistent, and there is much solitary play. Also the children tend to play together but each along his own lines, sometimes 'talking at' or interfering with each other.[72] Real cooperative play, with sharing of toys and activities, seldom emerges until four years and upwards; and it depends to a considerable extent on the amount of experience the children have had of playing with one another.

There are of course many individual differences between children. Some are generally out-going, and may show frequent sympathetic action but also occasional aggression.[73] Those who have had free, easy and affectionate relations with parents and brothers and sisters adjust more easily to other children. Some children with domineering parents try to dominate the play of other children, and may bully the younger and weaker. Others are withdrawn and tend to solitary play; and thus they are often left out of group play. So also are the highly aggressive. The solitary children may be anxious and insecure because they have received inadequate care and affection from their parents. Or else they tend to cling to adults and do not mix easily with other children because their parents have been over-protective and have not allowed them adequate freedom of action. It has been shown that four-year-old children who exhibit much dependence on adults other than the parents in their play cooperate less well with children of their own age and are less well accepted by them.[74]

As children grow older, they desire increasingly to play with each other and to be accepted by children of their own age. At what has sometimes been called the 'gang age', beginning at about nine years, group play is almost more important than anything else, especially to boys. At the same time, as the result of their interaction with other children, they learn to control their innate tendencies towards self-gratification and their aggressive reactions to thwarting. They find that selfishness and quarrelsomeness lead to disapproval, ostracism or direct retaliation. Thus increasingly behaviour is determined, not so much by what adults allow and approve of, but by what other children permit. Even a temporary isolation from the group strengthens this tendency towards conformity. Piaget found that by the age of 8–9 years, children's ideas of what is right and wrong were largely a function of what was accepted by the other children as 'fair', whereas previously they had been regulated mainly by adult sanctions.[75] From then on morality is increasingly determined by the opinions of the 'peer group', until the adult is able to accept those of society as a whole.

At the same time, attitude to adult authority is modified accordingly in children. They are no longer willing to accept this as paramount, not questioning it even if they disobey. They begin to say, 'If other boys do this, why shouldn't I?' And only if the conduct of adults sets a good example of reasonableness, friendliness and permissiveness, are the children willing to behave in like manner.

Children also as they grow older begin to take into account the motives of others, and to distinguish between intentional misdeeds and unintentional and involuntary ones; whereas younger children disregard the intention of an action, and judge it by its objective consequences, for instance, the amount of material damage produced. However, if such children are shown examples of conduct in which other people judge actions on the basis of intentions, and still more if they are approved for doing so themselves, they may learn increasingly to take intentions into account.[22] An example of modification of behaviour in the light of intention is given by the attitude to hitting others. Younger children have usually been forbidden by parents to hit anyone, and therefore think it is wrong. At school, the boys, though not the girls, find that a certain amount of hitting is socially permissible, especially if done in play. But excessive and unprovoked hitting is disapproved; and it usually disappears, except in very quarrelsome groups, to be replaced by 'name-calling'.

As achievement motivation develops, so also do competitiveness and rivalry. It was found that even in children of about five years, persistence in difficult tasks was promoted by competition between the children, to a greater extent than by adult praise.[76] Competition and rivalry are strongest in children who have been encouraged by their parents to succeed, and also by school teachers.

An interesting distinction has been drawn between motivation towards achievement and attainment for their own sakes, and towards obtaining the social rewards of achievement, such as approval and praise, and hence the enhancement of pride and the avoidance of social disapproval giving rise to shame.[77] Some light was thrown on this distinction by studying children's desires to perform publicly, for instance by reciting, and their self-consciousness and anxiety in front of an audience. There seemed to be considerable individual differences in these motives. It was suggested that they might be related to parental reward for achievement in itself, as against reward for obtaining public approval; or possibly to love-orientated as against 'shaming' techniques of administering discipline.

'Leadership' is another type of motivated social behaviour which emerges early in children, even at three years of age.[19] Commonly at this age the strongest and most dominant child tends to lead. But as social understanding develops, such children may no longer be accepted as leaders; and the leader will be one who shows some understanding of the wishes of others and ability to choose activities which all enjoy. He must possess reasonable intelligence, energy and initiative, and the capacity to make decisions and accept responsibility. But he needs also to be sympathetic and persuasive.

8. DEVELOPMENT OF SELF-AWARENESS

As children grow older, motivation is increasingly modified through diversification. Certain types of motivation become closely associated with the self, the enhancement of the self and its protection against threat and humiliation. This is contingent on the child's attainment of awareness of himself as a person and of his separate identity, which is related to his awareness of others, with their differing desires and fears. As an infant, he is conscious only of his own needs and the desire for their immediate satisfaction. Indeed, he may scarcely distinguish between internal needs and emotions, and the environmental stimulation which impinges on him from without. However, he becomes aware of external objects as such, and begins to differentiate them from his own limbs and body which he can move and manipulate at will. Also he perceives people as a unique class of object, who are separated from him yet respond to him and reciprocate his advances. He observes differences from others particularly when they thwart and fail to gratify him. Even his beloved mother, to whom he is so fiercely attached, shows that she is no longer a mere satisfier of his wants, but an independent person who may oppose and deny him. Increasing understanding of the independent actions and wishes of others is furthered through contacts with children of his own age. He learns to treat other people as individuals, and to respect and make allowances for them. So also as his conscience develops, an 'ego-ideal' is created, modelled in the first place on the behaviour and wishes of parents and other adults, and later upon what is approved and idealized by the peer group. But it is probably not until adolescence that full self-consciousness develops. The adolescent is both aware of himself as an independent person, who can will and control his actions; and also of the interaction of his will with the wills of others, in conformity or disagreement. Repeated experiences in a variety of situations which necessitate different forms of social response will enable the adolescent to develop a consistent yet adaptable personality.

The early growth of the idea of the self appears in the child's language. Before about two years of age he tends to refer to himself by name or as 'you'.[78] From two years, he is greatly concerned to assert himself over other children, and to safeguard his possessions from them; and the words 'I want' and 'mine' appear frequently in his speech. However, although most children, by the age of three years, are aware of their independent self-hood, this does not mean that their motivation is now associated with the enhancement of a conscious self. Nor does the boasting which occurs so frequently in children of this age: 'I say, I am the captain on horseback; I say, I've got a horse and a gun as well.'[79] These sayings constitute simply an assertion of superiority over his playmates.

Only later develops what McDougall terms the 'self-regarding senti-ment':[80] the system of motives and emotions attached to the conscious self which endeavour to enhance it and protect it against threats, particu-larly of some impairment of self-esteem. In later childhood, and still more in adolescence, the individual experiences personal success, and his feelings of self-esteem are enhanced. If they are thwarted, especially by some social obstacle or frustration, then he may feel humiliated and inferior. To avoid this experience, which tends to cause considerable anxiety, he may either strive harder, and perhaps more aggressively, to achieve success; or adopt various methods of 'ego-defence' which we shall discuss in Chapter 9. Younger children show less tendency to experience success as a source of achievement for the self, and failure consequently may be less bitter and less permanently resented. Their 'level of aspiration' is less pronounced, and they do not seek for high achievement. Their goals are immediate satisfaction of desire rather than delayed reward. Thus when children were asked to choose between a small piece of chocolate now or a larger piece the following week, 80 per cent of the seven-year-olds chose the smaller piece now, but only 20 per cent of the nine-year-olds.[81] Again, older children are more ready than younger ones to attempt difficult tasks, good performance of which is a demonstration of their achievement, and probably also of their personal involvement, and enhances their self-esteem. Willingness to persist in self-imposed tasks also increases above the age of ten years. However, feelings of self-esteem do not depend only on age. They are greater in children who believe that their parents value and approve of them; and less in children who have been unloved or rejected. Self-esteem is also affected by social group relationships. It tends to be highest in those of higher social class who have done well at school and have been leaders of clubs, etc.[82]

3

THE SATISFACTION OF THE
BIOLOGICAL NEEDS

I. HOMEOSTATIC MOTIVATION

We must now consider adult motivation, and firstly the motivated behaviour which is necessary to maintain life through satisfaction of the biological needs; and in particular the preservation of homeostasis, the conservation of the internal equilibrium of the body, based on a constant chemical composition, oxygen content and temperature of the blood stream. Although this is achieved to a considerable extent by the automatic operation of physiological mechanisms, such as breathing, digesting, sweating, etc., there must additionally be behavioural components taking the form of search for and attainment of air, food, water, and suitably warm or cool surroundings. If the supply of these is threatened or denied, there is increased striving for it, or withdrawal to more favourable surroundings. If neither of these courses is successful, the individual may relapse into a state of apathy and quiescence which constitutes a final attempt to maintain homeostasis by the conservation of bodily resources.

Little controlled observation has been made of human behaviour in states of acute air or oxygen lack. It would seem that if individuals are aware that they are being suffocated, their behaviour may become disorganized and panic-stricken. On the other hand, a mild degree of anoxia may produce elation. Again, people may be unaware of a rise of carbon monoxide in the content of the air, and breathe it in until death results without any apparent struggle or attempt to avoid it.

Exposure of the body to exceptionally high or low temperatures produces first the physiological processes of sweating, with heat, or shivering from cold. But in general these are supplemented by appropriate behavioural activities. In heat, there may be a reduction of bodily activity; the individual removes hot clothing and seeks a cool place. Food intake may decrease, but water intake increases to offset the loss from sweating. In cold, activity may be more energetic; heat loss is prevented by wearing warm clothes; the individual seeks shelter and supplementary heating; he may even migrate to a warmer climate. He tends to increase his food intake. But if such precautions are not sufficient to regulate heat production or heat loss, his capacity to work may be affected. And if the body temperature rises or falls excessively, death occurs, preceded by a state of apathy and quiescence. Thirst gives rise to more and more violent effort, until physical exhaustion supervenes. The onset of hunger is more gradual and its effects less disruptive, presumably because the body can tolerate food deprivation much longer than water deprivation. If food is completely withheld, hunger pangs and restless search for food increase for a period of three to four days, and then largely cease; and the individual becomes quiescent. But a continued very low diet, in semi-starvation conditions, maintains a constant desire for food and striving to obtain it. Thus descriptions of life in concentration camps during the 1939-45 war emphasized that the desire for food predominated over all others. Sexual desire and friendly social feelings entirely disappeared. The only restraint on snatching and stealing food from other prisoners was the fear of being killed for so doing. It has been reported that in a primitive society, the Sirono, where there was a persistently inadequate food supply, food was stolen whenever the opportunity arose and devoured immediately.[1] Again other motivated behaviour, including sexual activity, was at a minimum.

It is clear that in these cases the behaviour which occurred was motivated not only by food deprivation but also by acute fear of starvation and death. A study of the effects of food deprivation from which such fears were absent was carried out experimentally on 38 young men of good physique who volunteered to undergo a semi-starvation diet for six months.[1] But there was no danger to their health, because they were under constant medical supervision. Nevertheless, they became depressed and irritable, emotionally dulled, apathetic and incapable of effort. They lost interest in anything but food, and some lost self-control and stole it. Social intercourse became minimal.

Even comparatively short periods of food deprivation may affect the individual's perceptual and thought processes. Thus pictures of food or objects related to food, such as knives and forks, were seen increasingly more readily as the interval since the last meal increased—but only up to a certain number of hours, after which cessation of any response tended to occur.[2] Atkinson and McClelland have argued that when an individual is unable to satisfy his needs by some form of overt behaviour, these may appear freely in imaginative responses which are not limited by the reality of the situation. To demonstrate the occurrence of these imaginative responses in connection with various types of motivation, of which hunger was one, they administered the Thematic Apperception Test,* which consists of a series of pictures related in some way to the type of motivation to be investigated; in this case to food, food-getting, etc.[3] For instance, one picture showed an old man and a young man with a

* This and similar tests are described in more detail in the Appendix.

piece of meat between them and a knife beside it. People deprived of food for varying periods are asked to write a story about each picture, describing what is happening in it and what is likely to happen subsequently. Their stories are then scored for the number of references to desire for food, and also for activities related to food-getting. References to food increased up to 16 hours of food deprivation, and also to activities related to food-getting; but references to eating decreased. With pictures presenting food satiation, references to food also decreased. In other words, those who took the test became pre-occupied with activities designed to satisfy hunger, but were inhibited by their state of deprivation from thinking of satisfaction through eating. However, another experiment indicated that this inhibitory tendency decreased after 6–7 hours' deprivation; and responses related to eating increased.[4]

Even mild states of food deprivation may produce concomitant emotional effects. In particular, irritation and anger are likely to occur in hungry people in situations in which they would not normally appear, as was shown in an experiment by Gates.[5]

There has been considerable controversy as to what actually stimulates food-seeking behaviour. At one time it was thought to be instigated by the hunger pangs caused by muscular contractions of the stomach. However, studies have been made of animals in which the stomach has been removed, and of men in whom the nervous connections of the stomach to the brain have been severed; and in these desire for food and eating were normal. Thus it is now supposed that the effective stimulus is provided by changes in the chemical composition of the blood which are produced by food deprivation. It would appear that such a change rapidly stimulates a special centre in the hypothalamus of the brain,* which in turn stimulates eating or the desire and search for food. Another centre stimulates the cessation of eating when food satiation has occurred. There are separate centres in the same area for thirst and drinking.

However, food deficits may be qualitative as well as quantitative; that is to say, a satisfactory diet must be well balanced and contain the ingredients necessary to maintain the body in health. It is found that animals such as rats, offered a wide variety of foods, normally select those which make-up a well-balanced diet. It has even been claimed that young children do the same, but this claim must be accepted with some caution. Older children and adults appear to be guided more by taste, or food preference, and by habits of eating certain food substances. Thus a preference for sweet substances seems general, and indeed appears even in animals. In spite of their tendency to select a balanced diet, they may also

* The hypothalamus is a nucleus of brain cells situated at the base of the cerebral cortex, through which passes a large number of sensory and motor nerve tracts to and from the cortex.

consume a substance such as saccharine which has no nutritive value, and relieves no physiological deficit, in preference to a nutritive substance such as casein.[6] Infant rhesus monkeys, brought up apart from their mothers, soon developed a consistent preference for bananas and grapes rather than bread.[7] They were even affected by the colour of their food, preferring coloured to uncoloured cubes of banana. Thus these preferences are in part innate; though they develop more quickly through learning in infant monkeys brought up in contact with their mothers.

Food preferences in human beings are in all probability largely acquired by learning through social customs. Thus many people consume more sweet and starchy substance than are good for them. Again, they may prefer white bread to wholemeal, though the former is less nutritive. Among adult Americans and Englishmen, and also English children, potatoes are the preferred vegetable, while spinach is disliked because it is slimy and bitter.[8] Some people may even go hungry rather than eat food they dislike. Mexicans insist on eating 'corn' (maize) and refuse other foods; while Puerto Ricans will not eat fruit.[9] Sometimes certain foods are refused as the result of religious beliefs; for instance, pork by Jews and Muslims, beef by Hindus. The religious tradition is stronger than hunger. Other foods are eaten only on certain special, social and ritual occasions, and never at other times.

Appetite for food is also a function of a number of food habits. Food preferences are to a considerable extent habitual, that is to say, they are affected by familiarity. People tend to prefer the types of food to which they have become accustomed since childhood; except perhaps in cases in which they were forced to eat food such as tapioca pudding which they disliked then and have refused to eat ever since. Not only are there considerable differences in food preferences between different societies, but also between different social classes. But to some extent these may be due to the fact that working-class people have been unable to pay for the more expensive and recherché types of food, and thus have never become familiar with them. It is often extremely difficult to persuade people to eat new foods to which they are unaccustomed, and special techniques of persuasion may be used. This was shown by Lewin during the 1939–45 war.[10]

We also acquire habits of eating in a certain manner, at certain times and in certain places. Thus we feel hungriest at the approach of habitual meal-times, although the food deficit may be only slight. Appetite is commonly stimulated by the company of others, in a social setting. Again, we cease eating when we have eaten the accustomed amount, though this need not coincide with physiological satiation.

Thus we may conclude that in extreme states of food deprivation a man's behaviour may be determined to a great extent by his attempts to obtain food; and even in less extreme states, his thoughts may centre on it. Other motivation may be reduced in frequency and intensity. But in ordinary everyday life the biological need for food is a relatively unimportant form of motivation. Food-directed behaviour is largely a function of taste and habit, which are to a considerable extent determined by social customs. But such behaviour may be directed towards the attainment of food which is not necessary for maintaining bare subsistence; for instance, 'good' food which constitutes a pleasure and even a luxury. People work not only in order to keep themselves alive, but also in order to obtain such amenities; and they are much influenced by social custom and the desire for social display. The value placed on these amenities appears particularly in cases of downward social mobility—in people who have had to accept less well paid occupations than those to which they were accustomed—one of whose miseries is having to give up amenities to which they were habituated.

Thus we see that even simple homeostatically motivated behaviour may in man become complicated, diversified and modified through interaction with tastes and habits of eating and food seeking which are to a considerable extent acquired and maintained through social pressures.

2. SEXUAL BEHAVIOUR

There is another type of motivated behaviour which is often classed as supplying fundamental biological needs, namely, sexual behaviour; though the need is for preservation of the species rather than of the individual. But although sexual desire and sexual activity are innate in origin and universal in all animal species, they do not in man necessarily lead to reproduction. Sexual desire seeks satisfaction quite independently of desire for reproduction.

Even if sexual behaviour is instinctive and biologically necessary, it is in no sense homeostatic, and no physiological deficit is produced by lack of sexual satisfaction; nor is there any relation between degree of sexual desire and period of abstinence. Indeed, it may be that desire increases with frequency of sexual intercourse. However, sexual motivation is not only innate, but also is related to internal physiological processes, the secretion of hormones, the androgens and oestrogens in the testes and ovaries. (Other hormones are also involved, but it is not necessary to consider them here.) Among the lower animals, sexual behaviour depends on hormone secretion, which stimulates a special sexual centre in the hypothalamus; and such behaviour does not occur in their absence, for instance, if the testes or ovaries are removed.[11] This is not so in man. Some sexual behaviour begins before puberty, as we noted in Chapter 2, and continues in women after the menopause, when secretion of oestrogens terminates. In men, sexual desire may decline with increasing age before there is any decrease in androgen secretion. Although full sexual behaviour does not develop if castration or ovariectomy are carried out before puberty, it may function normally if these are performed after puberty. Impotence and frigidity are caused largely by psychological factors; and though it is sometimes supposed that they may be remedied by the injection of androgens or oestrogens, the effect may be largely one of suggestion. There is no evidence of a deficiency in androgens in the majority of homosexual males, or of oestrogens in homosexual females, nor does injection of these hormones have much effect on homosexuality. Whereas in animals the female is receptive to the male only during 'heat', when ovulation takes place, women do not show this behaviour. Indeed, there is some evidence that they experience the greatest sexual desire before and after ovulation.

In man, sexual behaviour is dependent to a far greater extent than in other animals on direct stimulation provided by the opposite sex; and on what he imagines and has learnt. Even coitus may not be performed proficiently, especially by women, until there has been some experience of this. In monkeys, it was found that those reared in social isolation without contact with parents or other monkeys of the same age did not show normal sexual behaviour when subsequently they encountered another monkey of the opposite sex.[12] Males tended to fight with normal females; and females sometimes fought males, or repelled or even hid from them.

The learning of sexual behaviour is of course under the control of the cerebral cortex, and sexual behaviour cannot occur in man unless the cortex is functioning normally; whereas in other animals the sub-cortical mechanisms may be adequate to instigate and control it. The patterns of sexual behaviour, particularly in sub-mammalian species, are often rigid and stereotyped; we encountered an instance of this in Chapter 1. In man, patterns of sexual behaviour, including courtship and sexual foreplay, are exceedingly complex and variable. Although there are some uniformities in all human societies, nevertheless there are also extensive differences, especially between civilized and primitive societies. Thus social customs affect sexual behaviour greatly. But also of course there are variations between individuals within societies.

These varieties have been described at great length by Havelock Ellis, Kraft-Ebing and many others. The most extensive coverage, at least for the U.S.A., appears in the Kinsey Report. But studies of primitive societies are numerous also. It is not possible here to consider this information in detail; but some interesting and important data have been given by Ford and Beach, who compared the sexual behaviour of animals with that of primitive and civilized human societies.

Coitus is less frequent among American married couples than it is in many primitive societies, frequency being governed by social convention. In most societies the male plays the initiating and more active role, but not apparently because he is more active and aggressive. In animals these roles are equally distributed between the sexes; therefore in man sex differences appear to be socially determined. The actual pattern of coitus varies considerably in different societies, and so does the amount and type of foreplay. Some stimulation of the genitals is frequent, but the incidence of kissing and stimulating the breast varies considerably. It was found to be greater in upper-class American males than in lower class.

Patterns of courtship vary greatly both in nature and extent. The cult of 'falling in love' and its various accompaniments is most frequent in Western societies and indeed may be disapproved in some others. Attraction seems to be based mainly on physical beauty in women, and on strength, courage and skill in men. But few societies have exactly the same criterion of beauty; in some, for instance, the important feature may be excessive fat.

Marital relations are strictly established according to a particular pattern, which is strongly reinforced by custom, in any one society; but the pattern varies greatly between different societies. There is almost always a single male who is responsible for the maintenance of the women and children, and polyandry is very rare. However, in some societies this male may be the mother's brother and not the natural father. Incest is almost universally taboo, because it would interfere with the stability of the family. But extra-marital sexual relations appear to occur in all societies. In some they are permitted, at least with certain types of kin; in others they are discouraged or prohibited, especially in women.

Among the perverted forms of sexual behaviour, homosexuality and masturbation are widespread, and even bestiality occurs not infrequently. Some societies are more permissive than others of perversions, and may indeed consider them to be normal forms of sexual behaviour. In others, for instance the Trobriand Islanders, they are regarded as ridiculous. It is difficult to understand why they should be treated with such disapprobation in our society when they are so widely practised; presumably the condemnation originates in religious sanctions.

Homosexuality may be due in part to the possession by many men and women of the capacity for sexual relations with either sex; it is social custom which limits them in our society, whereas other societies permit them. Homosexuality is most common in adolescence, and more frequent in men than in women. It is also quite common in monkeys and apes, and indeed in other animals, especially if deprived of contact with the opposite sex. As we have said, it does not depend on hormone secretion. But in men it may occur when there is a tendency towards passivity, dependence and feminine interests; and in women with masculine interests and aggressive tendencies which may be repressed.

Masturbation appears to be more common in civilized than in primitive societies, and is frequent in adolescence, especially in males. In primitive societies, it tends to be regarded as infantile. But it does occur in monkeys and apes.

Although opportunities for sexual satisfaction are widespread and varied, yet it appears that every society imposes fairly strict limitations upon these. Such limitations are considered to be essential in order to prevent sexual jealousy and strife, for the maintenance of good social relations, and especially of family life. But varied as are the patterns of sexual behaviour in different societies, it seems that psychological attitudes to sex may be even more varied. Social anthropologists have shown that in some societies, such as the Trobriand Islanders, sexual relations in marriage are highly valued, marriage itself being considered to be an index of adult social status. In others, such as the Arapesh, sexual intercourse is regarded as of much less importance than the enduring affectionate relationship between husband and wife. But among the Manus, marriage is a contract with important economic implications, and sexual relations are without affection or enjoyment.

Possibly all these attitudes and many more occur in Western societies. But it would seem that only in them has the idealization of sex in the form of romantic love reached such an excessive pitch that the desires of adolescents and young adults are largely centred on it, and their thoughts obsessed by phantasies of it. Moreover, social tradition encourages and reinforces the importance of romantic love and sex, while at the same time social custom condemns pre-marital and extra-marital sexual behaviour. The outcome is a conflict of motivation in which desire is increased, and accompanied by frequent and sometimes excessive anxiety and guilt. Consequently sexual behaviour has acquired an attractiveness altogether out of proportion to its actual pleasure and its biological importance. This importance may well be increased by the desire for achievement of social status; in adolescent males, for the status of adult sexuality, and for females, that of marriage. Again, for men sexual activity may provide opportunities for the display of aggression and of power, in the exercise of masculine potency, such opportunities being severely limited in our society in other directions.

The arousal of conflict by sexual stimulation, and the inhibition of conscious sexual desire, were illustrated in experiments with the T.A.T. At first sight the results were curious. A group of young men, shown photographs of attractive nude females, wrote fewer T.A.T. stories with sexual contents—stories about sexual intercourse, kissing or courting—than did those not aroused in this manner.[13] However, a group tested at a beer party, when their inhibitions were removed by alcohol, produced more sexual stories after arousal; moreover, their stories were more openly and less indirectly sexual. In another experiment, the test was administered to some men by a stern authoritarian individual in his sixties; to others, by a young man who treated them informally.[14] The sexual content of the T.A.T. stories of the former was distinctly less than that of the latter. There is a tendency in some people to feel anxiety and guilt over sexual arousal. Such people may give fewer sexual T.A.T. stories to pictures with a sexual content than do those who are less prone to such feelings. But also the former are less able to repress these responses when sexual tension has been released by recent orgasm.[4] Again, those who tend to repress sexual anxiety may instead express anger and disgust after reading sex stories.[15] But other people, sometimes termed 'sensitizers', may be quite conscious of their heightened anxiety.

It may seem difficult to account for the prominence which sexual behaviour and its accompaniments have attained in our society. However, the Freudian theory of instinct postulates that all human behaviour is based upon the operation of two primary instincts, termed the 'life' and 'death' instincts. The first of these (also known as the 'libido') includes all behaviour aimed at self-preservation and also all sexual, social and love relationships. The second is concerned with the termination of life, both in the self and in others, and all forms of aggression are based upon it. These instincts, and the desires and emotions to which they give rise, originate in the most basic part of the human personality, the 'id', the contents of which are wholly unconscious. It is the function of the 'ego', which is partly conscious, to keep them under control. This it does partly by repressing them into the unconscious mind; and partly by directing them into activities which are realistic, and which may lead to successful achievement of aims which afford some gratification of instinctive tendencies. There may be some degree of instinctive transformation, in which the individual learns to respond to new environmental stimuli by new forms of motivated behaviour. Nevertheless, these are still basically linked to the id, which supplies the energy for their performance. Also there is a continuing conflict and struggle between the id, seeking direct gratification of its instincts, and the ego which realizes the impossibility in real life of its complete satisfaction. Hence a considerable degree of anxiety may be generated and experienced; but it may be controlled by the mechanisms of ego defence, described in Chapter 9.

Sexual expression and gratification proceed through a series of stages in infantile development. The first of these is the oral stage, in which pleasure is obtained through sucking at the breast; the second, the anal, in which pleasure is centred on the excretory processes. During these stages, erotic feeling is directed towards the self, and they are therefore termed 'autoerotic'. At the third, the phallic stage, the libido becomes directed outwards upon loved objects, which are differentiated from the self, the ego. Next the Oedipus stage appears, in which the boy desires to obtain sexual relations with the mother, and consequently hates and wishes to destroy his rival, the father, who prevents these. However, fear of retaliation from the father, and particularly of castration, causes these desires to be repressed. The commands and prohibitions of the parents are internalized or 'introjected' to form the 'super-ego', which subsequently develops into the conscience. The conscience expands to include a positive admiration for the father in the 'ego-ideal'; and later to incorporate the commands and prohibitions of society in general. But any infringement of its sanctions arouses anxiety and guilt. The girl is said to go through a corresponding stage, sometimes called the 'Electra' phase, in which she desires sexual relations with her father, and particularly to give him a baby. Her fears of her mother's punitive reactions are reinforced by her perception that she has no penis; therefore she believes that she has already been castrated. Nevertheless, introjection and super-ego formation take place in her also, though possibly in a more complex manner.

Normally the child proceeds fairly smoothly through these stages. But if he is unduly punished, frustrated or deprived of affection by parents, he may become 'fixated' at one or other stage. Excessive conflict is set up, which cannot be successfully repressed. These conflicts may continue to have repercussions in consciousness at a later age, producing excessive anxiety, behaviour disorders or even neurosis, which are not under conscious control. However, the ego may be preserved through the operation of the mechanisms of defence, and especially by the sublimation of the libido into non-sexual activities (see Chapter 9).

This is only a very brief outline of Freudian theory, which is enormously more elaborate and cannot be discussed here in detail. If it were accepted *in toto*, it would provide an adequate explanation for the importance of sexual motivation and behaviour, and for the frustrations and conflicts associated with it. That it is not generally accepted, even by psychologists, would be attributed by the Freudians to the resistances in the ego and super-ego to the admission of its full implications. Indeed, much of the apparently fanciful nature of the theory could be explained in terms of a dramatic representation of processes which cannot even be formulated in rational language, let alone discussed logically. Nevertheless, there are certain reasonable objections to the theory, the most important being that of cultural variation. Freud based his theory mainly on the ideas and behaviour of neurotic patients suffering from conflicts arising in the strict social taboos experienced by the middle and upper classes of nineteenth-century Europe. These people were not faced by the threat of economic want and insecurity, or of physical danger. Thus the principal frustration they encountered was sexual; and this was probably related to over-strictness and lack of parental affection in childhood. Some of the first doubts cast on the theory were voiced by social anthropologists such as Malinowski, who investigated the very different parental and marital relationships of primitive peoples and their different sexual behaviour.[16] Other psychologists, notably Horney, have suggested that the primary conflicts in young children are caused by insecurity rather than parental sexual taboos.[17]

However, there are many important features of the Freudian theory including the concepts of conflict, unconscious in origin, and the effects it may produce in anxiety, guilt and neurosis. Though Freud certainly did not say the final word on these, he did originate their investigation. We shall return to this matter in Chapter 9.

3. MATERNAL BEHAVIOUR

Maternal behaviour is attributed by some writers, including McDougall, to an instinctive origin; and it can indeed be supposed to be essential for the preservation of the species, like sex. However, as Lorenz pointed out, no single instinctive tendency appears to be involved, even in the maternal behaviour of animals, but rather a number of different but coordinated behaviour patterns.[18] These include behaviour aimed at feeding and protecting the young, and also aggression against predators.

In mammals, a very important process is lactation, which depends primarily on the secretion of the hormone prolactin in the pituitary gland occurring from the ultimate stage of pregnancy. This physiological process, and also of course the processes involved in the egg-laying of birds, etc., is said to indicate the operation of basic physiological drives. Another instinctive activity which occurs in many species of insects, birds and mammals is some type of nest building; and this behaviour may follow a complex stereotyped pattern similar to those described on p. 6. In rats and other mammals another instinctive type of behaviour is that of retrieving the young if they fall out of the nest or wander from it. This may continue in rats until the sixteenth day after birth.

In most species of monkey and ape, maternal care is very marked during the early months of infancy. While the animals are moving about, the mother usually carries the infant with one arm until it is strong enough to support itself by clinging to her hair. In gorillas, carrying continues until the infant is three years old.[19] Rather older infants sit astride the mother's back until they are old enough to walk and run. When the animals are stationary, the infant crawls about in close proximity to the mother who retrieves it if it wanders too far. Frequently it learns from copying her movements what food to select. When it is old enough to begin playing with other young animals, it may scream and rush to her protection if it is frightened. But it becomes largely independent of her from the time it is weaned. The extent of care varies between different species, and even between different mothers of the same species. Those who have had no previous offspring may be less attentive and careful, indicating that maternal behaviour is to some extent learnt.

In human beings, maternal behaviour is even more variable. Lactation itself appears to be in part psychologically determined, and many mothers are unable even from birth to feed their infants themselves. Moreover, a study by J. and E. Newson of child-rearing practices in this country showed that among the 700 mothers they interviewed, about 50 per cent were still breast feeding their infants at a month after birth; 29 per cent at three months; and only 13 per cent at six months.[20] These numbers are considerably less than those found in earlier surveys, suggesting that breast feeding has declined appreciably in recent years. The usual explanation given in the above enquiry for cessation of breast feeding was that milk was not adequate in amount or constitution; but it was clear that often the mothers simply did not like breast feeding, a dislike which appeared to be associated with modesty and embarrassment at exposing the breast. But it is also true that modern methods of preparing the bottle ensure a more consistent and adequate supply of milk. And indeed maternal care may show itself in the trouble taken by the mother to prepare the bottle properly.

If we consider other aspects of child rearing in which maternal care is involved, it is clear that they also vary greatly between different mothers, and are affected by experience and by social custom. Studies by Margaret Mead and other social anthropologists of child rearing in primitive societies have shown very wide variations, which accord with the general pattern of culture of the society. Thus among the Arapesh of New Guinea, care and attention are centred upon the development of the child, who is brought up with great tenderness and affection by both parents.[21] Children are not weaned from the breast till upwards of three years. But among the Mundugumour the child is treated with harshness from birth upwards. He must struggle to suck at the breast, and is roughly weaned at the first opportunity. Thereafter he must fend for himself, with little care or affection shown him. Among the Balinese, the infant is treated indulgently until the age of about a year, but thereafter he is teased by the mother and his demands repelled until his frustrations make him withdrawn and unemotional.[22]

There are many other such variations between different societies, indicating that child care is largely determined by social culture. This is also true of our society. Mothers are often guided by the advice of their own mothers, but also they are influenced by current social custom; and, particularly in the case of middle-class mothers, by the advice of child welfare services and similar authorities, including Dr Spock! Some social class differences in child-rearing and in upbringing generally were discussed in Chapter 2. Other studies have indicated that there is little relationship between social class and the amount of care, protectiveness and affection shown to young children.[23] But working-class fathers do appear to treat their children more forcefully than do middle-class fathers; and their wives also. This exercise of power may be passed on by the mothers to the children, in the form of coercion. Possibly children are treated more permissively today in all social classes, though this again is more apparent in the middle classes, where also there is less overt physical punishment. The amount of tenderness and affection given to children has on the whole increased in recent years; homes are 'child-centred' to a greater degree than they were earlier in the century and in the last century.[20]

But the mother's behaviour to her children, and the degree and type of care and affection she gives them, differs between individuals and undoubtedly depends greatly on her own personality. Affectionate behaviour varies with the mother's personal needs; aggressive mothers tend to have a less close relationship with their children and to express affection less freely.[24] It may also be harder for the mother to show affection openly to her children, though not necessarily to feel it, if she experienced lack of affection in childhood. This is particularly likely to occur if she herself became anxious and withdrawn, through the influence of unstable or neurotic parents. Again, she may be preoccupied by anxieties arising from environmental difficulties, poverty, over-work, etc.; or caused by difficulties in marital relations. Mothers who have learnt to accept themselves are also more accepting to their children.[25] Some anxious mothers may be over-protective, apparently continually afraid that the child may meet with some harm or develop some illness. Finally, the warmth and affection shown by the mother seem to vary with the responsiveness and 'out-goingness' of the child's display of affection; thus the behaviour of both is reinforced by their mutual interaction.

It is clear that maternal behaviour in women is so far removed from the instinctive maternal care of the lower animals as to belong to an entirely different category. Indeed, it might more properly be regarded as one of the forms of socially motivated behaviour, to be discussed in Chapter 7, for tenderness and protectiveness to the weak and helpless are not peculiar to mothers, but occur extensively in childless women and in men, culminating in the altruistic behaviour we shall consider presently.

4

MOTIVATED BEHAVIOUR IN THE
EMERGENCY REACTIONS

I. FEAR AND AVOIDANCE

It is obvious that for the maintenance of life the individual must not only supply adequately the physiological needs of the body, but must also preserve it against injury and hurt. We possess types of motivated behaviour, sometimes called the 'emergency reactions', which appear to be innate and to emerge in early childhood. They arise in response to external stimulation, and not to physiological conditions in the body, although commonly they are associated with certain typical physiological manifestations. This behaviour includes avoidance or flight, and fight, which enable us to protect or defend ourselves from danger and injury. Avoidance and fight are characteristically associated with the emotions of fear and anger respectively, and the relationship is so close that frequently it is impossible to distinguish motivated behaviour from emotion. Indeed, some writers have supposed that the behaviour is caused by the emotion, which was first aroused by the appropriate threatening stimulus. However, we shall discuss this question in more detail in Chapter 5.

The primary causes or stimuli of avoidance behaviour range from the mildly unpleasant or the extremely novel and unexpected to those situations in which pain, injury, danger or death may be encountered. The behaviour which occurs in response to these situations, and which may or may not be accompanied by fear, includes withdrawal, which may be a spontaneous reflex action; avoidance by means of complex patterns of activity under cognitive direction and control; disrupted and uncontrolled behaviour and aimless movement, culminating in panic flight and escape; and a state of general inhibition and rigidity, as in animals 'shamming dead', when escape is impossible. The uncontrolled behaviour may be accompanied by a variety of physiological symptoms: rapid heart beat, sweating, muscular tension and tremor, even involuntary urination and defaecation. These we shall discuss more fully in the next chapter. There may even be loss of consciousness, followed by a decline into a condition of 'catatonic stupor'.[1] Generally speaking, the more severe the threat, the more violent, uncontrolled and disrupted the behaviour; but it is also affected by differences in age, intelligence, personality and previous experience. Quiescent states tend to supervene when active escape is frustrated; and fear may be more severe in so far as no definite course of action is available.

It is sometimes found that mild states of fear actually improve performance. They may increase alertness and produce greater caution and carefulness. Such behaviour is under full cortical control, and may be directed also towards intelligent avoidance of disagreeable and hurtful situations, perhaps by some form of detour behaviour. But if danger increases or is prolonged, behaviour becomes increasingly impulsive and even stupid, quite ineffective in avoiding the dangerous situation. An instance is the orderly retreat from a building on fire which turns to panic flight involving injury and death to many of those involved. Quite clearly these two forms of behaviour differ; the problem is whether they are based upon different psychological processes. One possibility would be that the tension set up by attempts to control and restrain overt action increases steadily as the duration and threat of the situation increases, until fear becomes unendurable. Restraint suddenly breaks down and violent action supervenes. Or it may be precipitated by an additional stimulus, such as the cry of 'Fire!' or the sight of someone running amok.

Fear is particularly likely to arise as the consequence of some unexpected catastrophe, such as a fire or a flood. If the event is one from which there is a possible escape, panic behaviour may occur such as that described above. All normal socially cooperative behaviour disappears, and extreme fear causes every individual, or at least the majority, to attempt to escape from the scene as rapidly as possible by struggling, fighting, even trampling others underfoot. Such behaviour seems to begin in a few excessively panicky and uncontrolled individuals, but rapidly spreads to others. However, many catastrophes are so sudden and overwhelming that no escape is possible, and their effects must be suffered. The first reaction of the majority may be a kind of numb bewilderment, in which they hardly realize what is happening.[2] They may feel little actual fear, though its physiological concomitants may appear. A small number may be panic-stricken, crying and screaming. When the first emergency has passed, acute fear may be felt, and sometimes anger at the causes of the incident. But behaviour becomes more realistic, though also there is repetitious discussion of the event, and a good deal of crying, especially by women. The after effects include anxiety and fatigue, sometimes almost psychotic behaviour.

In time of war, fear may be intense, prolonged and repeated. Members of the Armed Forces are of course trained to control their behaviour, but this does not prevent them from being afraid. An enquiry among American airmen in the 1939–45 war showed that almost all of them felt afraid at some time; in some cases most afraid at their first mission, and in others, towards the end of a tour of duty.[3] They experienced many of the physiological symptoms described above; and, in some cases, feelings of irritability, unreality, inability to concentrate, even loss of memory. Although these men were sustained in the control of their behaviour by Service morale and by the comradeship of other men in their units, nevertheless the fear of failure and cowardice was often added to that of danger. When they were able to take some immediate effective action to help themselves, fear was relieved; but when, as often, they felt themselves to be helpless in the face of danger and unable to adjust to it, then fear was reinforced. This occurred in prolonged field fighting, and its effects were observed by Mira during the Spanish Civil War of 1936, when, in addition to fear of the enemy, men feared to run away lest they should be shot by their comrades.[1] Sometimes stuporous and catatonic states occurred, to be followed by extreme excitement and panic.

During the 1939–45 war, civilians in Britain were exposed to frequent danger from bombing, sometimes very severe, in a manner which had never occurred previously in war-time. It had been anticipated that, since they were in no way trained to meet danger and were not helped by Service morale, there might be acute terror and panic behaviour. This did indeed happen in some of the most severe air raids, the so-called 'blitzes'. If unable to escape during the raid, people might show the type of immobility described above; and as soon as the raid was over, rush madly away to find any place of safety, hardly knowing what they were doing. Frequently this behaviour was followed by a period of amnesia, repression and forgetting of the experience. Sometimes effects were delayed and did not appear until weeks or even months later. This was noted after the destruction of Rotterdam.[4] There might be a complete psychotic disintegration of personality. The prolonged state of fear of arrest, imprisonment and even death which occurred in countries occupied by Germany such as Holland, often produced physical and mental exhaustion. Owing to the very high morale of the Dutch, this was followed in many cases by recovery and resistance. But among those who could not endure it suicide was frequent.

However, in Britain panic behaviour as the result of recurrent air raids was in fact much less frequent than had been anticipated. Apart from the type of behaviour described above, there were cases of uncontrolled behaviour, including excessive weeping, in some of those in buildings destroyed by bombing. This was followed by states of bewilderment, depression and apathy lasting several hours.[5] But repeated experience of bombing by those in less acute danger tended to produce some degree of acclimatization, and even the ability to sleep through air raids. However, general moods of irritability, depression or lethargy were often experienced, though there was little neurotic breakdown. Social factors were very important in relieving prolonged anxiety; the general social attitude of courage and acceptance expressed in the saying 'Britain can take it', and the social contacts with others, for instance in air raid shelters, especially those under good leadership.[6] Social-directed activities, such as those of Civil Defence workers, often overcame fear, though sometimes these workers broke down after prolonged stress and sleeplessness. It seemed that people possessed the capacity to adjust to enduring threat provided that they were not exposed to great hardship of other kinds. But a general breakdown in the normal way of life, loss of homes, etc., sometimes produced more disturbance than fear of bombing; for instance, prolonged states of apathy.

A study of attitudes in war-time showed that the long-term effects of bombing might be an increase in cooperative activities, such as voluntary war-work.[7] Although people tended to become less cheerful and often more critical of public authorities and their methods of protecting civilians, hostility to the enemy was on the whole less than in those who had not been exposed to bombing. The former were in general more realistic and less subject to irrational beliefs. These observations again indicate surprising resilience and adjustment in the face of real danger, as compared with the deterioration which may result from internal fears which have no objective cause.

Behaviour in less terrifying situations has been studied experimentally in parachutists[8] and in soldiers stationed in the neighbourhood of an atomic explosion.[9] The former were given the T.A.T. test (see Appendix), and also they were presented with words of varying relevance to parachute jumping, while their skin resistance was tested.* The latter response became greater just before parachuting, and the number of T.A.T. stories relating to parachuting increased. But there was also in some cases a denial of fear, and anxiety-producing words were mis-read. Thus some of the men were fully conscious of their fears; others tried to control them through repression. The same alternative effects appeared in the soldiers. In some cases, descriptions of two pictures, one of men looking into the sky, the other of a ruined city, contained more episodes of behaviour aimed at coping with threats of danger immediately before and after the atomic explosion than at other times. But in other cases, these episodes were fewer at this time, indicating the repression of fear. Even a discussion of the dangers of war had the effect on some people of making them repress their fears and fail to express them in T.A.T. stories written subsequently.[10] It was clear that these people were trying to avoid consideration of fearful incidents.

It has been suggested that the main initial cause of fear lies in experi-

* The resistance of the skin to an electrical current passed through it decreases in states of emotion and of general arousal, through increased secretion of sweat (see p. 87). This is sometimes termed the 'G.S.R.' (galvanic skin response).

ences of pain, and indeed that avoidance of pain is a primary drive and fear arises secondarily as a reinforcement of this. Thus anticipation of pain is associated with fear, which leads to withdrawal and avoidance. Now it is true that infants show a reflex withdrawal from painful stimulation which persists throughout life. But it appeared that fear arises in infants from causes other than pain avoidance, for instance in reaction to sudden unexpected events. Though fear of pain may continue to stimulate withdrawal tendencies, social custom encourages children and adults to inhibit this withdrawal, especially in socially approved situations such as encounters with doctors and dentists. Nevertheless, they cannot altogether inhibit the distress and suffering caused by the experience of pain, nor the fear aroused by its anticipation. Thus when someone has been informed that he will receive an electric shock, in an experimental situation, his ongoing activies become increasingly disrupted and his internal physiological reactions greater as the moment of shock approaches. Moreover, the greater the probability that he will receive the shock and the more severe the pain he anticipates feeling, the greater his fears.

But the actual experience of pain and the emotions of suffering and distress caused by it are very complex and variable. Some experimenters have stated that the onset of pain, whether from pricking, burning or electric shock, is related solely to the intensity of stimulation, in a manner which is fairly constant in different individuals. Recent experiments have cast some doubt on this view. But it would appear that variations in the emotional reactions to pain, of suffering and distress are much greater; though naturally these reactions tend to increase with the severity of pain. These variations are in part a function of the expectations of the sufferer. Thus it was shown that, even in experimental conditions, the pain experienced by individuals who expected it, on the basis of instructions, 'I want you to report as soon as you experience pain', was greater than if individuals were merely told to report the nature of their sensations.[11] On the other hand, when people who had experienced severe shocks were asked if they would volunteer for a second experience of the same kind, they felt less pain and showed less physiological reaction to pain on the second occasion than on the first.[12] Although no explanation was given them as to the reasons for asking them to repeat the experience, they were ready to bear the pain, which appeared to lessen it. That pain may be minimal when it is not expected is also shown by the fact that the administration of placebos (neutral preparations) may relieve post-surgical pain almost as well as that of drugs such as morphine.

Pain may be more severe and distressing to those who are already frightened. Women in Western countries who are afraid of pain in childbirth appear to experience it more acutely than do women in primitive societies who may hardly pause from their work to give birth. But the former, if they can be induced to relax from their fears, may feel less pain also. An understanding of the cause of pain may also bring relief; still more if attention is directed towards other satisfying experiences. Thus wounded soldiers sometimes experienced comparatively little pain because of their relief at escaping from battle.

The effect of prior experience was shown in experiments on dogs and chimpanzees.[13] Young dogs were reared in isolation until eight months of age, without any contact with painful stimuli, or with other animals experiencing pain. Subsequently, when pricked or burnt with a lighted match, they exhibited reflex withdrawal, but did not escape from these stimuli, nor show any signs of pain or fear. A young chimpanzee, reared in the same way until 31 months, also exhibited no pain or discomfort when pricked by a pin.[14] It has been suggested that young children tend to feel pain more readily when their parents are obviously frightened and distressed; and indeed that such influences may affect their capacity to suffer minor injury for the remainder of their lives.

In adults, there is considerable individual variation in the amount of distress and suffering experienced in comparable degrees of severity of pain.[15] Those who are highly anxious or hypochondriacal appear to suffer more than do normal people; whereas in cases of psychotic depression, and sometimes of schizophrenia, suffering may be minimal. Again, inhibited and anxious individuals were found to respond with greater fear to a frightening film than to the threat of electric shock; whereas the more stable and extraverted showed a greater response to the threat of shock than to the film.[16] In the former an imaginatively caused fear was more potent than the anticipation of real pain.

Somewhat similar differences have been observed in connection with the 'phantom limb' experience.[17] After a leg has been amputated, the patient may continue to feel that his limb is still there, as the result of sensations from the scar tissue. These may be painful; and in some patients the pain seems to become worse with time, rather than decreasing, and even spreads to other parts of the body. But their complaints may be intermittent, and may arise in connection with other unpleasant emotional experiences. These patients also tend to be highly anxious and hypochondriacal.

Individual differences in distress caused by pain are also associated with differences in anticipatory fear. Those who attempt to repress unpleasant experiences may be more disturbed by the anticipation of a painful electric shock than are those who fully admit them to consciousness.[18] The former try to avoid thinking about the impending shock, which seems to make matters worse. People who were only moderately frightened before a surgical operation experienced less distress afterwards than did those who were extremely frightened, and who tended to develop acute anxiety or depression.[19] But those who showed little or no fear beforehand were often hostile and aggressive subsequently to the hospital staff, whom they blamed for the pain and discomfort they experienced. It would seem that they had avoided thinking beforehand about the possible consequences of the operation, and then attributed them to the negligence of the hospital staff.

Fear and distress may also be caused by witnessing the pain and suffering of others. They may be particularly marked in situations in which people believe that they have themselves caused pain. In an experiment, individuals were instructed to deliver more and more severe electric shocks to others, supposedly to test the effects of punishment on memory.[20] In actual fact the victims received no shocks, but they pretended to react to them by pounding on the partition wall between them and those who delivered the shocks. Many of the latter, though not all, although they were assured that the shocks were not harmful, nevertheless showed signs of great emotional disturbance; they sweated, trembled, groaned and clenched their fists, and sometimes almost collapsed. One third of them became excessively agitated and refused to give the most severe shocks; and some walked out of the room, expressing their disapproval of the experiment. It would seem here that the emotions were aroused by the conflict between conformity to the experimenter's commands, and the distress caused by the imagined pain of the victim; and some people tried to avoid the consequent anxiety by actual withdrawal.

All these data suggest that fear, pain and the distress caused by pain interact with each other. Thus fear not only anticipates the experience of pain, but also aggravates it, and the suffering caused by it, though to a greater degree in some people than in others. But there are many other fears which are not directly associated with pain, or even with acute danger. Many people may not have experienced such fears to any great extent. But there must be few who have not at one time or another feared a loss of security. It would perhaps be said that the possibility of such a loss arouses a state of anxiety rather than of fear. It is difficult to differentiate fear and anxiety at all precisely. Fear is in all probability innate in origin, and arises suddenly and acutely in experiences of danger or pain; whereas anxiety is a long-term mood of less intensity, often caused by some condition within the individual himself, and acquired especially in the anticipation of failure or punishment. Anticipation may provoke more anxiety than does the actual realization of these, because it is associated with doubt and worry as to how to respond appropriately. Particularly in social situations, the individual is anxious and uncertain how to behave, and expects to receive social disapproval, rejection or contempt and consequent humiliation, if he behaves in a manner not in accordance with social custom. Thus the fundamental basis of the experience is a fear that the 'self' will be in some way impaired. Because anxiety is internally caused, and also to some extent shameful, people may prefer to experience it in solitude; whereas fear, caused by an external situation, they usually like to confront in the society of others experiencing the same emotion;[21] or even more in a group dominated by a protective leader.[22] Indeed, the example of calm behaviour by another person may itself reduce fear, for instance of snakes.[23]

Whether a possible loss of security arouses fear or anxiety, the conditions producing insecurity may be real enough: poverty, want, unemployment, accident, assault. People may be subject to constant and prolonged fear of these for themselves and for those they love. Thus, as we shall consider in Chapter 8, they may enter occupations which they hope will enable them to avoid such insecurity; and parents often advise their children to choose similar occupations. However, the fear of environmental causes of insecurity is often reinforced and even replaced by fear of social insecurity. We noted that in young children insecurity arose in the physical weakness of the child which caused him to seek dependence on his parents. So throughout life most people depend to some extent on the support of others, in physical and also in social insecurity. Thus they associate with companions, and with a variety of social groups who may help them in difficulties, and who strengthen their capacity to resist, not only actual danger, but also the dominance or oppression of other persons or social groups which may threaten their livelihood, independence or self-esteem. Although membership of social groups acts as a support, an added anxiety may then arise as to the possibility of the withdrawal of such support through social disapproval, ostracism or rejection. Again, both the child and the adult constantly need to feel secure in the affections of others, and much anxiety may be experienced if they believe themselves threatened by the loss of these. Thus a very important type of motivation, to be considered in detail in Chapter 7, is that which impels people to behave in such a way as to retain the support and affection of others.

2. FIGHT

We noted that the second type of emergency reaction to the threat of danger, and particularly to overt attack, was defensive fighting. But fighting and other forms of aggressive action occur in situations in which defence is not involved. There has been endless controversy as to whether fighting, and aggression generally, are instinctive, as McDougall and Freud supposed; or whether they are acquired, not only as a response to threat of attack, but also to interference, thwarting or frustration, especially of human origin. The American 'behaviorists' have tended to support the latter theory. On the other hand, Konrad Lorenz has deduced from his studies of animal behaviour that aggression is spontaneous and instinctive, in man as in other animals.[24] He regards it as an instinct the operation of which is necessary for biological survival, and for the maintenance of strength and efficiency in the species, since the weakest do not survive. Fighting is employed in the food-getting activities of carnivorous animals; and in the defence of almost all species against predators, in self-protection and the protection of the young. In defence, aggressive action need not necessarily result in the destruction of the attacker.

But in many animals aggression is directed not only towards other species but also within the species towards other members. It is this form of aggression which is most dangerous in man, and which is the most difficult to explain. However, Lorenz considers that within-species aggression also has important biological functions. In many animals it is most apparent in the defence of a 'territory' which the animal regards as its own. The existence of territories is essential to prevent over-population of an area by more animals than can obtain adequate food supplies from it. Again, aggressive action against other members of the species often occurs in order to obtain dominance in gaining food or females in mating. Sometimes actual fighting takes place, but without much injury being caused. Thus male red deer often fight in the rutting season, but they may merely push each other with their horns; even if they wound each other, the injuries are seldom severe. Fighting to the death is infrequent, except in animals confined in highly restricted conditions. Often actual fighting is replaced by threatening or warning behaviour; bird song and the bright colours of certain fish act as warning signals. Or there may be displacement behaviour, such as that described on p. 7. New patterns of behaviour may appear in ritualization, for instance in some type of display.

In the establishment of dominance also there may be more threatening than actual fighting. The snarling of dogs, their stiff gait and erect tails, act in this manner. Although actual fighting may follow, more commonly one will give way and run away, or show appeasement, crouching and wagging its tail to demonstrate its submissiveness. The general tendency is for the weaker animal to withdraw in such situations.

Many animals flock together in groups, often in order to protect themselves against predators. Thus small birds combine together to 'mob' predators. But these groups can persist only if aggression against other members of the group is controlled or inhibited. Ritualized activities may enable aggression to be displaced; Lorenz instances the ritualized posturing of lizards and certain fish. Again he suggests that 'bond behaviour' may develop in the form of individual attachments in prolonged matings, care of the young, even a type of friendship. Thus small groups of friendly geese greet one another with appropriate cacklings. However, strong attachment to members of the group may be associated with considerable hostility to other groups, and even fighting, as between rival wolf packs. But again actual fighting may be replaced by threat or display. Lorenz has described most amusingly the behaviour of a flock of geese which perform a 'triumph ceremony' of cackling, extending the neck and beating the wings, when they have successfully repelled intruders.

Earlier studies of monkeys and apes living in captivity, in highly restricted conditions, had suggested that they showed considerable aggression both between groups and also between members of the same group. But more recent studies of animals living in natural conditions indicated quite the contrary.[25] Some species occasionally kill other animal species for food, and also show defensive aggression against predators. Baboons in particular may attack animals which threaten one of their number, though more often they bark at them. Many monkeys live in fairly large organized permanent groups; but these seldom come into real conflict with each other. Groups possess 'home ranges' over which they forage. But in some species, such as the baboon, two or more groups may intermingle, for instance while drinking at a water-hole; they largely ignore each other. In other species there may be a core area at the centre of the home range. When another group approaches this, it may be warned off by shouting, barking or howling (particularly in howler monkeys). Occasionally, in rhesus monkeys, if one group suddenly meets another and the latter does not retreat sufficiently rapidly, there may be fighting and severe wounding. But this behaviour was observed in rhesus monkeys living in the neighbourhood of Hindu temples in Uttar Pradesh, where the area was somewhat limited.

In apes, groups are usually smaller.[26] Gorilla groups, which are fairly stable in membership, may approach each other and intermingle briefly. Occasionally an adult male from one group may charge and even bite another, which then retreats. In spite of the legends of their ferociousness, gorillas are on the whole extremely peaceable. Their curious behaviour of beating the chest with both hands may be a warning signal, or a displacement activity resulting from a conflict between attack and retreat. Chimpanzees show even less group aggression. Groups again are small, but unstable, frequently changing their membership. They travel about foraging over large areas, and often aggregate and intermingle. There is much vocal interaction, in grunts, barks, hoots and also drumming of trees with the hands; but these are forms of communication, producing interaction, and never a warning aimed at separation.

Aggression between members of groups is also slight. Most monkey groups have dominance hierarchies, that is to say, orders of dominance; and the more dominant males obtain more food and females than the less dominant. But dominance is often not at all obvious. In baboons, two or more adult males may act aggressively together to maintain dominance over the group. But in most species threatening gestures, grunts and barks are more common than actual attack; even when biting occurs, it does not produce severe injuries. Less dominant animals usually avoid the more dominant, or behave submissively, for instance by 'presenting' their hind-quarters.* Occasionally there is minor quarrelling and fighting in which dominance is not involved, especially between younger males. Among gorillas and chimpanzees also quarrels sometimes occur, with short-lived fighting, biting and screaming; but little damage is done., Chimpanzees exhibit minor status differences, but there is no fixed dominance hierarchy.

One must conclude from these observations that either monkeys and apes possess no instinctive tendency towards aggression; or that the instinct is normally latent, and aroused only by the mutual interference. which occurs in restricted living conditions. This behaviour contrasts so strongly with that of man, who not only hunts and kills other animals for food but also shows such highly aggressive behaviour towards his own species, both within and between groups, that one is almost compelled to believe the Biblical story of the 'fall'! Human aggression appears in fighting, violence, cruelty, destruction and war. As we noted, there has been much discussion as to whether this aggressive behaviour is innate and instinctive in origin; and whether, if this is so, war between groups is inevitable in human society. It would seem that war has played a prominent part in the lives of many, if not most, primitive peoples, and occurs in the majority of human societies. However, as Mead and others have shown, there are considerable cultural differences in this respect. The friendly and peaceable Arapesh of New Guinea, who do not fight and have little personal possessiveness or desire for power, may be contrasted with the Mundugumour, who live in much the same environment, but are highly aggressive, continually fighting each other and other tribes.[27]

In many primitive societies hostility may be aggravated and reinforced by aggressive rituals such as human sacrifice, head hunting and cannibalism; though it may be displaced to some extent in phantasy—in rituals imitating sacrifice and fighting, or even popular myths. In more advanced societies, religious persecution has been frequent, involving torture and widespread and cruel forms of killing. These types of behaviour suggest that fighting between groups is the result of natural aggression, and is not carried on simply in order to obtain more territory and better food supplies.

The causes of war between modern civilized societies are exceedingly

* 'Presenting' is primarily the sexual gesture of the female inviting the male to copulate with her; but it appears to be used as a substitute activity by males also to indicate submissiveness.

complex; but the main cause would appear to be not so much the fear of dangerous attack or the attempt to obtain the territory necessary for biological survival as the struggle for wealth, power and prestige. Thus the Nazi fight for '*lebensraum*' was really intended to gain power. Often, as in this case, the principal agents in making wars have been ambitious despotic rulers or powerful ruling cliques. Many of their subjects do not participate in the fighting and are unwilling to do so. And frequently they experience only mild degrees of aggressive feeling against the enemy. But wars are ritualized forms of group conflict, and they are stimulated and maintained by propaganda and appeals to group prestige and loyalty. Moreover, group solidarity and conformity are always enhanced by the real or fancied threat of external attack and danger, and aggression is also increased by these means. Nevertheless, it is doubtful if war between nations can be attributed to the innate aggression of their members, or that there is any innate individual disposition to make war.

But there are many other acts of group violence within national groups in which aggression is general and widespread, such as rebellions and race riots. This behaviour is seldom related to territorial aggression; and though it more often occurs in urban than in rural environments, it is not directly related to overcrowding. Those who participate in these activities are generally stimulated by resentment against the unjust dominance and oppression of more powerful groups; thus they attempt to overthrow them and obtain their power. Indeed, this resentment may have a very real cause, in the deprivation and frustration of poverty, unemployment, etc. Again, criminal violence may be carried out by those who feel themselves to be a deprived minority—a 'sub-culture' which is segregated from society and unjustly denied the opportunities which are enjoyed by the more fortunate. Even youth groups, resenting the dominance of the old and detesting their customs, may revolt against them by civil disobedience and sometimes actual violence.

Yet it is not only the deprived, oppressed and under-privileged who behave aggressively. Almost any group of people who feel themselves threatened in any way tends to adopt hostile attitudes towards the real or imagined source of this threat. Sometimes a mere divergence in the customary ideas and behaviour of other groups may appear in some way to undermine the importance, the permanence and stability of traditional customs in one's own group. Religious and ideological differences are particularly effective in this respect. Strong and cohesive solidarity within the group may actually increase aggression against other groups. Moreover, there is a tendency for permanent states of prejudice to arise against other groups, which are reinforced by fears that the latter will deprive one of livelihood, in competition for jobs or houses; of amenities, by noise, dirt and overcrowding; or through sexual seduction of or assault on women. Prejudice may exist as an attitude of hostility without necessarily giving rise to aggressive action or overt attack on the group against which prejudice is felt. But there is a latent tendency for such behaviour to erupt, which may be directly stimulated to action through rumour or propaganda. The latter was most effective in religious persecution and in Nazi Jew-baiting. Sometimes attacks seem to result from entirely independent threats to livelihood; thus it appeared that the number of Negro lynchings in the southern states of the U.S.A. increased when the value of the cotton crop fell.[28]*

Modern civilized societies do provide certain socially approved methods of expressing aggression between groups, such as economic competition and rivalry, and also competitive sports. Unfortunately, however, when mutual rivalry between nationalities arises in the latter, actual fighting may break out; for instance, between different football teams and their supporters, if they believe that they have been unjustly treated.

These societies also take steps to control and suppress within-group aggression between individuals by means of their laws, and through the encouragement of social conformity to these and of the desire for social acceptance. Again, substitute activities are available, such as competition in the achievement of power, status and wealth; and in dangerous and competitive sports. Even indulgence in viewing plays and films of violence may act to some extent as a substitute, though it is possible that these aggravate rather than relieve aggression (see p. 69). In spite of these substitutes, however, individual acts of violence and cruelty are all too frequent. The causes are too complex for elucidation here.

It is impossible to give more than a sketchy and highly speculative outline of these complex events. But it would appear that human beings possess an innate tendency to attack both those who assault them, and also anyone who seems to threaten their lives, their livelihood, their independence and the supposed 'rights' of themselves and of groups of which they are members. As we shall see in the next section, non-physical assaults and restriction of independence and of 'rights' may also give rise to forms of aggression other than actual fighting or violence. However, we shall see also that there are means of controlling these. But the relationship between the tendency to physical and non-physical aggression and the making of war is a remote one. War is an ancient social institution, which arises from a complex of social traditions and customs that lie outside the scope of this book. We have seen that many of those involved may themselves possess little or no aggressive impulse against the enemy.

* This study has been criticized on the grounds that the statistical method employed artificially elevated the correlation between number of lynchings and value of the cotton crop. But there has been some disagreement on this criticism.

3. OTHER FORMS OF AGGRESSION

In our society aggressive action is constantly occurring in forms other than overt physical attack and defence. We saw in Chapter 2 that aggression first appeared in infancy, in response to interference with and restriction of movement, and took the form of wriggling and screaming, and later of temper tantrums. Conflicts with parents and other children over restriction and interference continued to produce aggressive actions, but kicks and blows were eventually replaced to a great extent by angry words. In adults, the main causes of aggression are psychological and not physical assaults: verbal insults and slights; domineering and arbitrary commands; annoyance, interference and obstruction, either open or concealed; and a host of similar types of injury. Now since aggression appears to arise frequently as the result of frustration of some on-going action, it has been suggested that frustration is its primary and fundamental cause. Thus Miller and Dollard formulated the 'frustration-aggression' hypothesis: that frustration always gives rise to aggression, and aggression is always caused by frustration.[29] But many objections were raised to this hypothesis, and it was subsequently reformulated as follows: 'Frustration produces instigation to a number of different types of response, one of which is some type of aggression.'[30] In this form, the hypothesis has been widely accepted, and much experimental evidence has been cited as to its validity.

Nevertheless, it must be noted that aggression is likely to occur only when the aggressor feels personally involved in the frustrated activity, and the frustrating person is perceived as initiating a psychological threat to the self of the aggressor and to his feelings of pride and self-esteem. Interference by another is felt as humiliating, and there is a resort to aggressive action to remove inferiority and restore self-esteem. In other words, it is the wanton attack of one individual on another which typically produces aggression, and frequently anger also. Some people are particularly prone to regard any kind of interference or obstruction as a personal insult.[31] But if an injury is perceived as excusable, then it is unlikely to arouse aggression. Thus it has been argued that attack and annoyance rather than frustration are the real causes of aggression, or at least of the type of aggression aimed specifically at harming another person.[32] It has been claimed that experiment shows that frustration alone may arouse little aggression.[33] The latter appears particularly in the defence of the self; and also it enables an individual to reach the goal of motivated behaviour by continuing attack and overcoming interference. But frustration in itself is relatively unimportant—if, for instance, it arises in circumstances in which there is no personal attack; and it will be followed by non-aggressive reactions (these will be discussed in Chapter 9).

It is difficult to determine the exact relationship between anger and aggression. Some psychologists have supposed that anger invariably arises first, and that it may or may not lead to aggression. Sometimes rage may be diffuse and unfocused on any particular object towards which aggression could be directed; activity may then be restless and unspecific.[34] But it would seem that in some circumstances aggressive actions occur immediately in response to attack, and that there is little anger unless direct action is inhibited, for instance through fear of retaliation or punishment for aggression. It is clear, however, that anger and aggression frequently accompany each other. In many of the experimental findings described below, little distinction is made between the occurrence of aggression and anger. Both anger and aggression, if prolonged, may give rise to more or less permanent states of hostility.

The frequent occurrence of anger, especially in certain people, was shown many years ago in a study by Gates.[35] Fifty-one women students were asked to record their experiences of anger over a period of one week. The number of experiences per student varied from 0–10. Though they were more frequent in states of hunger, sleepiness, cold and fatigue, they arose most often in social situations in which frustration or interference were encountered. There were occasional physical assaults, such as slapping; but the most frequent responses were angry exclamations and retorts, restless behaviour and sulking. Impulses towards physical attack were numerous, but were usually controlled.

It would seem therefore that anger was primarily caused by frustration and interference which were felt as personal attacks. Moreover, aggression arose in similar circumstances, though it was not always expressed openly. This is more likely to happen in so far as the assaults of the attacker become more frequent or more unpleasant. Thus in an experiment in which students were told that they had failed to perform card-sorting tasks satisfactorily, they made a variety of responses in the early stages including greater effort, apology for incompetence and attempting to give up the task, as well as aggressive behaviour towards the experimenter.[36] But as he increased his derogatory remarks and reproaches and his attacks on their self-esteem, there was an increase of anger and violently expressed aggression. Again, if there is an anticipation of friendliness which is not forthcoming, but unfriendliness is encountered instead, then more dislike is aroused than if there has been no such expectation.[37] Repeated experiences of interference may appear as attacks, and may give rise to increasingly aggressive responses.[38] This occurred in nursery school children who played a game of moving a toy car along a road, encountering a toy car moved by the experimenter in the opposite direction.[39] Behaviour became more aggressive as the experience was repeated.

To a considerable extent aggressive behaviour is stimulated by the example of others, and from childhood upwards is more frequent when others are perceived as acting aggressively. Thus even if aggression is instinctive in origin, it is reinforced by social example; and also the type of aggressive action is learnt to a considerable extent by imitation. Children tend to copy the behaviour of quarrelsome and aggressive parents, and to indulge in aggression themselves if it is permitted and not controlled by the parents. They may also imitate the example of other adults who are behaving in an aggressive manner. Thus, in an experiment, children who witnessed an adult attacking a toy doll subsequently attacked a doll in their own play; and also struck other toys with a mallet and showed generally uninhibited aggressive behaviour.[40] But children who had seen an adult playing quietly with the doll did not behave in this way. Aggressive behaviour was particularly likely to occur if the adult was a man, presumably because physical aggression is regarded as more acceptable in men than in women. Adults may show similar imitative behaviour. People were shown to be offended and angry when they witnessed a scene in which one man attacked another verbally for his opinions in a very aggressive way.[41] But if a third person censured the attacker, or apologized for his behaviour, the witnesses not only expressed themselves as less angry, but even felt anxious or depressed.

Aggressive behaviour may be stimulated by participation in the actions of a group of people who behave in such a manner. In mob violence, the members of the mob are encouraged by one another to perform aggressive and destructive acts which they would never dare to do singly. Even the opportunity to talk to other people who have been offended by the behaviour of a superior may produce a rise in hostility to him.[42] This is especially likely to happen if the people are well known to one another. Again, individuals participating in an experiment in which they had been told that they would find each other congenial to work with made more hostile remarks about an experimenter who insulted and criticized them than did other individuals who had not been told this.[43] Indeed, those who feel that they have some mutual bond may combine together in counter-attacks against an outsider who is perceived as attacking one of them.

There is little doubt that there are considerable individual differences in the tendency to behave aggressively, and that some people do so much more readily than others. The former react aggressively to a variety of different forms of attack: physical attack, direct or indirect verbal attack, hostile attitudes, signs of anger. It would seem that there may be some temperamental basis for such aggressive tendencies, which may be inherited from aggressive parents. Aggression may be related to physique, but although it is on the whole commoner in strong active men, some small men are extremely aggressive, possibly as a compensation for feelings of inferiority. Again, some people are innately more impulsive and less controlled in their behaviour than are others, less able to tolerate attack or interference or to postpone the gratification of their desires. They may also be lacking in the ability to make social relationships of a friendly nature. Some delinquent boys have been found to be of this type.[44] It has also been suggested that unduly aggressive adults show inadequate personality development, lack of ego-strength and of self-esteem. Thus they may try to 'boost' themselves by behaving aggressively. However, no matter what innate motivation is involved, aggressive behaviour is greatly affected by social example and control and, as we have seen, especially by parental treatment.

Differences in aggressive behaviour are also found between the two sexes, again partly through their innate tendencies but probably even more through cultural differences in upbringing. Males commonly show more overt aggression and even physical aggression than do females, who use verbal and indirect means of attack. Males are physically stronger and more active; and possibly also they are stimulated by the male sex hormones. But in addition social custom condones aggressive behaviour in men and disapproves of it in women. Thus boys may be encouraged by their mothers to stand up for themselves and fight other boys, whereas open aggression is discouraged in girls, though 'cattiness' and 'name-calling' may be permitted. Long-term studies of children growing up into adult life showed that aggression was a more consistent and persisting tendency in males than in females.[45] The latter, as the result of social pressure, tended to repress aggressive action. Adult women might be as prone to anger as men, but they feel more anxiety and guilt at the open expression of aggression and therefore may inhibit it.

It is probable that working-class children, especially boys, are more openly aggressive than are middle-class children. The aggressive behaviour of the former may be more socially permissible, and may be stimulated by that of parents and neighbours. There may be less control of aggression by parents; and if they do punish it, they may use corporal punishment which is a further stimulus to aggression. Middle-class parents tend to discourage open aggression, and less frequently use corporal punishment. Moreover, they often adjust the severity of punishment in accordance with the perceived intention of the child, especially at adolescence; whereas working-class parents are more concerned with the overt consequences of the aggression, and punish it accordingly.

Clearly social prohibition or control of open aggression is essential, both to protect society from the consequences of actual violence, and also to make social interaction more friendly and agreeable. But it has sometimes been argued that it is better from the point of view of the individual himself that he should be allowed to express his aggressive impulses in some way, rather than 'bottling them up' inside him. If aggression is not expressed openly, it may not be eliminated but may result in a persistent state of hostility and resentment. Thus in an experiment in which students were sent insulting notes, supposedly by other students, those who were permitted to send notes in return were slightly less hostile subsequently to the senders than were those who were not allowed to send notes, and were therefore obliged to inhibit the expression of aggression.[46] The effect was greater for those low in self-esteem.[47] The open expression of aggression may dispel it to some extent if opposition or attack is short-lived and relatively weak, but not if it is prolonged. One experiment showed that people interrupted in performance of a task by the experimenter recovered more quickly from the aggression aroused if they were permitted to give him electric shocks.[48] But this result has not been confirmed by other experimenters.[49] It would seem that the expression of aggression may be satisfying only if it produces the successful removal of interference or restores self-esteem. Thus students angered by a teacher's violation of established rules were permitted to write notes to him complaining of his behaviour.[50] When he then proceeded to act according to the rules, less hostility was felt than when he did not read the notes at all. In the latter case, they felt slighted; in the former, their self-esteem was restored.

Nevertheless, there is danger that indulgence in open aggression may prolong rather than reduce it, particularly if those against whom aggression is directed retaliate in kind, and mutual recrimination develops. There is also the possibility that if aggressive acts are frequently repeated and go unpunished, they may become habitual, and result in a permanently aggressive disposition. Therefore it is not surprising that from childhood upwards open aggression is controlled and socially disapproved.

What courses therefore are open to those whose aggressive impulses have been aroused by the many real or fancied attacks of others? One way of reacting is to avoid when possible those who are likely to make such attacks, or situations in which they arise. If this is not possible, and disapproval, punishment or retaliation are feared, open aggression may be inhibited, and anger is likely to be felt. This may be shown by the physiological changes of the type we shall discuss in the next chapter. Inhibition may be reinforced by moral condemnation, either by one's own conscience or by others. Moral condemnation is especially feared and avoided from persons of authority and high social status. Thus students who had been insulted by the experimenter were subsequently allowed to express verbal aggression either towards a member of the academic staff or towards another student.[51] Considerably more aggression was expressed towards the latter. But a similar control of aggression may occur in situations in which approval or friendship is sought. Even nursery school children inhibited aggressive responses when it was made clear to them that these prevented their social acceptance by other children.[52]

However, there are certain methods of avoiding both open expression and also complete inhibition. One frequently employed procedure is a resort to some form of substitute action. The greater the punishment for aggression anticipated, the more likely is this to occur. One form of substitute behaviour is the expression of moral indignation against the behaviour of others, which may be stigmatized as unjust or anti-social. It is possible that many social reformers are instigated by some such displaced aggression, as seen in the energy they display in attacking those who oppose them. Moral indignation tends to arise more frequently in women than in men; the former are more ready to condemn violation of social codes of behaviour which they themselves may have found disagreeable.

Another type of displacement is the direction of aggression towards someone who is not its initial cause. Thus aggressive boys who have been severely punished by unaffectionate fathers may behave aggressively towards their teachers, particularly if the latter treat them in an authoritarian fashion.[53] However, if there is great fear of punishment, the aggression may be directed against a more distant agent and appear in the form of anti-social behaviour, aggression against society. A very distant object from which little retaliation need be feared is the Government; and we are often inclined to attribute the blame for our disappointments to this. We noted that in war-time many people in Britain were more inclined to feel hostility towards the Government for not protecting them adequately than against the Germans. Possibly this was partly because they expected better treatment from the former!

We noted on p. 60 that permanent states of prejudice might exist against social groups which appear to threaten or deprive the group of which one is a member. But such prejudice may also be felt against groups which are not harmful. Aggression against someone who is invulnerable or punitive may be displaced and directed against minority groups such as Jews or coloured people, which are powerless to retaliate. The prejudice may then be justified by attributing potentially harmful characteristics to the minority group, saying, for instance, that coloured people are noisy, dirty and immoral; and that they compete unfairly for jobs and houses. Jews may be accused of plotting to obtain undue wealth and power by underhand means. Such a justification may be related to an actual experience. One noisy family of coloured people or one piece of Jewish sharp practice serves to condemn these groups as a whole. But in some cases there may appear to be no connection whatever between a fancied injury and aggressive behaviour. Thus we noted that the number of Negro lynchings in the southern states of the U.S.A. increased when the value of the cotton crop fell. [28] Presumably the aggression arising from this injury to livelihood was displaced since there was no obvious cause against which it could be directed. Another instance of displacement towards a totally irrelevant object was demonstrated in an experiment in which young men at a summer camp were promised that they could attend a gambling session in the evening.[54] Instead, they were compelled to carry out a long series of dull and difficult tests, which obviously aroused their anger against the experimenter. Before and after these they were required to rate the favourable and unfavourable qualities of several nationalities including Mexicans and Japanese. Fewer favourable qualities were assigned to those on the second rating than on the first. It should be noted that a number of experimental studies has failed to give evidence of this type of displaced aggression; and it may be that it operates principally in strong and deeply rooted prejudice.[55]

It has been observed that members of a group against which there is strong prejudice may sometimes themselves express this prejudice, perhaps in an exaggerated and excessively irrational form.[56] This seems to be due to a form of displacement by means of identification with the aggressor. The individual is diverting his counter-aggression from someone whose aggression he fears, into a form which will bring acceptance and social approval from the latter. Thus he is averting the danger from himself and finding a safe means of expressing his aggressive tendencies. This course of action has been observed in Jews and in Negroes who express anti-Semitic and anti-Negro prejudice.

It is sometimes supposed that aggressive tendencies may be lessened by various forms of substitute activity, including aggressive sports. But there is no evidence that these actually reduce aggression, and some observations have suggested that they may increase it. It would appear from the favourable effects of play therapy on maladjusted children that the open expression of aggression in this relieves and benefits them. But the effect of the therapy may be due in part to the understanding it imparts to the child of what is troubling him. However, as we noted in Chapter 2, phantasy or make-believe play appeared to afford a substitute satisfaction for aggression. Thus children who were encouraged to play freely with teacher and pupil dolls frequently introduced aggressive acts, especially against teacher dolls, such as putting one on the stove and another with its head in the toilet.[57] Both highly aggressive and weakly aggressive children gave more of these aggressive responses than did children in the intermediate category; moreover, the aggressive responses of the former increased during the play period. Presumably those who showed little aggression outside the play situation had repressed it; and their inhibitions were released by the permissiveness of the play. But it cannot be assumed that aggression was significantly reduced by this release.

The same may also be true for phantasy expression in the stories told about the T.A.T. pictures. It does appear that aggressive tendencies may be expressed in these. In one experiment, the greater the degree of overt aggression among a group of working-class delinquent boys, the greater the number of aggressive acts in their T.A.T. stories.[58] However, this relation did not always appear in middle-class boys, whose aggressive tendencies had presumably been socially discouraged; and they were inhibited even in T.A.T. expression. But boys whose mothers had condoned if not encouraged their aggression showed both overt and T.A.T. aggression.[59] In adults who have no specially strong aggressive tendencies, aggression may be aroused by hostile criticism, and appear subsequently in response to T.A.T. pictures of aggressive and frustrating incidents.[60] But again there has been considerable disagreement as to whether the writing of such stories decreases aggressive reactions subsequently. It appeared in one experiment that those who were allowed to carry out the T.A.T. after being insulted by the experimenter made fewer hostile comments than those who had not done so.[60] Moreover, the greater the number of aggressive acts described in the stories, the fewer were such comments. However, it has been suggested that anxiety and guilt were aroused by the T.A.T. expression of aggression, and these inhibited its appearance subsequently. Another experiment indicated that for those who frequently indulged in day-dreaming, a period of day-dreaming reduced aggressive feelings towards an insulting experimenter as effectively as did the performance of the T.A.T.[61] But also inwardly directed hostility increased; thus aggression was displaced from the experimenter towards the self. However, it is possible that in some circumstances phantasy expression might relieve long-repressed aggressive tendencies by enabling the individual concerned to realize their nature, as we noted in connection with the effects of play therapy on children.

It has also been suggested that watching scenes of violence in films and television programmes may act as a relief to the aggressive tendencies, and that people may live out their aggression in the emotions aroused by these. It is true that people with strongly aggressive dispositions appear to enjoy such scenes of violence, but there is no evidence that their aggression is in any way weakened by viewing these scenes. Indeed, it is possible that children may be incited to aggressive acts if these seem to receive social sanction through their appearance in films and television programmes.

There is one further consequence of the inhibition of aggression when it can find no outlet in substitute or displaced form. We noted that those who were afraid to display open aggression might direct it inwards upon themselves, and experience a considerable degree of guilt. They may indeed feel guilty not only after attacking others, but even at the thought of doing so. Such guilt may appear in T.A.T. stories. It is particularly likely to be felt when aggressive impulses arise against loved persons, for instance in children who come into conflict with loving parents. Men who have had close affectionate relations with their fathers tend especially to experience guilt. Guilt also occurs in those with strong punitive consciences, living in societies with high moral standards which prohibit overt aggression. It is felt especially when there seems to be no justification for aggressive behaviour. However, it is less likely to occur if hostile feelings can be expressed indirectly and even anonymously. In an experiment, students were encouraged to describe their true feelings about their parents and to express any resentment against them openly, in a discussion with other students; and apparently they found this to be a great relief.[62] Free expression was felt to be permissible because the students paid relatively little attention to each other's statements, and did not think their own would be remembered against them afterwards.

However, guilt may often be recurrent, and may be accompanied by considerable anxiety lest the individual may be unable to inhibit his aggressive impulses. But guilt and anxiety may be countered by employing one of the 'mechanisms of defence' (see Chapter 9), such as for instance 'reaction formation'—behaviour completely opposite in nature which is submissive and outwardly friendly.

We have discussed at some length the various forms of aggression, which range from overt violence through verbal attack, substitute and displaced behaviour to more or less complete inhibition. We have noted some of the circumstances in which these different forms arise; but clearly there are individual qualities and experiences which strongly affect the particular behaviour adopted. These are partly a function of innate temperamental disposition, but even more of parental treatment and of other forms of social condonation and control.

5

THE EMOTIONS

I. THE FUNCTIONS OF THE EMOTIONS

It is clearly difficult if not impossible to dissociate the behaviour occurring in the emergency reactions from the accompanying emotions of fear and anger. Indeed, one could almost say that the most persistent and unchanging characteristics of these states were the emotions felt; whereas the behaviour varied according to the situation. We are therefore faced by the problem: Are emotions themselves motivating? Or is motivation invariably accompanied and reinforced by characteristic emotions? We have seen that McDougall adopted the second of these hypotheses, and attributed an accompanying emotion to almost all his instincts or propensities; not only flight with fear and aggression with anger, but also curiosity and wonder, self-assertion and elation, parental instinct and tenderness, and so on.[1] However, he himself in his later writings placed less stress on these relationships; and few modern psychologists would accept them. Indeed, some would altogether eliminate the psychological concept of emotion, believing that it has no functions other than those covered by motivational drives.[2] Others suppose it to be a hypothetical intervening variable, the existence of which is merely an inference from observed behaviour. Yet whatever the origin and function of emotion, it constitutes a unique form of direct experience. However uncertain people may be as to the exact nature of their motives, they are seldom in doubt as to whether they are experiencing emotion; and usually they know well enough what emotion it is. Therefore, to abandon the concept of emotion would be to set aside a large area of normal human experience which is as worthy of consideration as any other human experience.

Several psychologists, on the other hand, such as Arnold and Bindra, have postulated that emotions themselves are motivating, and indeed that no distinction can usefully be drawn between motives and emotions.[3] Arnold considers that all perception of objects and situations is accompanied by appraisal of these as to whether they are attractive and beneficial, or repulsive and harmful. This appraisal may initiate a tendency to feel a specific emotion, accompanied by the impetus to perform specific actions. Thus the emotional appraisal would appear actually to motivate us to action. The view is indeed fairly widespread, as we have noted, that anger is the cause of aggressive action, even if it does not invariably lead to it.

However, Arnold states that certain emotions do not necessarily impel action; in joy we merely try to prolong the existing state of affairs, and in grief we have given up hope of improvement. There are other complex and subtle emotions which do not necessarily lead to any specific course of action. Thus sympathy may be little more than a passive registration of the emotions of others, accompanied by corresponding emotions; whereas compassion stimulates us to take action to relieve the unhappiness of others. Yet all emotions enable us to evaluate objects and events, and judge their significance to us. They may even enable us to understand more fully than reason alone, especially in situations involving the desires and actions of other people. Furthermore, they make possible the evaluation of our own actions, thus stimulating us to persist in certain courses of action which seem valuable to us, while desisting from others which are useless or harmful.

Not all motivated behaviour involves specific emotions, though there may be more diffuse feelings of pleasure or unpleasure (disagreeableness). Behaviour aimed at satisfying the basic physiological needs is of this kind. Some psychologists, of whom Dewey was perhaps the first, consider that emotion is typically associated with frustration in goal-directed activity.[4] If the latter proceeds without let or hindrance, little emotion is felt. Thus if we can escape promptly from a dangerous situation, we may feel little fear, compared with what is felt if we are prevented from escaping. Many people have experienced such occurrences. Again, if we are attacked and overcome the attack immediately by well-directed aggression, we feel far less angry than when aggression is thwarted. It has also been suggested by the Freudians that the cause of anxiety, or at least of morbid anxiety, is the damming up of the libido, which cannot be permitted to find immediate satisfaction, and is indeed repressed from consciousness. We shall discuss this further in Chapter 9.

The theory that emotion arises through frustration of motivated behaviour may be applicable to the unpleasant emotions, especially fear and anger, but it does not appear relevant to the pleasant emotions such as joy and elation. On some occasions these may occur when frustrations and obstacles are overcome; and indeed they may be stronger in such situations than if no frustrations had been experienced. But it would be difficult to prove that they never occur except in conjunction with the removal of frustration. They would seem often to have a positive stimulating effect in reinforcing behaviour such as that occurring in purposive activity aimed at the achievement of long-term goals.

Another suggestion is that emotions are felt whenever we perceive a change or contrast in the amount, probability or immediacy of potential satisfaction or dissatisfaction.[5] Thus we anticipate that a situation will be agreeable, and are consequently disappointed and resentful when it is not. Or we think that it may be difficult and unpleasant, and are joyful and elated when things go well. Furthermore, the stronger our expectations and the greater or more sudden the contrast with the experienced situation, the greater will be the emotion felt. The emotional reactions to a situation may vary according as to whether it is in prospect, in present experience or in retrospect. Thus when people were asked what they would feel if, for instance, they missed their railway connection on their way to an important visit, they reported that beforehand they would feel anxious as to whether they would make the connection; when they found they had missed it, they would be angry; afterwards, as anger abated, they would feel unhappy and sorrowful.[6]

In many of the arguments as to the nature of emotion, there has been a tendency to classify experiences into the categories of pleasant and unpleasant, and to pay comparatively little regard to the characteristic patterns of feeling, though clearly the behaviour with which they are associated is in general differentiated in accordance with these specific patterns. The argument that our behaviour is largely determined by attempts to maximize pleasure and minimize unpleasure—the old hedonic theory—also has its modern supporters, notably P. T. Young.[7] However, his argument is based mainly on two sets of animal experiments. The first of these demonstrated that rats would learn to run through mazes more quickly to obtain certain preferred kinds of food than to obtain others less well preferred. This preference may operate even in hungry rats, which will choose saccharin rather than cheese, because they prefer the taste of the former although it has no nutritive value. The other more recent experiments were initiated by Olds, who was able to insert electrodes into different areas of the rat's brain, and implant them there permanently.[8] The rat could then stimulate its own brain electrically by pressing a bar which closed the circuit through the brain. Olds found that rats would continue to stimulate certain areas of the hypothalamus and limbic* regions of the brain an almost indefinite number of times, presumably because the effects of stimulation were pleasurable. Moreover, they would learn to perform tasks with 'self-stimulation' as a reward, preferring this to food even when they were hungry. However, stimulation of other areas was unpleasant, and produced avoidance reactions.

The argument was therefore that rats were stimulated to perform

* The 'limbic area' is situated within the cerebral cortex. It is the primitive part of the cortex, sometimes known as the 'old brain', which is relatively more prominent in animals other than man, in whom the 'new brain' is extensively developed; and it appears to be the centre in the cortex most concerned with the experience of emotion.

certain actions because their outcome was pleasurable, and to avoid situations which were unpleasant. This hedonic theory has been extended to cover human motivation, notably by McClelland.[9] He suggests that pleasure and unpleasure arise spontaneously, through innate disposition, in situations in which there is a discrepancy between what the individual expected to encounter, and what actually occurs. The individual learns to make responses which maximize pleasurable feelings and minimize unpleasurable feelings, thus developing patterns of goal-orientated behaviour characterized by approach or avoidance. This type of theory can be applied fairly readily to appetitive behaviour, such as obtaining agreeable food and avoiding unpleasant food. But McClelland goes further, and employs it in connection with motivated behaviour in general, stating that this is characterized by the individual's expectations of achieving certain particular types of pleasurable experience, or avoiding particular unpleasurable experiences. We shall discuss one important application, in 'achievement motivation', in Chapter 8.

Now it may be recognized that most of us, at least at times, tend to seek agreeable rather than disagreeable situations—social acceptance, for instance, rather than social isolation or rejection. But it is possible that the pleasure is a secondary reinforcement which we have learnt to expect we shall experience in conjunction with certain courses of motivated behaviour and their outcome. It has been postulated additionally that difficult and strenuous functioning, associated with continued muscular contraction, is inherently unpleasurable or even painful; whereas smooth functioning or muscular relaxation is intrinsically pleasurable and satisfying.

Although certain emotions are generally classified as intrinsically unpleasurable, situations arousing them are not necessarily avoided on every occasion. Thus as regards anger, moral indignation may be more pleasurable than unpleasurable, presumably because it creates a feeling of moral superiority. Possibly something the same is true of the fear encountered in dangerous occupations and sports, such as mountain climbing; the individual experiences self-enhancement through his ability to control his fears. But this hardly applies to the liking for ghost stories and horror films; the only explanation for this would seem to lie in the contrast between imagined fright and actual safety!

It might be supposed that some light could be thrown on the relations between emotion and pleasure–unpleasure by studies of the effects of direct stimulation of the brain in human beings. In fact, electrodes have been implanted in the brains of human hospital patients, some psychiatric cases, others with disorders such as intractable pain.[10] It was found that stimulation of certain centres in the limbic area did indeed reduce anxiety, and sometimes produced pleasurable feelings, which might be related to sex and to agreeable sexual memories. Intractable pain could be relieved by such stimulation. Stimulation of other centres produced unpleasant feelings, even the emotions of rage and fear. When self-stimulation was permitted, patients chose to stimulate the former rather than the latter centres. However, there is no evidence as to whether self-stimulation of this kind could motivate other types of behaviour. And indeed it has been argued that pleasure is an essentially passive state, no more than an accompaniment to the achievement of homeostasis and the relaxation of tensions.

In contrast to the theories of the motivation of behaviour by emotion, some psychologists, notably Young, consider that emotions, as distinct from feelings of pleasure and unpleasure, actually disrupt and disorganize positive activity and render behaviour maladaptive.[7] Young is referring principally to the more violent forms of unpleasant emotion, such as strong fear or anger; and, as we have seen, panic and rage undoubtedly lead to extreme disorganization and to behaviour which may be quite inappropriate to the situation. But it may be the excess of emotional excitement which is disruptive—the 'over-arousal' described in the next chapter. Mild degrees of fear and anger may stimulate and reinforce well-planned adaptive behaviour. However, it has been suggested that even comparatively slight degrees of emotion may narrow the range of attention, which becomes funnelled and concentrated upon some central event, while peripheral events are ignored or overlooked.[11] This may have the effect that an individual performs better than normally the main task upon which he is engaged; but if it is necessary occasionally to respond to peripheral cues, performance of these responses will deteriorate. If emotional stress increases, more and more aspects of an activity will be affected until finally it becomes completely disorganized. This is particularly likely to happen in anxious individuals; whereas confident and well-motivated individuals may maintain organized behaviour in conditions of great stress.

It is difficult to say whether the same effects occur in the pleasurable emotions. It would seem that we often act more effectively when we are 'on top of the world'. Great love and devotion may enable people to perform feats of which they would otherwise be incapable. But perhaps here also it is the central activity performance of which is improved, while other peripheral aspects are disregarded.

2. EMOTIONAL EXPRESSION

There are certain types of activity which appear to accompany emotion as such, though they are not necessarily involved in other forms of motivated behaviour. These have been studied extensively. The first is emotional expression, in facial expression, gestures and modifications of speech. Certain of the simpler emotions, fear and anger in particular, are associated with quite specific and characteristic patterns of emotional expression. There are also other patterns, perhaps less clearly definable, in joy, surprise, sorrow, disgust, contempt, etc.

It is difficult at first to understand what functional significance emotional expression may have—what use it is to the individual other than perhaps giving him a means of 'letting off steam' and decreasing internal tension. Darwin, in *The Expression of the Emotions in Man and Animals*, postulated a direct biological utility for emotional expression.[12] For instance, the angry dog bares its teeth and growls, and its tail stiffens and hair bristles, thus making it more frightening to its enemies. It expresses the opposite emotion, friendliness, by antithetically opposite expressions, crouching, drooping the body and wagging the tail. Though possibly an angry man also looks more frightening and a submissive man more ingratiating, the theory is nevertheless distinctly fanciful.

It is possible that the most important function of emotional expression is the communication of emotion to others. When other people recognize that someone is angry or afraid, a child particularly, they may do something to relieve his emotion. They may help him to escape or to overcome obstacles. At least they may be sympathetic and consoling, for instance at the sight of sorrow. This implies that particular facial expressions, gestures, etc., uniformly express the same emotions in everyone, and that they are easily identifiable. This is probably true of the simpler emotions. Thus typical in anger are flushing, frowning, clenching of the fists and teeth, a rise in the pitch and intensity of the voice. A man with whom the author was acquainted could always be seen to be annoyed from the pink flush that spread over his bald head. But sometimes only the raised voice is noticeable. Fear is perhaps identified by blanching and sweating, dropping of the corners of the mouth, starting of the eyeballs, rigidity, a thin high-pitched voice. In joy, there is relaxation and smiling.

However, some experimenters have suggested that emotional expressions cannot easily be recognized by others if the situation which is stimulating emotion is not apparent. Emotional states shown in photographs are not always identifiable, though markedly different emotions such as love, fear, anger and disgust can usually be distinguished.[13] But it is possible that in real-life situations we may be able to recognize the whole moving pattern of facial expression, gesture and voice, which provides far more evidence as to the nature of the emotional state than does a photograph. It should also be noted that if someone is posed for a photograph, they are apt to assume what they suppose to be the characteristic expression, the conventional appearance of a 'ham' actor simulating an emotion.

There has also been considerable disagreement as to whether these emotional expressions are innate and develop spontaneously, or whether children acquire them by imitation. It would seem, however, that even blind infants, who cannot imitate, express the simpler emotions such as anger and sadness in much the same manner as sighted infants, though perhaps somewhat less clearly.[14] It is possible therefore that emotional expression becomes to some extent stereotyped by imitation. In the expression of the more complex emotions, imitation may play a greater part. Thus it is stated that these modes of expression differ in different cultures.

3. PHYSIOLOGICAL PROCESSES IN EMOTION

A great deal of theorizing and experiment have been devoted to the physiological changes which take place internally in emotion. We are often aware in strong emotion that breathing and beating of the heart become quicker; the muscles become tense; we begin to sweat; and there is a fluttering or churned-up feeling in the abdominal regions. It should be noted, however, that different people vary in their awareness of these sensations. Nevertheless, one of the earliest theories as to the nature of emotion, the James–Lange theory, was based upon this awareness, together with awareness of the expressive gestures. William James and the Swedish physiologist, Carl Lange, postulated at about the same time, though with somewhat different emphasis, that our sensations of the bodily changes following the perception of an emotional stimulus in fact constituted the emotion.[15] Thus the experience of emotion was a pattern of sensations, and no other feelings were involved.

Now however important these sensations, it is obvious that emotional experiences differ quite clearly from each other, and that we have no difficulty in discriminating even between the unpleasant emotions such as anger and fear. Yet the bodily processes, and the sensations derived from them, may be very similar. Moreover, as Cannon pointed out, animals may continue to show overt expression of emotion even when the nervous connections between the brain and the internal organs have been severed.[16] Later evidence has shown that human beings may also continue to experience emotion after spinal injury has cut off internal sensation. Moreover, the experience of emotion commonly begins before the bodily changes are well under way.

Cannon investigated many of the physiological changes which normally accompany emotion, and particularly the emotions of fear and anger. He studied these in animals, for instance, in cats confined by a harness or confronted by a barking dog. He concluded that such stimuli aroused the emergency reactions and the accompanying emotions of fear and anger. In these situations, nerve impulses from the hypothalamus were conveyed by the sympathetic nervous system to the internal organs of the body. The sympathetic nervous system is one branch of the autonomic nervous system which, as its name conveys, is not under voluntary control as are the nerve impulses producing movements of the limbs, etc. Thus automatically the heart beat faster and more deeply, increasing blood pressure; digestion was stopped in order that its blood supply could circulate to the muscles and brain. Furthermore, the suprarenal gland was stimulated to secrete a substance, adrenalin, which circulated in the blood stream. This not only reinforced and maintained the same processes as the sympathetic nervous system, but also caused a breakdown of glycogen in the liver, which was conveyed as sugar to the muscles, to supply them with a source of energy. Other concomitant changes were an increase in the rate of breathing, pupil dilatation and the secretion of sweat.

When the emergency had passed, the parasympathetic nervous system, the other branch of the autonomic nervous system, came into action. Nerve impulses to the internal organs slowed down breathing and the action of the heart, and restored digestion and the storage of glycogen in the liver. The parasympathetic nervous system also operated in pleasurable states, including sexual activity.

The biological utility of the physiological emergency reactions is obvious. A threatening stimulus mobilizes the energy of the body to take immediate action, by flight or fight. The muscles and the brain are well supplied with blood containing the oxygen necessary for liberation of energy. If, however, these are not utilized in immediate action, the continued physiological processes may arouse sensations which reinforce the emotional patterns associated with action or frustrated action.

However, Cannon's theory was too simple. Extensive later experiments have shown that not all the physiological processes described occur in every state of strong emotion, even in every state of fear or anger.[17] Or some may occur to a greater degree than others. Some experimenters have found that blood pressure increases more in anger than in fear, but heart rate increases more in fear than in anger. Others have shown that in fear increase of blood pressure is produced by constriction of the blood vessels; in anger, by faster pumping of the heart. Again, although sympathetically induced changes may predominate, parasympathetic processes occur also. In anger there is flushing of the skin caused by dilatation of the blood vessels of the skin, which is usually attributed to parasympathetic activity. Some experimenters have found that the blood supply to the digestive organs may be increased. Fear, accompanied by blanching due to constriction of the skin blood vessels, is supposed to involve mainly sympathetic activity. Yet it would seem probable that even if this is the case in violent avoiding activity, such as panic flight, the 'sham dead' reaction must involve parasympathetic activity, which also gives rise to urination, defaecation and possibly vomiting. Another theory is that the responses occurring in fear and anxiety are produced by adrenalin secretion; whereas those in anger are due to nor-adrenalin, also secreted by the suprarenal glands, or to mixed adrenalin and nor-adrenalin secretion.[18]

Clearly there is much disagreement as to the cause of these physiological reactions in emotion. Moreover, they may differ in different persons. Thus it was found that individuals judged by psychiatrists to be more prone to anxiety than to aggression tended to show relatively high adrenalin secretion after harassment; whereas those more prone to aggression than to anxiety had relatively higher nor-adrenalin secretion.[19] Again, whereas sympathetic activity was found to predominate in both rage and fear in normal individuals, parasympathetic activity predominated in neurotics who were more prone to withdrawal than to violent action.[20]

Other emotional and motivational states show similar mixed patterns of sympathetic and parasympathetic activity, for instance sexual behaviour. In pain, there are some sympathetic processes, increased blood pressure and decreased skin resistance due to sweating, but others are missing. In sorrow, a relatively passive emotion, parasympathetic activity seems to predominate, and the same may be true of joy. But when the latter leads to actively joyful and euphoric behaviour, sympathetic activity becomes predominant.

Some experimenters have found that the pattern of physiological changes differs to a greater extent in different individuals in the same situation than in the same person in different situations. Thus Lacey found that one individual might show consistently little change of blood pressure and skin resistance, but great change of heart rate and great variability; another, almost the reverse pattern; a third, little change in heart rate but great changes in blood pressure and skin resistance.[21] In a later experiment, Lacey and Lacey showed the occurrence of characteristic patterns of change in blood pressure, heart rate and skin resistance which were consistent for some individuals in pain (caused by putting the foot in icy water), and in performing two tasks, mental arithmetic and word association.[22] But there were no consistent differences between situations, except for a very small number of individuals. One generalization could be made: those who showed a marked increase of blood pressure and decrease of skin resistance in anticipation of the painful stimulus, possibly as the result of fear, had comparatively small changes when it was actually applied.

However, there is one considerable objection to these studies of variation in physiological processes, which is that reports were rarely obtained as to what emotion was actually felt in the various situations.

Thus we have seen that even the threat of pain may produce different emotional reactions in different people. Again, when an experimenter seeks to arouse aggression through attack and frustration, the result in some people may be greater effort, in others anger and aggression, in still others anxiety. Thus it is possible that recorded variations in physiological processes may in fact be due to individual differences in emotional reaction. This is supported by observations which indicated a rise in heart rate in those who responded aggressively to critical attack; but no rise in those who reacted submissively.[23]

According to Cannon, these physiological processes, and also those associated with emotional expression, are mediated principally by the hypothalamus.[16] This centre not only controls these processes, but also imparts the peculiar quality of emotional feeling to the internal sensations. Normally emotional activity is under cortical control, but this is released in violent emotion. Cannon's evidence was that when the hypothalamus was severely injured, emotional feeling was impaired; but if the nerve tract between the cortex and the hypothalamus was injured, cortical control was released and excessive emotionality occurred. However, subsequent experimental evidence has shown that this theory also is too simple.[20] Although emotional expression and the physiological processes may be organized by the hypothalamus, cortical mechanisms in the limbic and other areas stimulate and control these. Thus it has been shown that injuries in certain parts of the limbic area may lead either to rage or to increased docility both in man and in other animals. Direct electrical stimulation may also produce emotional states, though there is considerable disagreement as to the nature of these and as to the areas stimulated. That other cortical areas are also involved was shown in a striking experiment by Klüver and Bucy.[24] They found that surgical removal of large areas of the temporal lobes, and parts of the associated limbic area, destroyed normal emotional reactions in monkeys. Not only did the animals show lack of fear and anger; but also they appeared to lose the capacity for evaluation and selectivity of objects. They were restless and hyperactive, and attended to everything that came their way, examining it and putting it in their mouths. Moreover, their sexual behaviour also became quite undiscriminating. It would appear that, even if the affective and motor aspects of emotion depend on the functions of the hypothalamus and the limbic area, emotional evaluation of environmental stimuli involves other parts of the cortex. Thus it has been hypothesized that there is a hierarchy of nerve centres in operation, including the temporal and frontal cortex, the limbic area, the hypothalamus and the reticular formation. The functions of the latter will be discussed in the next chapter.

Further evidence is given by the experiments of Schachter as to the primary importance of the higher brain centres in perceiving and evaluating the emotional significance of situations.[25] In his experiments, people were first given an injection of adrenalin which, as we saw, stimulates and reinforces the action of the sympathetic nervous system in producing the physiological changes characteristic of certain emotions. Some of these people were told that the effect of the injection might be to increase the heart rate and produce flushing of the face. Others were incorrectly informed that they might experience numbness of the feet, itching sensations and a slight headache; while a third group was given no advance information. In half of these cases, each individual was taken into a room in which a confederate of the experimenter proceeded to behave in a euphoric manner, with various kinds of tomfoolery. In the other half, each individual was confronted by a confederate who behaved angrily and aggressively. Those who had been given no advance information, and still more those who had been misinformed as to the effects of adrenalin, experienced euphoria in the euphoric situation and anger in the angry situation; and they behaved in the same manner. Those who had been correctly informed as to the effects of adrenalin showed this behaviour to only a mild extent. In all cases there was in fact an increase in pulse rate as the result of the adrenalin injection. Another group of people were placed in the same situations after having been injected with a salt solution instead of adrenalin. They conformed to some extent to the behaviour of the confederates, but without the strong emotional feelings and with no increase of pulse rate.

Schachter therefore concluded that a state of arousal or emotional excitement may be produced by adrenalin, and the consequent activation of the sympathetic nervous system. But the nature of the emotion experienced depends partly on what an individual expects to feel, and partly on the type of emotional stimulus to which he is subjected, particularly when this stimulus is provided by some kind of social situation. Other experiments have also shown that emotional moods are determined to a considerable extent by the social situation one encounters.

In the next chapter we shall consider the processes of arousal and excitement which occur not only in emotion, but also in other situations.

4. COMPLEX EMOTIONS

Some emotional states appear to be compounded of simpler emotions, reinforcing or conflicting with each other. One such is jealousy, which as we saw might appear as early as the second year of life. It seems to be compounded of fierce and possessive love for a particular person—in early years the mother—together with fear that she may withdraw her love; and anger against some person who is the cause of this withdrawal.

Thus a child of about two years and upwards may be jealous of a new baby when he fears that his mother has withdrawn her love from him and is giving all her care and affection to the baby. This jealousy is closely related to separation anxiety.

In other complex emotions, it is difficult to discover any simpler concomitants. Thus the experiences of, for instance, admiration, respect, gratitude, sympathy, compassion, pity, contempt, envy and so on are readily identifiable, but they cannot be analysed into constituent simpler emotions. In some cases they are associated with particular types of behaviour; we instanced above sympathy and compassion (p. 72). They may occur in conjunction with some type of social motivation, to be described in Chapter 7. In some cases they have characteristic modes of emotional expression. But it is not possible to state whether or not they are associated with any specific physiological changes other than those caused by general arousal. Nevertheless they are of great importance in reinforcing social motivation, the more so that they themselves are more closely identified with the self than are emotions such as fear and rage. The latter we feel often as temporary emotional outbursts, belonging as it were to the primitive part of the personality which is normally kept under control. Subsequently we may wish to dissociate ourselves from them.

Two important emotional states normally associated with some type of emotional conflict are shame and guilt. Shame appears to be the more primitive of the two, engendered by a fear of exposing weakness or inferiority, or of showing childish impulsiveness and lack of control, in a manner which invites social contempt, and thus constitutes a threat to prestige and social status. The criterion appears to be what is socially approved and admired. Guilt, however, relates to the abrogation of moral values. The individual is conscious that his impulsive tendencies have led, or may lead, him to transgress against the moral standards maintained by the super-ego or conscience. Whether or not the latter, as the Freudians postulate, arises through introjection of parental commands and prohibitions to forestall retaliatory punishment, it would seem that guilt is caused by actual or imagined disobedience to the demands of an internal monitor incorporated within the self, and not merely to some external authority. Moreover, there would appear to be a close identification of the internal monitor with parental standards, since it is particularly forceful in children who are treated lovingly by their parents, and feel strong affection for them, but are fearful of losing their affection as the result of disobedience; for instance, if in their words or behaviour they appear to threaten with the loss of their love. Guilt feelings may be alleviated as the child grows up in so far as he identifies himself with a positive 'ego-ideal', and imitates the behaviour of admired persons, thus reinforcing his moral standards. But if the childish conscience is retained, with a severe and punitive enforcement of moral prohibitions, guilt may be frequent and excessive, and may inhibit activity of a kind which is seldom disapproved socially, except in very Puritanical circles. It is also likely to be associated with anxiety, a fear of retaliatory punishment for wrong actions. As the child grows up, his moral standards become based, not simply on the commands and prohibitions of the parents, but on those of society generally. However, he cannot avoid guilt, as he can shame, by mere outward social conformity, because the criterion and judgment of good behaviour are internalized. As we noted, it is particularly likely to arise in connection with repressed aggression and morally disapproved sexual activity.

Many people are prone to experience emotional moods or dispositions. That is to say, they are not continuously conscious of a particular emotion, but they are readily aroused to it by some very slight stimulus. This need not be an external event; it may be a recollection or a thought. Some of the commonest moods are: cheerfulness, irritability, depression. Anxiety may also occur as a mood of prolonged diffuse fear, often experienced when it has no obvious cause, and characterized by continual attempts at or hopes of avoiding social punishment or disapproval, rather than the avoidance of physical danger. We shall consider it again in Chapter 9.

There are cases in which these moods are engendered by temporary physiological states. Thus anxiety and depression occur in illness, or perhaps more often during the period of recovery from illness. But more commonly they are associated with the temperamental disposition, that is to say, the innate emotionality, which is not greatly modified by learning. It has been found that there are characteristic individual differences in temperament. Some people are readily aroused to feel emotion, and their emotions are strong and difficult to keep under control. Others are more placid, and their emotions are relatively weak. Again, there are temperamental differences in prevailing mood, and in particular between the predominantly cheerful or irascible, on the one hand, and the fearful and depressed, on the other.[26] It would appear that the former persons tend to be more active and outgoing, readily showing overt expression of their emotions. The latter are inwardly directed, with emotion which may be strongly felt but not openly expressed. This is of course much the same as the introvert-extravert dichotomy. However, it should be emphasized these are highly simplified classifications or types of temperamental tendency, and the majority of people fall into intermediate classes, varying in their emotionality and the manner of expressing it according to the situation. For the same reason, the associations which have been suggested between temperamental types and types of physique must also be regarded with caution. Even if on the whole the extroverted or sthenic tend to have short rounded bodies with a good deal of fat, while the introverted or asthenic are thin and scraggy, the correspondence is not very close. Neither has Kretschmer's hypothesis, that the rounded body is related to the violent mood swings of manic-depressive insanity, and the thin body with the withdrawal and emotional poverty of schizophrenia, been substantiated by later enquiry.[27] Equal caution must be maintained in accepting the more elaborate classification of Sheldon, which associates a rounded body with cheerfulness and pleasure-seeking, a strong muscular body with activeness and aggression, and a small thin body with timidity and withdrawal.[28] Moreover, in these cases the appropriate type of behaviour may have been acquired; for instance, the strong muscular individual is more likely to be successful in active pursuits.

Attempts have also been made to associate temperamental disposition with predominance of internal secretion of certain hormones; for instance, prevalence of nor-adrenalin secretion with impulsiveness and aggression, and of adrenalin secretion with fearfulness. Again there is no reliable evidence for such an association; and it could equally be true that the frequency of aggression causes the prevalence of nor-adrenalin secretion, and vice-versa.

Finally, these temperamental dispositions do not necessarily have any very close relationship to individual differences in predominant motivation, at least of the more complex and highly developed type to be discussed in the following chapters.

6

ACTIVATION, AROUSAL, EXPLORATION
AND COMPETENCE

I. ACTIVATION

There has been greatly increased interest in recent years in the general
activation of the body which is essential, not only in emotion, but in all
waking behaviour as contrasted with sleep. There is in fact a continuum
of levels of activation from sleep and drowsiness through increasing
degrees of attention and activity to extreme effort and violent emotional
outbursts. A high degree of activation occurs in strongly motivated
behaviour; and it has been equated with general drive state (see Chapter
1). Fundamentally degree or level of activation depends on the physiological metabolism of the body, and the amount of energy it can supply.
Thus, when food supply is reduced below a certain level, activation and
capacity for work decrease. But how this energy is applied, and how
activation develops in particular circumstances, is controlled largely
through the brain, which determines what is needed and what is appropriate. This direction of energy is associated with arousal or alerting to
particular situations and activities. Although the terms 'activation' and
'arousal' are often used synonymously, it is convenient to apply the
former to the utilization of energy in various forms of behaviour; and
the latter to direction of attention and activity.

Comparatively recently it has been discovered that there exists a special
centre in the brain which is the controlling mechanism for activation and
arousal. This is the reticular formation, a mass of nervous tissue in the
centre of the brain stem. It appears to regulate the extent to which consciousness is aroused to attention, and also the amount and type of bodily
activity appropriate for reaction. It interacts with the cortex, which perceives and determines the meaning and significance of sensory stimulation
both from the outside world and also from the body itself; and with the
limbic area and the hypothalamus, which are involved in emotional and
motivational processes. Adrenalin and other hormonal secretions may also
affect reticular activity. Any injury to the reticular formation, and the
effects of drugs such as the barbiturates, dull consciousness and may induce
long periods of sleep. Direct stimulation of the reticular formation increases alertness, and may make perception more rapid and more sensitive.
It is particularly alive to novel or changing stimulation, whereas it may

cease to respond to monotonously repeated or unchanging stimulation. It may also provide prior entry to the cortex of certain kinds of sensory stimulation, especially pain, while inhibiting response to stimulation of relative unimportance.

Thus in the waking state the brain is aroused to receive and react to incoming stimulation. The degree or level of arousal of the cortex may be assessed directly by recording the electroencephalogram (EEG), which shows the rhythmical waves of nervous activity in the cortex. On arousal from sleep, the long slow wave formations of sleep are replaced by the rather quicker and less profound but still rhythmical alpha waves. But if the individual then begins to make any mental or physical effort, the alpha waves disappear, and there appears a complicated pattern of more rapid, less strong and desynchronized discharges, the beta waves. Thus it is possible to judge when an individual is in a relaxed state, and when he begins to attend to anything at all closely. Thereafter, varying degrees of activation and energy mobilization may take place.

Duffy in particular has been concerned to demonstrate the manner in which all motivated and emotional behaviour is characterized, not only by its direction—in hunger, sex, fear, etc.—but also by its degree of activation in terms of energy mobilization, forcefulness, excitement, and so on.[1] Activation varies with the degree of stimulation provided by the existing situation, and also with the individual himself and his psychological appraisal of the situation. Thus any task which is arduous or difficult for *him*, or anything which prevents him from achieving motivational goals, produces a high degree of activation. Those with a high level of achievement motivation are more highly activated than are those with a lower level, especially when they expect success; they mobilize more energy throughout the performance of a task.[2] It would seem possible that there are other important differences in activation associated with differences in motivational strength.

Sometimes, particularly in frustration and fatigue, mobilized energy is directed towards emotional display, rather than into task performance. In general, behaviour is most effective at moderate levels of activation, and sensitivity is also greatest. The optimal level varies for different activities, and appears to be somewhat lower for intellectual and highly skilled activities than for others. At low levels, there is sluggishness; at high levels, intense excitement and the inappropriate disorganized type of behaviour described in the previous chapter. Thus it could be suggested that emotionally determined behaviour ceases to be adaptive at the point at which activation rises above the optimal level. However, Bindra has suggested that the degree of organization of emotional and motivated behaviour may constitute a dimension independent of activation.[3]

Levels of activation cannot be directly measured; still less is it possible to determine exactly what is the optimum level in any given case. But change in level may be assessed from the changing internal physiological processes described in the last chapter. Important are the changes in circulation of the blood, in blood pressure and heart rate. But it is often difficult to determine the significance of these in terms of general activation, and as we have seen they tend to vary according to the situation and the individual. Thus one hypothesis is that increase in heart rate results from emotional involvement in any motivated behaviour. That this is partly but not entirely true seems to be shown by the changes in heart rate of individuals who discussed their philosophy of life with someone who criticized it and attacked them abusively; subsequently, they could defend themselves against this criticism.[4] The heart rate rose considerably through excitement in anticipation of this discussion; it remained at much the same level throughout the criticism, although this usually aroused anger; and rose to a still higher level when they subsequently defended themselves aggressively and with considerable verbal forcefulness. This rise did not appear in those who responded submissively. Thus the greatest effect was produced by the activity rather than by the emotion.

However, other observations have suggested that an increased heart rate accompanies the rejection of unpleasant stimulation, and also concentration on mental work such as mental arithmetic; whereas a decreased heart rate occurs when the individual is viewing or listening to external environmental stimuli, or is pleasantly affected by them.[5]

More reliable measures of activation as such are: the degree and fluctuation of tension in the muscles of the limbs; and the electrical conductance or resistance of the skin of the hands (see footnote, p. 52). Thus muscle tension increases and skin resistance decreases in states of alertness and of interest; and in difficult tasks when these require effort. In fact, there may be decreases of resistance in response to any task which is seen to be challenging. Again, it has been found in motor car drivers that a decrease occurred whenever some event took place which required attention and appropriate responses, such as the perception of traffic lights or of traffic turning in from a side road.[6] Such changes also occur when annoyance or anxiety are stimulated, for instance in pilots landing or taking off aircraft.[7] But muscle tension also tends to be high on beginning a task, and to decrease as the individual becomes more familiar with it, or achieves his goal. Emotional and unstable individuals are quickly aroused, showing more rapid and more variable changes in the physiological indices than do more placid and stable individuals, and also taking longer to return to the resting level of activation after emotional stress. But in the very placid, activation may be inadequate to perform monotonous tasks with efficiency. The actions of the unstable tend to be impulsive and erratic, as the result of over-activation; whereas those of the more stable are well controlled and coordinated. But even in the latter, activation is regulated more appropriately when behaviour is directed towards a well-defined goal; whereas there may be disorganization when there is a conflict of goals. Activation may be increased by a strong incentive. Thus although the work output of German civilians during the war was in general limited by the amount of energy available to them from their limited food supplies, it did increase when they were promised cigarettes as an incentive.[8] But in consequence their body weight fell.

We may perhaps conclude that much of the observations on internal physiological changes which we considered in the last chapter relates in fact to this process of activation. But activation produces not only the excitement of emotional states, but also the energy on which motivated behaviour is based, including the performance of interesting and strenuous tasks.

2. AROUSAL

Extensive investigations have been carried out into the various causes of increase in arousal and attention. Intense, novel and changing stimulation is the primary cause. We saw that even the infant 'oriented' towards sudden and unexpected stimuli, such as noises and bright lights, often showing a startle response. This type of arousal appears throughout life. But a selective arousal also begins early in life, first towards stimuli which are meaningful to the infant, such as the mother's voice; and secondly towards novel stimuli. However, if they are excessively novel, they produce over-arousal and fear responses. Repetition of an initially fear-provoking stimulus may lead to decrease in fear and the appearance of attention and interest, but this is not always so (see footnote, p. 21). Finally, habituation, with loss of interest and attention, may supervene. Something novel in a familiar situation is likely to produce arousal, but again there may be over-arousal, as in the case of Hebb's chimpanzees who were terrified by the appearance of their keeper in strange clothes.[9]

As the child grows up and his range of familiarity broadens, the circumstances of arousal and fear naturally change. Arousal continues to be caused by novel and intense stimuli, and by movement and variation. But again meaningfulness and interest are important, and also unexpectedness—a discrepancy with the familiar and what was expected to occur. Such stimuli may cause also a shock of surprise, perhaps followed by pleasure at something new and interesting, and then failure of interest if the stimulus is indefinitely repeated. This was demonstrated in an experiment in which a sentence completion task followed the presentation of an unexpected number series; the sentences were completed to have pleasant meanings.[10] But when the number series was expected, the sentences were completed to have relatively unpleasant meanings. Similar effects appeared in studies of adult chimpanzees. They were presented with pairs of objects for short periods of time; and they usually looked longer at the more changeable and movable objects, and manipulated them more extensively.[11] But also they changed frequently from one object to another. And whenever a totally new set of objects was introduced, or even the colours of the objects altered, examining and manipulation increased in amount.

The effects of lack of variation on arousal are demonstrated in the performance of tasks which lack any intrinsic interest, but involve responding over long periods of time to repeatedly appearing signals. Such situations have been investigated in 'vigilance' tasks, which test ability to maintain vigilance or awareness and alertness. The prototype experiment was carried out by Mackworth, in his 'clock' tests. A pointer rotated on a disc like the face of a clock, in a series of small jumps.[12] But every now and then, at irregular intervals, the hand made a double jump, and a reaction was required to each of these by pressing a key. After about half an hour individuals began to miss these signals; and the number of omissions increased steadily over a two-hour period. The increase was due partly to the irregularity of the signals, so that it was impossible to anticipate when they would appear; and partly to the fact that they were not very noticeable. But also it was shown in this and in subsequent experiments of the same kind that, if some incentive was introduced, there was little or no decline in vigilance. One incentive was to inform the observer whenever he had missed a signal, thus telling him if he were doing well or badly. Thus arousal decreased in the monotonous and uninteresting task, but the decrease was prevented by an increase in motivation. A recent study showed that the EEG rhythm decreased in frequency as vigilance declined.[13]

The most striking illustration of decrease in arousal occurred in the so-called 'sensory deprivation' experiments carried out at McGill University.[14] Here each experimental observer was paid at a high rate to remain confined alone in a small chamber continuously for several days. He lay flat on a bed, with goggles over his eyes which transmitted only a blur of light; he could hear only a steady hum of noise; and his hands were covered so that he could touch nothing. For a while he slept much. But then sleep became difficult; he became bored and restless, and was unable to think continuously or to concentrate. Thus his intelligence test performance deteriorated. Subsequent experiments showed that this completely unvarying type of stimulation produced greater and more disagreeable effects than did complete darkness and silence. Nor was a random pattern of lights much preferable, because it was meaningless.

The EEG rhythm decreased in frequency and the incidence of alpha rhythm and even slower rhythms increased, indicating a decline in arousal. It is likely that activation in general declined in many of these experiments as the result of restricted movement, for the effects of such restriction seemed particularly severe. The restlessness which appeared, and is indeed frequent in any boring situation, may have indicated an attempt to raise activation. But there were considerable individual differences. Some people appeared able to relax, follow their own trains of thought, and tolerate a low level of activation. Others however reacted by sudden increases of activation, shown in desynchronization of the EEG, accompanied by emotional outbursts which might become so panic stricken that the individual was obliged to give up the experiment. This happened particularly in the highly active, or the anxious and emotionally unstable; whereas more placid, stable and dependent individuals could continue to tolerate the conditions. Studies of men living in the Antarctic have shown a similar lack of resistance to the monotonous conditions of life there in the over-active and unstable.

The effect of long-term sensory deprivation was demonstrated in monkeys reared in complete darkness or unpatterned light for 16 months from birth.[15] Thereafter they showed an exceptional eagerness in pressing a lever which opened a door giving them a view of their surroundings.

A milder reaction to monotony appeared in an experiment in which the T.A.T. was used, in the same manner as described previously. After listening to a dull and repetitive story, individuals who experienced this as monotonous subsequently included an increased number of references to the desire for novelty in their T.A.T. stories; but the latter exhibited less novelty and originality than after more stimulating activities.[16]

3. PLAY AND VARIETY

The experiments just described demonstrate the unhappy state of those who are confined like prisoners or restricted to very monotonous living conditions. Fortunately most of us are able to live in surroundings which provide us with an adequate amount of variation and interest. It would appear that the need for variety may express itself in three different ways: (1) the desire for environmental conditions that in themselves afford novelty and variety, which are then experienced relatively passively; (2) curiosity appearing in active exploration of the environment; and (3) active use of the cognitive processes, and especially the imagination, to provide unusual, original and stimulating ideas. In an experiment using the T.A.T., it was found that the appearances of these tendencies were relatively uncorrelated.[17] Thus it would seem that some people are able to create variety and novelty for themselves, either by exploring the environment or by producing their own interesting ideas. But others who cannot do this are dependent on variety in conditions which come to them.

We noted that young children not only welcomed novel experiences, but also actively investigated and explored their surroundings, and especially any unfamiliar objects they contained. Some older children and adults continue to show exploratory behaviour and to exercise their imaginations; but others may desire to be provided with variety and novelty. If they are not, they may become listless, apathetic and lacking in effort; or they may revolt against such situations by constant change of occupation or even by destructive activities. Undoubtedly there are individual differences in the desire for novelty and variety. Whereas some people seem to desire continual change, others seem to prefer the unchanging and the familiar. But it is possible that in many cases they have in childhood been restricted or over-protected and not encouraged to be adventurous and independent.[10] Or they have lacked security and affection, and are therefore likely to be fearful of the strange and unfamiliar.

But as we saw (p. 22), play activities in children did not depend solely on exploration of the novel, but occurred in so far as objects and situations afforded diverse possibilities for bodily activity, manipulation, etc. It may be that play in adults also depends on the possibility of making slight variations in familiar modes of action. But usually there is in the play activities of adults, as in those of children, a relaxation of tension, and therefore perhaps a decrease of activation; whereas it is high in the initial investigation of novelty. And it would seem that play activity is enjoyable for itself and is an end in itself; it does not lead to the expression and satisfaction of other motivational tendencies, even curiosity. Hence little motivational tension is involved. So also we may either actively and purposively seek for original images and ideas; or employ them playfully. But these playful activities may serve as substitutes for more realistic motivated behaviour, and enable us to discharge tensions arising from frustrated motivated behaviour (see Chapter 9).

4. EXPLORATION AND COMPETENCE

Though exploratory behaviour may in part be aimed at obtaining novelty, its principal function seems to be to gain an understanding of the environment, and the capacity to make use of it more effectively. In the first place, people appear to be motivated towards the acquisition of information which reduces uncertainty as to the nature of their surroundings, and resolves any conflict between competing interpretations. Thus it was found that in experimental situations people shown pairs of patterns spent more time looking spontaneously at complex irregular patterns than at simple regular ones, since a longer examination was needed to perceive fully the shapes of the former.[18] The same behaviour occurred with incongruous material, such as pictures of the head of one animal attached to the body of another; prolonged inspection was needed to resolve the incongruity. Moreover, such persistent perception might be necessary to overcome a conflict between competing responses, since the individual until he was certain what the stimulus was would not know how to respond to it. This motivation towards achieving an understanding of the nature and causes of events appears, as we have shown, particularly strongly in the curiosity and exploration of children. It tends to die down at adolescence, and to remain at only a moderate level in the lives of most adults. But in a relatively small number of people it remains high throughout life, appearing in a strong and persistent interest in invention, discovery, scientific research and the pursuit of truth.

Manipulative behaviour, as we noted, may also be employed in attempts to discover the nature and properties of objects. But it leads additionally to constructive activities to which certain people are especially strongly motivated; for instance, carpenters, machine makers, engineers, architects and painters. Indeed, the writer may be said to enjoy constructing in words, and the composer in musical sounds. But everyone is to some extent concerned to develop the capacity to manipulate the objects in his environment. Indeed, Woodworth, in his 'behaviour primacy theory', suggested that the most fundamental type of motivated behaviour takes the form of attempts to deal effectively with the environment.[19] Such behaviour is not random, but directed, selective and persistent. On the same idea is based White's concept of 'competence': that directed and persistent behaviour is carried on in order to interact effectively with the environment and to master it.[20] Indeed, he supposes that the growth and maturation of the ego depend on the successful development of competent activity. This behaviour includes not only investigation, exploration and manipulation, but also the employment of strength and skill in the control of the environment and of the body.

However, it is not possible, at least at present, to trace any direct relationship between arousal and activation on the one hand, and exploratory and manipulative behaviour on the other. It may be that strong exploratory motivation is associated with a high capacity for arousal and activation; or it may be that in some people activation is employed in such motivated behaviour, rather than in other forms. As we shall see in Chapter 8, certain people with outstanding interest and skill in scientific discovery appear to possess both marked exploratory motivation and also a high degree of energy and persistence in pursuing such discovery. Perhaps in less outstanding cases, there may be interest and skill but less activation of energy. In those in whom activation is low, exploration is replaced by desire for relatively passive experience of environmental variation; for instance, by going on a cruise rather than undertaking an adventure! However, these suggestions are highly speculative. But it would appear to be generally true that exploratory and constructive activities are satisfying in themselves even when there is no immediate achievement of the ends foreseen. Indeed, one achievement is likely to lead on to others. Thus the behaviour is self-perpetuating, and is not terminated by any specific consummatory acts such as food consumption or the avoidance of danger. And by pursuing this behaviour for itself and not for the attainment of any specific goal, intelligence and personality are developed, enlarged and strengthened.

7

SOCIAL MOTIVATION

I. MEMBERSHIP OF SOCIAL GROUPS

We have considered the early stages of social behaviour in children, and have seen that almost every kind of behaviour is affected by social relationships. In general, children and adults are motivated to behave in such a way as to seek the society of others and to attain social approval and acceptance, and to control and inhibit behaviour which is disapproved by others, and which may even be punished by them, although it may be personally desirable and satisfying. The universality of such motivated behaviour would suggest the existence of innate, or at least fundamentally based, motivation. This would include both the tendencies to seek social contacts and to live in the society of others; and also to obtain their acceptance and approval. Thus something more than mere gregariousness is involved.

There are occasions on which human beings associate and act together in large unorganized groups which have no permanent existence, such as mobs or crowds, in situations arousing extreme rage or panic fear; for instance in lynching mobs, or in panicking mobs in situations of great danger such as that of a theatre on fire. There are no social attractions or social relationships between the members of these mobs; they combine together, sometimes under a leader, to react by violent action to the emergency situation in which they find themselves, behaving in an uncontrolled manner of which they would be incapable in normal situations. Such mob behaviour is sometimes deliberately prolonged by means of propaganda, as Hitler prolonged and aggravated Nazi mob behaviour, over a considerable period of time.

Rather more normal social attraction operates in crowds, such as audience crowds, members of which collect together to witness some exciting event. Undoubtedly their interest in the event is heightened by their social participation, the feeling that they belong to a large aggregate of people showing common emotions. Nevertheless, such aggregates also have only a temporary existence; and the motivated behaviour of their members is nearer to that of the animal herd than to that of members of the more organized and permanent groups which are such an important feature of human social activity. In the latter there is not mass action, but an interaction between individuals in which they accommodate their

94

behaviour to each other, and often work together to attain a common goal.

Many species of monkey live in permanent and cohesive social groups, as we noted in Chapter 4.[1] Those of baboons are particularly remarkable. They move about large tracts of country in organized groups, mothers and infants in the centre protected by adult males, with other males scouting ahead and protecting the rear. In some cases, 'sentries' are posted to give warning of attack. In this and other species, organization is based on dominance hierarchies, the older and stronger males being at the summit of the hierarchy. Although the cohesiveness and permanence of these groups varies in different species—they are relatively weak in chimpanzees—yet social organization appears to be a prominent characteristic of the sub-human primates. Undoubtedly this social behaviour serves to protect individuals, and especially the young, from the danger of attack; but its permanence and complexity would indicate that social attraction is also directly involved.

It could be argued that the similar tendency of human beings to form and belong to social groups is aimed fundamentally at the attainment of security, as we noted in Chapter 4. The individual becomes securely embedded in the group which supports him in need and protects him from danger. Clearly the helpless human infant would stand little chance of survival unless he were incorporated in the family group. Again, amid the bewildering complexity of modern civilized life, individuals find their roots in family, neighbourhood and national groups. That group membership does provide security is perhaps shown in the increase of group solidarity in groups faced by a common danger. We noted in Chapter 4 that individuals were enabled to tolerate their fears in war-time through their awareness that others were threatened by the same or greater danger. Fears might be lessened by actual social contacts; for instance, in air-raid shelters during bombing. Still stronger was the encouragement derived from active attempts made by groups of people, such as Civil Defence workers, to alleviate the situation and to protect themselves and other sufferers. Membership of small organized social units, such as Air Force squadrons and Army tank crews, increased feelings of participation and belongingness still further, and the consciousness of equally shared hardship and danger maintained morale.[2]

But group membership undoubtedly affords much more than protection against insecurity; it gives positive satisfaction and pleasure. People feel that they 'belong' to a human group and in so doing have a real place among their fellows, with recognized social status. This occurs irrespective of personal feelings of affection and friendship for individual members of the group, though these also may be important. But the loyalty and belongingness inculcated by membership of large institutional groups such as trades unions and political parties may be considerable even though there is little or no personal contact between many of the members. The stronger the feelings of belongingness in group members and of attraction to the group, the more cohesive and permanent the group is likely to be.

Finally, there are many activities carried on by groups which attract people to membership. Indeed, many social groups arise initially with the purpose of performing an activity in which members have a mutual interest. Such are the clubs and societies for sport, drama, music, social and charitable activities of all kinds. Motivation is enhanced, action is more enduring and effortful, satisfaction is increased, when people combine together to promote such activities. Indeed, it might be said that for the majority of human beings such social participation is the most valued and enjoyable part of their lives.

2. THE EFFECTS ON MOTIVATED BEHAVIOUR OF DIFFERENT TYPES OF SOCIAL GROUP

Among all human groups the family is most fundamental, since it moulds the behaviour of the child at his most malleable age. It is not surprising that he grows into family life, and in most cases endeavours to perpetuate it when he is adult. Moreover, as we have noted, the long period of helplessness of the child necessitates prolonged care and protection—though this could of course be carried out by a larger group as it is to some extent in the Israeli Kibbutzin. Nevertheless, the family group appears to be universal in human society, but it does not occur in monkeys and apes. Though the tie between mother and infant is close in these species, pairing between male and female is in most cases impermanent. It was thought at one time that the formation of 'family groups' of one adult male, females and young, was a characteristic feature of group structure in monkeys and apes, but this seems to occur rarely when they are living in the natural state. Moreover, males seldom pay much attention to their offspring, though a baboon may attack anyone who threatens a mother and its infant.[1] However, in many species, notably the langur and baboon, other females are most attentive to and solicitous of an infant, touching, holding and passing it from one to another.

The human family, by contrast, contains not only a mother and children, but also a man, usually the father, whose function it is to maintain and protect them. The period of infancy and helplessness is much longer in humans than in monkeys and apes, and therefore children require protection and support for longer. As we saw in Chapter 2, the influence of family relationships on motivated behaviour, and its adaptation through learning, are far-reaching. The child learns to adapt his behaviour not only to the personal interactions between himself and his parents, but also to the customs of society in general as transmitted to him through their observance of these customs in guiding and controlling him. It is not surprising therefore that in different human societies the manner in which the child is reared and the behaviour he learns from his parents replicates the general pattern of culture of that society. We noted in Chapter 3, for instance, that, according to Margaret Mead, the Arapesh showed great care and tenderness towards their children.[3] These grew up gentle, affectionate and cooperative; but also timid and lacking in initiative, because of their great dependence on their parents. The Mundugumour child, on the other hand, who had never known anything but harshness, became aggressive and individualistic, incapable of much social cooperation. An interesting situation arose in the Samoans.[4] There children were kindly treated, but without much personal affection from the mother. She might from time to time give the infant to other women to look after. And as soon as he was old enough to walk, he spent most of his life in the care of other children. If he was tired of his own family, he might go and live with another. Thus when he grew up, his capacity for social cooperation was considerable, but he lacked the ability for close ties of personal affection. Also he took life as it came, and showed little individual initiative.

There are many examples of such differences in prevailing motivational tendencies in primitive societies. We noted that in our society also there were differences between social classes, for instance in the importance attached to achievement, individual effort, the capacity to postpone immediate gratification for future success, the control of behaviour by internal conscience. There are other differences in internal family relationships which may considerably affect the personalities and motivation of their members, such as the structure of authority within the family. In many European countries, including this country, the enforcement of authority by the father over his wife and children was a marked feature of family life in the past. Families were more closely knit than they generally are today, and the children were dominated over by the father, while the mother was the principal source of care and affection. Hence the Oedipus situation! But nowadays relationships are more egalitarian. Husband and wife may both go out to work and earn; both may share authority, care and affection for the children. But the children may also have more freedom and be more independent of their families than in time past. By contrast, studies of people living in slum areas have shown that there the real head of the family may be 'Mum', who dominates not only over her immediate family, but also over her married daughters' families.[5] This may have an unfortunate effect in restricting their activities and interests, even producing considerable immaturity of personality and lack of personal motivation.

Although the influence of family relationships on the child's motivated behaviour is fundamental and far-reaching, he is also affected from early years by interaction with his contemporaries, as we noted in Chapter 2. Play groups are a prominent feature in the life of monkeys and apes also. The young animal enters one of these as soon as it is able to leave its mother, and lives almost entirely in such a group until it is old enough to mate. In this it acquires a great deal of social learning; and indeed young monkeys do not develop normally if isolated from such a group. So also the human child increasingly conforms in his behaviour to the example of his peers. But the influence of the peer group is often modified by interaction with adults, especially when the child goes to school; and here again social class differences may play a part. He may be educated at a school in which he encounters teachers or children of a different social class. The working-class child may have difficulty in adjusting his behaviour to what is required by his teachers. But, especially if he goes to a school where he mixes with many middle-class children, he may gradually acquire middle-class values, including the emphasis on achievement. The middle-class child may experience a conflict between the behaviour he has been taught at home and the roughness, bad language and dislike of intellectual effort of his working-class companions. Which type of behaviour finally prevails may depend on the occupation which he enters on leaving school, since the social class hierarchy operates again as between professional and similar occupations on the one hand and manual occupations on the other.

But the influence of social group membership operates not only through social class differences. There are many other groups which affect behaviour. There are the adolescent, teen-age and young adult groups, with their 'sub-cultures', which inculcate types of behaviour that often seem weird and repugnant to their elders, as for instance with the 'flower people' and the 'hippies' of 1967. There are institutional groups such as the Churches. Some of the Protestant sects, for instance, impose a strict moral code of behaviour on their members, discouraging not only the sexual freedom which is now so general in society but also the pursuit of pleasure, drinking, gambling and so on. Finally, there are great differences in customary ways of behaving between different regions and countries, so much so that 'national character' differences have been supposed to exist. For instance, it is said that the British and Americans are more apt than are other nationalities in creating and maintaining small social groups of a voluntary character, such as clubs, and encouraging the personal give-and-take and the cooperative activity these necessitate. In other countries, individual activity and self-gratification are restrained, either by family influences, as in France, or by regulation by the state as in Russia.

It is difficult to define specifically what are the exact differences in motivated behaviour arising in these different social groups. Moreover, cutting across them are the influences of personal relationships, in friendship and marriage, and of membership of small informal groups: the groups of men in factory workshops described by Elton Mayo;[6] the clubs and societies; the pub and street groups. There is a tendency in all these for members to conform to a social 'norm' of acceptable behaviour. But as the individual moves from one group to another, and from the 'role' or part he plays in the activities of one to that in another, his socially motivated behaviour varies accordingly. However, to a considerable extent he can choose to become a member of groups in which he can play roles which accord with his interests and other motivational tendencies. It may be only the very withdrawn or the highly aggressive individual who is unable to find a congenial outlet for these. Some sociologists have gone so far as to suggest that personality consists largely in the social roles played by people in their membership of different social groups. But this overlooks the fact that some forms of motivation appear consistently in particular individuals throughout their lives and indeed seem to direct people in the first place to adopt certain social roles by choice.

Finally, motivated behaviour is affected not only by direct social pressure exerted by the groups of which people are members, but also by the immense body of traditions, beliefs and opinions conveyed to them through their families, companions, etc., in childhood; and through the influence of mass media—the press, television, films and books—from childhood upwards. The long-term goals of motivated behaviour are largely determined by interests and sentiments, the aims of which derive in the first place from all these social sources.

3. THE STUDY OF SOCIALLY-MOTIVATED BEHAVIOUR

Although the influence of differences in social group membership is so variable in modern civilized societies, nevertheless certain types of motivated behaviour have been observed to occur fairly generally among their members. These may not appear in everyone, and there is great variation between different individuals in their strength. Some of these individual differences seem to originate in innate temperamental disposition. Others may be the result of upbringing and family relationships, and in some cases it is possible to suggest how this has occurred. Still others may be caused by the social group memberships of adult life; but these at present are little understood.

The most extensive list of types of socially motivated behaviour was drawn up in an investigation of personality characteristics by H. A. Murray and his colleagues.[7] These he labelled 'needs', though they are in fact psychogenic motivational tendencies which must be distinguished from the biological and homeostatic needs, called by Murray 'viscerogenic'. The psychogenic motivational tendencies are directed towards social behaviour and certain other forms of behaviour such as constructiveness and curiosity. Murray does not claim that they are innate, though he would allow that temperamental disposition may be involved; and they do not all occur in everyone. The needs in Murray's list (the terminology of which is sometimes obscure) may be classified as shown in the following table:

H. A. MURRAY'S LIST OF 'NEEDS'

Viscerogenic needs

These are for: air, water, food, sex, lactation, urination and defaecation; for avoidance of danger, unpleasant stimuli, excessive heat and cold; for sensuous gratification; for rest and sleep.

Psychogenic needs

These are not fundamental biological needs, though some are innate, and include:

A] Needs pertaining to prestige and enhancement of the self; superiority (ambition); achievement; recognition (demanding respect); exhibition (showing off).

B] Needs pertaining to the defence of status and avoidance of humiliation; defensiveness; counteraction (overcoming defeat).

C] Needs pertaining to the exercise of power or acceptance of the power of others; dominance and submissiveness; independence; contrarience (trying to be different); aggression; abasement and resignation; avoidance of blame.

D] Needs pertaining to affectionate relations with others; affiliation (friendliness and cooperativeness); rejection (opposite of affiliation); nurturance (protectiveness and sympathy); succorance (demanding protectiveness and sympathy).

E] Needs pertaining to inanimate objects; acquisition; conservance (preservation against damage); order (arranging things, keeping them tidy); retention (keeping things); constructiveness.

F] Needs pertaining to cognition; needs to explore, ask questions, acquire knowledge, satisfy curiosity.

In drawing up this scheme, Murray and his colleagues were considerably influenced by Freudian theory, and they included some of the Freudian concepts, such as the super-ego and ego-ideal, narcissism or self-love, etc. Other important characteristics included emotionality, impulsiveness, anxiety, extraversion and introversion.

Needs are not necessarily conscious, and they may give rise to behaviour the origin of which is not immediately obvious. Needs are often inter-related, each reinforcing or conflicting with each other. Different types of behaviour may be employed by different people in satisfying the same need. Moreover the needs are related to certain situations which may stimulate them to occur in response to the 'press' or force they exert on the individual. For instance, some types of social relationship will stimu-late affiliation, others nurturance, others aggression; but the effects they produce may differ in accordance with the different interpretations placed on the situations by different people. The extent and the manner in which an individual reacts to these stimuli appears to depend on previous ex-perience, especially in childhood. Such experience also influences the individual in such a way as to cause him to seek actively to encounter particular types of situation, for instance, people towards whom he can display nurturance or from whom he can obtain succorance. It would appear that patterns of press, need and action become developed and established within the personality which Murray calls 'themes'; thus press failure plus need achievement lead to continued striving for success.

Murray's scheme originated in the first place in general observations of behaviour in everyday life and in clinical settings. But he and his colleagues then proceeded to employ it in the investigation of the indi-vidual personality characteristics of thirteen young men. A variety of procedures was utilized: interviews, case histories and autobiographies; questionnaires; tests of ability and learning; tests of personality, including the T.A.T. and Rorschach tests; observations of behaviour in standardized situations. From the results of these a 'psychograph' was drawn up for each man indicating the main types of press to which he had been exposed throughout his life, the principal needs he possessed, and the types of behaviour he exhibited. Unfortunately the amount of data accumulated was so large that Murray was able to include only a single detailed case study in his book.

Other investigators have made use of Murray's scheme to conduct personality studies and to enquire into the occurrence of particular types of motivation corresponding to the needs. Thus in a study by Frenkel-Brunswik, a group of youths and girls aged 18 years was assessed by psy-chologists who had known them for a considerable period of time for the strength of nine of the needs, including achievement, dominance, aggres-sion, independence, affiliation, abasement and succorance.[8] These assessments were related to ratings on a variety of social qualities, based on observations of behaviour made two years earlier at a club-house. The psychologists' assessments of needs were closely related to measurements of these obtained from the T.A.T., but the relation to their overt social behaviour was more variable, depending to some extent on whether the individuals were well or poorly adjusted. Excessive aggression, abasement (self-blame) or succorance (desire for sympathy) occurred in different types of maladjusted individual; and some were socially quite successful. It was concluded that a given need might be related to different overt behaviour patterns in different individuals. Another difficulty which may occur in assessing social motivation from overt behaviour is that the latter may vary according to the type of interaction which one person may have with different associates.[9] Many people, for instance, show deference to those in authority and dominance to their subordinates. Again, these types of behaviour are likely to vary with the customary expressions of motivation which the individual has acquired during his upbringing. Middle-class people may conceal their motivation to a greater extent than do working-class people.

Recently it has been suggested that social motivation takes the following main forms: dependency (which may cover succorance also), affiliation, dominance, sex, aggression and self-esteem.[9] Nurturance is apparently not included in this classification. Observations are cited which seem to show that social motivation may vary along two main dimensions: dominance to dependency; and high affiliation, including sex, to low affiliation. Aggression may be linked with dominance and low affiliation.

4. AFFILIATION AND SOCIAL CONFORMITY

Many studies of particular types of motivation have been carried out by Atkinson, McClelland and their colleagues, of which one of the most important is affiliation. It was defined by them as concern with the establishment and maintenance of positive affectionate relations with other persons, and with the desire to be liked and accepted. In fact it would appear to have been in the main the type of motivation on which belonging and loyalty to social groups are based. This motivation was stimulated experimentally by testing students in their 'fraternity' houses rather than in a classroom; and by requiring them to rate the other members of the group tested on a variety of personality characteristics, and also to select the three with whom they would most like to be friends.[10] In general, the number of T.A.T. responses relevant to the attainment of friendly relationships, and the fear of isolation or rejection, increased in those stimulated in these ways. There would appear to be a difference between the positive desire for friendly relations and the negative fear of rejection, which shows up clearly in rather unstable and withdrawn individuals. The latter also appeared when students who had been rejected from fraternity membership were compared with those who had been accepted.[11] In another study, it was found that any form of situation intended to stimulate the need for affiliation, and especially doubts about popularity, aroused anxiety in those possessing a high degree of this need.[12]

It would seem that affiliation must include a willingness to subordinate personal motivation to what is accepted by other group members. Conformity to the behaviour customary within the group is essential if it is to preserve its existence without quarrelling and splitting. Undoubtedly social conformity is widespread, if not universal, in human society. It is the motive source which cements society together, causing individuals to keep under control much behaviour which would produce individual satisfaction at the cost of breakdown and strife in the group. The normal individual is able to establish a balance between his personal needs and the demands of social living, though as we noted in Chapter 2 this might create considerable internal conflict from childhood upwards.

Clearly people differ from each other in the extent to which they are willing to subordinate their own wishes to those of the groups of which they are members, or of society as a whole; and in the extent to which they possess independent opinions which they are ready to express in the face of social dissent or even disapproval. It has been suggested that these individual differences cannot be ascribed to the variations in a single motivational tendency to social conformity, but that a number of different motivational forces may affect the behaviour of conformity or non-conformity.[13] In particular, the two opposing tendencies to conformity or non-conformity towards the general customs and opinions of society must be distinguished from acquiescence to a current social pressure, as against resistance to this or independence of it. The acquiescent individual is easily influenced and tends to give way to any form of social pressure; thus his opinions and behaviour vary according to those of the people with whom he is in immediate contact, and he tends to do as they do. The independent may agree with others if it seems desirable in his own interests to do so. But on any issue in which he is emotionally involved, he may through conviction preserve his independent judgment against all attempts to make him change it.[14]

Though a moderate degree of conformity is reasonable and desirable in the preservation of normal social relations, excessive conformity to existing social customs and traditions may give rise to extreme conservatism and resistance to all social change. It may be associated with the attitude of authoritarianism in those who in fact are low in self-esteem, and therefore tend to cling to established authority because they are afraid to stand up for themselves. Thus they comply with the demands of others because they feel it dangerous not to do so. Non-conformity, on the other hand, may be due to aggression and rebellion against existing social custom, especially in the frustrated and deprived. It may assume pathological proportions in certain psychological disorders, taking the form of automatic and mindless negativism.

The excessively acquiescent may appear to possess a compulsive tendency towards the reduction of anxiety about acceptance by others. It is suggested that they are characterized by a strong 'approval motive'.[15] It was found experimentally that such people seldom exercised any independent judgment, but agreed with the judgments of the group in which they were situated, even if these were deliberately made illogical and incorrect. They would change their attitudes, even quite inconsistently, when the group appeared to change also. If required to perform boring tasks, they would do so if they thought that this would please the experimenter; and their performance improved greatly if they were encouraged by him, but deteriorated if he was discouraging. In situations of excessive frustration, they repressed all expression of aggression.

Those in need of approval were much affected by the influence of the social group, but exerted little influence on it. Their self-esteem was low, and they were prone to feelings of inadequacy. Though highly desirous of social approval, they had little expectation of success in obtaining it, and were constantly afraid of rejection. They liked to believe that they possessed personality traits of high social desirability, but had little confidence that this was so. Indeed, it was found that those who were actually most socially acceptable had real self-acceptance, and esteemed themselves highly for their socially desirable characteristics. Those who needed approval, although they appeared conventionally normal, were in fact rather maladjusted. They adopted defensive measures, such as the denial or repression of failure, to conceal their personal inadequacy even from themselves.

It has been argued that an excessive and undesirable degree of social conformity may be widespread in American society. Riesman considered that in primitive societies behaviour is largely determined by social tradition.[16] In civilized societies, in their early stages of growth, individuals become motivated by goals and ideals, such as the achievement of personal success, controlled by conscience which sets up internalized standards of morals. But as society becomes stabilized, this 'inner-directedness' tends to be replaced by 'other-directness', in which the chief motive is conformity to the customs of the social groups with which the individual has some personal contact. He is then concerned to behave as they appear to wish, and to obtain their social approval through easy personal relations with them; and he may feel considerable anxiety lest he be unsuccessful. Thus as he moves from one group to another, he takes on the colour of each in succession; and since he has no over-riding standards, his behaviour becomes variable and even his personality fragmented. His political behaviour may show no consistent pattern, and he may become bewildered and finally indifferent to general political and social issues.

A similar type of behaviour has been stigmatized by W. H. Whyte as characterizing the 'organization man', whose main desire is not for individual achievement but for fitting in with the organizations to which he belongs.[17] Thus he has no opinions or ideals of his own, but accepts those of the organizations. It has also been noted that as the older 'entrepreneurial' type of small business gives way increasingly to large bureaucratic organizations, so also their members are less affected by feelings of guilt if they do not work well, and are directed more by their sensitivity to social pressure.[18] A similar distinction between middle-class and working-class attitudes towards work has also declined; that is to say, all are increasingly affected less by personal standards of good work than by the opinions of others. It has been suggested that 'other-directedness' is increasing among skilled industrial workers in this country also.[19] On the other hand, more than one study has indicated that American children are oriented more towards their peers than are children in certain European countries, and depend on their standards at an earlier age.[20]

McClelland, however, does not conceive of 'other-directedness' as incompatible with personal effort and achievement.[21] He regards it as an important constituent of the capacity for efficient business management and salesmanship. Managers and salesmen must be able to take into account the desires and needs of those with whom they are associated if they are to succeed in their enterprises. However, as we shall see in Chapter 8, individuals must also possess a high degree of achievement motivation to be successful. Thus McClelland's concept of 'other-directedness' does not relate to the kind of dependence and subservience to the opinions of others postulated by Riesman and Whyte.

Very closely associated with social conformity appears to be motivation directed towards the establishment, maintenance and improvement of social status. Most people desire to be accepted and respected by members of the social groups to which they belong. By becoming incorporated within certain particular groups, an individual achieves the status of an accepted member; he feels valued and needed by other members of the group. And his status in society in general is determined partly by the place within the social hierarchy of the groups to which he belongs; and partly by the role or function he performs in these groups.

The significance of social status and roles has been recognized more clearly by sociologists than by psychologists. There is little doubt, however, that most people attach great importance to social valuation which relates to status, though there are of course individual differences in this. People seek to belong to a group because it has high social status;

because its members belong to the middle or upper classes rather than to the working class. Moreover, they conform in their behaviour to what they believe to be the behaviour customary in that social class, or the particular social groups within that class with which they hope to be associated. Vance Packard has described amusingly, though perhaps with some exaggeration, the attempts made by people to maintain or improve their social status.[22] Many of the objects which people seek avidly to acquire—wealth, possessions, amenities, luxuries—are sought mainly because they emphasize the social status of a privileged class. But status is associated also with birth, parentage, education and many other factors.

One of the most important of these is occupation; a man's place in the status hierarchy is largely determined by the occupation he carries on and the functions he performs in it. Some people are mainly concerned to preserve their existing status, and fear to lose it through inability to succeed or survive in their existing occupation. Others desire to improve their social status by obtaining a better job in a higher status occupation. We shall discuss this more fully in the next chapter.

5. POWER AND DOMINANCE

Closely related to the desire to improve social status is the attraction of power and of the opportunity to dominate over others; though the latter is perhaps less widespread than is the former. One of the forms of motivation studied by a colleague of Atkinson and McClelland, using the T.A.T., was the attainment of dominance or power, defined as concern with the control of the means of influencing people, and especially with attempting to command others. It was investigated by administering the T.A.T. using pictures depicting such situations, to students endeavouring to obtain office as student leaders.[23] Their T.A.T. stories were compared with those of students making no such attempts. It should be noted that potential leaders not only volunteered for office, but also they and their friends canvassed other students to support their candidature. Certainly they described more behaviour incidents of the kind noted above than did the others. The students were also assessed for individual differences in the desire for power on the basis of teachers' ratings for argumentativeness and attempts to convince others in class. Those producing larger numbers of T.A.T. power-related stories received higher ratings. They also tended to choose from a number of possible occupations those which gave opportunity for leadership.

Now it should be noted that the principal type of motivation studied here appears to have been for the attainment of leadership, including the influencing and control of the behaviour of others and trying to convince them by argument. It was claimed, however, that a general tendency to dominate was involved, and also attempts to avoid dominance and humiliation by others. But in fact some distinction should be made between dominance and leadership, since there are probably many people who desire to dominate, and indeed make aggressive attempts to do so, without wishing to exercise responsible leadership.* On the other hand, in many types of leadership, persuasiveness, understanding of the desires of the group and feelings of responsibility for seeking to implement them, are more important than dominance.

Maslow has related the desire for dominance to feelings of self-confidence and self-esteem.[24] His argument is that those who are secure in their self-esteem may be consistent and forceful in their actions, but that the latter may be cooperative rather than competitive. It is individuals who are less securely self-confident who need admiration and who constantly seek to reassure themselves by attempts to dominate over others. Actual behaviour aimed at dominance is also related to particular status relations with others. Thus in relations in which one individual believes himself to be of superior status, he may assume a position of leadership, and direct and determine the behaviour of the more submissive. But if he believes that his status is inferior, he may be resentful and aggressive, and behave defensively, especially if he is ambitious and craves the recognition he is not given. This kind of behaviour appears not infrequently in members of the middle and lower social classes who are unable to exert power over upper-class 'bosses'. However, there are undoubtedly people who are consistently submissive (non-dominant) in the majority of social relations. Women tend both to feel and to behave less dominantly than do men; and it is probable that the marriage relationship is more successful when the husband is more dominant than the wife. In spite of this, it has been found that indulgence in overt sexual behaviour by women is more closely related to a high degree of self-esteem and self-confidence than to strength of sexual desire.[25]

---

* It may be remembered that the British Prime Minister Stanley Baldwin accused the newspaper proprietor Beaverbrook of attempting to exercise 'power without responsibility, the prerogative of the harlot throughout the ages'. Another instance is the '*éminence grise*', the 'power behind the throne'.

8

GOAL-DIRECTED BEHAVIOUR

I. INTERESTS

It has been pointed out that much human behaviour, as distinct from that of the lower animals, is characterized by its organized, highly motivated, goal-directed nature.[1] It possesses an overall purposiveness; the individual is committed to a task and his activities are dominated by this. It is directed by rational thought, and relevant creative ideas emerge spontaneously, without effort or strain. Accompanying emotions are pleasurable; there is a minimum of anxiety and a high tolerance of effort and fatigue. But the activity may be disrupted by interference from secondary aims such as those of security, wealth, status and power.

Thus the goal-directed activity is controlled by a conscious intention to achieve certain aims by means of specifically chosen courses of action. This does not mean that people are aware of all the motivation which impels them to undertake these activities; indeed they may be largely unconscious of the operation of certain motivational tendencies. But probably they are quite clearly aware of the general aim towards which they work persistently and with great energy and endurance; and they employ their powers of thought to plan their activities in the most appropriate fashion. Furthermore, they are strongly 'ego-involved'; they identify themselves with these activities and feel the self to be enhanced by their performance and by the attainment of the aims of the activities. But achievement does not result in complete cessation of that kind of activity. On the contrary, the individual is stimulated by his own successful performance to continue the activity in order to attain further goals. In contrast, tasks which do not involve any kind of aim or achievement produce boredom, and, if they must be repeated indefinitely, the experience of satiation—feeling completely 'fed up'. People do not seek to prolong such tasks, and indeed they try to avoid them.

It must be admitted that although this type of goal-directedness tends to increase with age in children, it is not exhibited by everyone, and is more prominent in the behaviour of some people than of others. Nevertheless, it must be regarded as a very important type of human motivated behaviour, even if not of universal occurrence.

Some of these persistent long-term activities are directed by 'interests', which may appear in the choice of careers and occupations, of subjects of study and of leisure activities. An 'interest' usually involves some thought and study in the attempt to increase relevant knowledge within the sphere of interest; and often energetic action in pursuing it. Superficially, the interest is characterized by its topic; and many studies of interests leave it at that. But more intensive investigation suggests that interests may be deeply rooted and enduring tendencies which involve a variety of motivation as well as of ability and knowledge.

A number of studies of interests has been made in students and in other people. The usual technique has been to ask them a series of standardized questions about their interests, their preferred courses of study or occupation, their leisure activities, etc. The answers have then been submitted to a type of statistical treatment, factorial analysis, which has the effect of grouping these answers into certain categories supposed to be determined by the major prevailing interests of the group. Thus in a group of young women Guilford found the following: (1) vocational interests: mechanical, scientific, social welfare, aesthetic expression, clerical, business, outdoor activity, physical activity; (2) interests involving motivational tendencies, such as self-reliance *v.* dependence, expressiveness *v.* restraint; (3) interests involving partly motivational tendencies and partly directions of thought and activity: adventure, diversion (variety), precision, thinking, culture, orderliness, sociability, status-gaining.[2] The distinctions between these three categories are not altogether clear; but motivation not directly connected with what is normally regarded as a topic of interest appears to be involved in (2) and (3). Thorndike's classification of interests was simpler though somewhat similar: social intercourse, ideas, practical and realistic activities, music and art, outdoor sport, amusement and self-indulgence.[3] This last category, and those in Guilford's categories (2) and (3), suggest that the particular form of motivation which enters into performance of an activity may sometimes be more important than its more obvious centre of interest.

Another classification of interests in more general terms which has been widely used is that based on six main 'values' hypothesized by Spranger: theoretical (including scientific), aesthetic, religious, social, economic (earning a good living) and power-seeking.[4] It has been shown that a questionnaire based on these 'values' has some predictive capacity, and that answers are related to choice of studies and of careers.[5] Thus students of physical and biological science showed strong theoretical interests (values); students of literature, languages and art, aesthetic; students of economics and politics, social.[6] In the main, those with interests of these kinds were low in economic and power-seeking interests. Students who obtained good results in examinations in science and languages were particularly high in theoretical and aesthetic interests respectively. A factor-analytic treatment of the scores on the questionnaire suggested that the Spranger values could be grouped under three main headings:

(1) interest in utility and power, characteristic of those who chose business occupations; (2) interest in human relationships, shown by those taking up various forms of social service; (3) interest in abstract questions of truth and beauty (scientific and literary). Religious interests fell outside this classification; and indeed they may be different in nature, as we shall consider in the next section.

A rather similar and widely used questionnaire is the Kuder Preference Record, which lists seven major types of interest: scientific, computational (keeping accounts, collecting statistics), musical, artistic, literary, social service, persuasive (public speaking, selling).[7] This also is claimed to relate to the occupational choices of students, but it is not correlated with examination results in different subjects.

However, such investigations do not show the extent to which the interests affect behaviour and provide persistent long-term goals of action. A new light has been thrown on the basis of certain types of interest by Hudson's comparison of the bias towards arts or science subjects by intelligent school-boys, many of whom were subsequently followed up at the University.[8] In particular, he compared their performance on standardized tests of intelligence, which necessitate the use of strictly logical deductive reasoning towards a single correct answer, with that in 'open-ended' questions requiring a more diverse and imaginative type of thinking. These two types of thinking had been termed by Guilford 'convergent' and 'divergent' respectively; and the latter had been identified by other writers with original or 'creative' thought.[9] Hudson, however, considered that both convergent and divergent thinkers could show originality; but that the former tended to do so in scientific subjects, and the latter in arts subjects, such as history and modern languages including English. Moreover, he found that there were other typical differences in the interests, motivation and personality characteristics of convergers and divergers. The latter had a wide range of cultural interests, in literature, art, social questions and politics; the former, a narrower and more restricted range, chiefly in construction and machinery, in outdoor activities and in natural history. Although conventionally orderly, obedient and socially conforming, they were in reality somewhat detached from intimate personal relations, disliking emotional involvement and expression; they were more interested in 'things' than in people. The divergers were more imaginative, more free in emotional expression and intensely interested in the 'human condition'. However, Hudson suggested that they also tended to avoid personal involvement in human problems and relations and viewed them with a certain detachment, the better to understand and judge them.*

* Recent studies carried out in Australia showed that among school-boys and students in their first three years at the University, the number of convergers and

Studies of individuals with distinguished careers in later life showed that these differences continued to be important, but for the emergence of genuine creative ability other qualities were necessary.[11] In the case of distinguished physical scientists, an early interest in mathematics, physics and machine construction and a marked ability in relevant types of thought, developed as the result of great effort, persistence and drive, and a real devotion to the pursuit of scientific research and discovery. It would appear that these men were capable of a high degree of sustained activation in their work. They were also adventurous and curious, self-reliant and confident; somewhat aggressive and ruthless in following their aims. They were disinterested in social participation, and had little concern for personal achievement, social and professional status and wealth. Their parents, who were seldom either very wealthy or very poor, had encouraged their independence and their love of learning from childhood upwards.

Biological scientists had early interests principally in natural history, but also in literature. Though showing many of the same qualities as the physical scientists, they appeared somewhat less detached from social interaction and interest in human problems, and were perhaps less withdrawn and better adjusted. Social scientists such as psychologists and anthropologists were naturally well aware of human situations, and were not orientated towards things rather than towards people. Their early interests had been in literature, and to a less degree in social welfare and in natural history. They made their vocational choices later than did the physical and biological scientists, and were less independent in mind and less completely concentrated on a single line of interest. They endeavoured to view human problems with detachment, but were often uneasy and unsuccessful in social relationships, and tended to feel aggressive and guilty. It was suggested that they were still to some extent involved in rather difficult parental relations, whereas the physical and biological scientists had become completely detached from these. It would seem possible that historians and novelists have somewhat the same ambivalent attitudes of concern with as against detachment from human problems.

It would appear therefore that in certain people the pursuit of an interest is fundamental to the whole course of life; and that very complex motivation may be associated with the intellectual abilities involved. This will obviously vary according to the type of interest. Simpler types of

divergers among those specializing in science were about equal. But in the fifteen best students, who proceeded to an honours degree in their fourth year, 73 per cent were divergers and 23 per cent convergers. The former, taking several different science subjects, obtained better results in their final degree examinations. Thus it would appear that science students are more likely to do outstandingly good work if they are divergers.[10]

interest may occur in other types of occupation. For instance, the engineer, though like the physicist centred on things rather than on people, is more practical-minded, and concerned with constructive activities and competence in overcoming and manipulating the physical environment. Interests may also be involved in the performance of less high-grade industrial occupations. Probably they were more prominent in the work of craftsmen who exercised their skill and constructive motivation in carpentry, metal work, etc. than they are in modern industry; though they may well play a part in the work of highly skilled mechanics and technicians. About forty years ago it was found that even laundry workers experienced considerable pleasure in washing and ironing lingerie which looked nice in consequence.[12] It is doubtful if similar experiences exist today. Nevertheless, more recent investigations showed that pride in skill may be more general in industry than the outsider supposes. Even in routine machine work, some people feel considerable satisfaction in turning out quickly a succession of well-made articles. But 'pride in skill' may be related to achievement motivation rather than to interest.

But occupational and leisure-time interests depend considerably on the social pressures of fashion, and also vary with age. Thus among children, boys often want to become engine drivers or skilled mechanics because manipulative activities are generally popular among them. Interest in sport is widespread among boys and men because it employs physical activity and attracts social admiration. Older men identify themselves with such activities even when they are no longer able to perform them themselves. Girls and young women want to become hairdressers, 'models' or air hostesses because these occupations place a premium on physical attractiveness. These interests change with time, partly because adolescents and young adults are more fully aware than are children of the nature and extent of their abilities and opportunities, and are therefore more realistic in their aims; and partly because they understand better what are their personal desires and aspirations, and in consequence are less swayed by fashion. In middle and old age there is a natural decrease of interest in activities requiring physical skill and energy and departure from established habits and customs.[13] Quieter and more solitary occupations may be preferred to the more active and sociable. However, there may be an increase in those which involve instructing, directing and supervising other people.

2. SENTIMENTS

We have described the pursuit of interests as directed by complex patterns of thought, activity and motivation, organized and centred about certain aims. Other rather different types of organization have been termed 'sentiments'. McDougall stated that in sentiments ideas about particular objects, especially people and groups of people, have become linked through experience with one or more innate propensities, together with the corresponding emotional tendencies, in such a manner as to promote strong and persisting courses of action leading towards remote goals.[14] Sentiments differ from interests in that the emotional element is more prominent, and that the actions are directed and controlled to a less extent by rational thought. Their most salient characteristics are love of a particular object, person, social group or abstract idea; and strong motivation to support and promote this object, and to attack or overcome anything which threatens it. The earliest sentiments are those formed by the child about his parents and his home. These widen in scope to include his friends, his wife and children; social groups such as school, university, town, occupational and political groups, country; and finally abstract concepts such as those of religion, political ideologies and ideals, for instance, of justice and liberty. In some cases, a positive sentiment of love for these objects may be accompanied by a negative sentiment of hatred for anyone who opposes, harms or threatens to harm them. The harm may be largely imaginary, as in the dislike of and prejudice against the 'out-group'. People feel in this way towards groups to which they do not belong simply by contrast to their positive feelings towards those of which they are members.

Normally the nature of love for the object of a sentiment changes and develops as the individual matures. The dependent love of the child for his parents is replaced by companionate love for friends and compassionate and protective love towards the young, the weak, the unhappy and the sick. Some of the most important sentiments in adults are those associated with sexual relationships. In these there may occur all degrees of sexual desire, affectionate feeling, companionship, sympathy and protectiveness. Though in the young sexual desire may predominate, the other feelings play an increasingly important part as the relationship develops and matures; and it is unlikely that it will be stable and enduring unless this occurs. Some degree of mutual dependence is also involved; there will also be support, and the excessive, clinging and exclusive dependence of childhood is unlikely to produce a happy relationship. Though some aggression may occur, in so far as each partner is frustrated in obtaining all that he wants, the relationship may not be successful unless aggression is kept under control or displaced elsewhere. Sometimes undue aggression in one partner produces fear and withdrawal in the other.

Two experimental studies of sentiments have been carried out, using a variety of tests.[15] Certain objects of sentiments were selected, and those who carried out the tests had to describe their ideas and feelings about them, to answer questions about them, and to formulate arguments for and against them. These data were related to information obtained from case histories, interviews, T.A.T. and free association tests. The sentiments studied in most detail related to religion and its philosophical and social-political associations. The emotions included in the religious sentiment were love, awe, reverence, fear, specifically directed towards religious objects such as God, the Church and fellow men. There were of course great individual differences in the strength and nature of the sentiment, ranging from a high degree of maturity and a closely integrated hierarchical organization of ideas, beliefs, emotions and motivated behaviour down to a more or less unorganized collection in the childishly immature and the predominantly indifferent. In the first case, beliefs, ideas and behaviour had widened and become increasingly intelligent and rational through thought and study, and the understanding of personal experience and of the experience of others. But in the immature and indifferent, ideas, beliefs and actions were less clear and well-defined, and frequently conflicted with each other. The religious sentiment of some people appeared to have developed little since childhood. They maintained the simple beliefs derived from their parents, with little critical evaluation of these. Indeed, they were often deficient in the ability for rational thought, and lacked intelligent interests. They tended to classify all behaviour into the absolutely good or evil; but their capacity for social activities and social relationships was poor. Their emotions were strong and sometimes violently expressed; but they appeared to have been transferred with little modification from their parents to God. Still others possessed weak and chaotic religious sentiments, incorporating little strong feeling or motivated behaviour. Beliefs and ideas were vaguely idealistic and largely unorganized, and were often divorced from parents' ideas and beliefs. Some who were moderately religious combined this sentiment with strong social and political interests. But others had altogether changed the focus of their sentiment to philosophical ideas or social and political ideologies. These, in the more mature, were often highly organized, consistent and rational; indeed, they were more in the nature of interests than of sentiments. In some cases, there had been a complete revolt against parents' beliefs. But the effect of traumatic incidents in parental relationships in other cases resulted in a complete disruption of philosophical and religious sentiments.

Thus social and political interests and social work may be combined with religious sentiments, or may form a substitute for them. The interests and sentiments upon which social service work is based may involve complex motivated behaviour. The social worker and the social reformer may seek to know and to understand the type of service they perform and the people whom they serve. They may also regard them with love and compassion, which will energize and reinforce all attempts to help them and to improve social conditions. Nevertheless, they will preserve a certain detachment and independence of judgment, and not become unduly involved in personal relationships and reactions. Again, such activities are not necessarily entirely selfless. The social worker derives satisfaction from his performance of his task, and it may be related to his ability to bring about improvements in a manner of which others are incapable. This is still more true of the social reformer. Devoted as were people such as Florence Nightingale and Eleanor Rathbone, for instance, they were so fully identified with the objects of their concern as often to over-ride the interests of others in a dominating manner. Their love for the objects of their sentiments was accompanied by hatred of and aggression against anyone who appeared likely to frustrate the aims of their activities.

It would appear that sentiments in different persons may vary greatly in their strength and in their effect on behaviour. They may have developed and matured into firm, consistent and integrated organizations of intelligent ideas, controlled emotions and persistent activities directed towards long-term goals. Indeed, they may lead to the undertaking of hazardous and exhausting action and enormous self-sacrifice. Even when this does not occur, they may determine the individual's values to a great extent. Though these values are in the first place socially inculcated, individuals may adopt them and identify with them, and incorporate them into the 'conscience' which exerts a moral and ethical control on their behaviour.

But in others sentiments may be immature and emotional—indeed, 'sentimental'. They will be relatively superficial, unorganized and unrelated to the main purposive activities and therefore exert little effect on behaviour. Or they may retain an infantile dependency on and identification with the beliefs and opinions of the groups with which these people are associated. The good qualities of the object of the sentiment are irrationally exaggerated and its bad qualities minimized. Hence, 'My country, right or wrong.'

3. THE SELF-REGARDING SENTIMENT AND SELF-ACTUALIZATION

Whatever their other sentiments, everyone possesses what McDougall termed the 'self-regarding' sentiment—the organization of ideas, beliefs, emotions and motivated behaviour centred on the self.[14] Most people have some system of beliefs about the nature of their personalities and of their prevailing motivation, though they may be considerably mistaken as to the real nature of these. Most people act in such a way as would seem likely to maintain their pride, enhance their self-esteem and the esteem of others; and to protect themselves from contempt, disapproval and frustration. Since self-esteem depends to a considerable extent on the esteem given by members of the groups to which people belong, they seek to harmonize their behaviour and their ideas about themselves to accord with the opinions of others. They also attempt to use their abilities to the maximum, and in the most congenial manner. It sometimes seems that the maladjusted, perhaps because of parental discouragement or rejection in childhood, possess poor self-esteem, and go out of their way to appear inferior, or so helpless that they must depend on the support of others. Or they may continually adopt methods of 'ego-defence' to protect themselves from social disapproval. Thus their self-regarding sentiment seems more negative than positive. We noted in Chapter 2 the manner in which the self-concept and the related self-regarding sentiment developed and matured as the child grew up.

Maslow has suggested that the fundamental motivational tendencies (which he, like Murray, calls 'needs') are organized in a hierarchy.[16] At the bottom are the physiological needs; then safety; then love; then self-esteem and the esteem of others; and at the summit, 'self-actualization', the effort to realize the maximum fulfilment of all the potentialities and abilities, and especially the creative abilities. These needs develop in turn as the child grows up; but the higher appear and function only in so far as the lower are reasonably satisfied. The higher needs are not for the removal of deficits, or for producing relaxation of tension. Their expression in motivated behaviour is itself positive and pleasurable. It leads to continued activity and the search for new and higher goals, though satisfaction may be more readily postponed than in the case of the lower needs. The latter remain below the level of consciousness as long as they are reasonably well satisfied, but may emerge and dominate behaviour in conditions of deprivation or frustration. Thus we saw that in conditions of acute hunger, people were conscious of little else. Again, the need for safety is strongest in children; but it may also dominate the behaviour and emotions of adult neurotics, who have not developed the normal adult degree of security. However, maladjustment and imperfect adult development are more commonly produced by lack of love. But some people who have been unsatisfied in their need for love may seek satisfaction instead in obtaining esteem. And only the most mature and intelligent may reach the final stage of self-actualization, which is accompanied by the capacity to accept and depend on the self, to cease from identifying with others, to rely on one's own standards, to aspire towards the 'ego-ideal' and to detach oneself from social demands and customs when desirable. However, it should be noted the people who have reached this stage are relatively uncommon; Maslow was unable, in his studies, to discover more than a small number among his acquaintances. There is evidence to show that the majority of people are more ready to accept certain motives and characteristics of their personalities than others.

However, the greater the degree of acceptance of self, the greater the willingness to accept other people and the problems they present. Maslow also considers that, independent of his hierarchy of needs, are motivational tendencies towards obtaining knowledge and understanding, through the exploratory behaviour described above. He does not discuss those important types of motivation, towards independence and individual achievement; they may however be involved in the development of self-esteem, and are therefore transcended at the stage of self-actualization. As we have seen, many conflicts in life arise from independence and achievement motivation; and Maslow admits that, although reasonable satisfaction of the lower needs may be a pre-requisite for the attainment of self-actualization, nevertheless there must also be the capacity to overcome frustration and conflict. But it must be through realization and acceptance, not through escape and avoidance. Thus self-actualization could not be attributed to individuals such as those described in section 1 in whom an over-riding interest was joined with avoidance or repression of emotional difficulties and problems of social relationship. Rather in self-actualization there must be a harmonization of motivation relating to interests, personal achievement and involvement in human relationships. This is found in the truly great; notably, Einstein.

4. LEVEL OF ASPIRATION

We have considered some of the ways in which people consciously direct their behaviour and strive to perform certain types of activity, and to attain certain ends. It would appear that they frequently attempt to reach some criterion of excellence in so doing, and set themselves a 'level of aspiration', the standard they hope to attain. The act of setting such a level of aspiration may itself motivate the individual to try his best; though sometimes a knowledge of how well he has performed previously may be almost equally effective.[17]

Even in simple verbal or manual tasks performed in laboratory experiments, individuals may set themselves a certain standard of performance. This may be assessed by requiring several repetitions of the task, telling people each time how well they did in the last trial, and asking them to estimate how well they think they will perform at the next trial. Again, before they are informed about their previous performance, they may be asked to estimate what it was and then told whether they exceeded or fell short of their estimate. The majority of people tend to set their level of aspiration—how well they will perform in the next trial—slightly above their previous performance, and to continue to adjust the level in successive trials. That is to say, if they reach the level they previously set themselves, they raise it on the subsequent trial; if they fail, they lower it.

The greater the success, the stronger the tendency to raise the level; the greater the failure, the stronger the tendency to lower it. Moreover, these tendencies may transfer to other tasks performed subsequently, if they are of a similar nature.[18] These effects are more likely to occur in tasks in which people expect to improve with practice than in tasks which are complete in themselves, such as solving puzzles. Again, in a task which has been practised for so long as to have reached its ceiling, individuals may lower their levels of aspiration if they do particularly well on one occasion, arguing that this was a chance effect, unlikely to recur. In a task performance of which depends a good deal on chance and varies considerably from one trial to another, level of aspiration may not be closely related to performance, but may depend on particular motivation.[19] Thus the level will be high with strong motivation towards achievement and high hopes of success, but low if people fear they may fail—though there are certain exceptions to this which will be discussed later.

Any very easy success tends to discourage effort and to produce a low and static level of aspiration. But the value placed on the task and its estimated difficulty may also affect level of aspiration. Boys set their level of aspiration lower for a highly valued task than for one of less value, because they thought they were less likely to succeed in the former.[20] Again, the level of aspiration may be affected when expectation and performance are found to differ. If people succeeded in a task which they expected to be difficult, and in which they thought they would fail, their experience of success and satisfaction was greater, especially if they could attribute success to their own intelligence and efforts, than if they expected to succeed.[21] But if they failed in a task in which they expected to succeed, their experience of failure was correspondingly greater, unless they could attribute their failure to the unforeseen difficulty of the task, or to circumstances beyond their control. Their level of aspiration was likely to rise with unexpected success, and to fall with unexpected failure. But a moderate amount of failure may stimulate the individual to try again and try harder. Continuous and marked failure tends to produce a decline in level of aspiration; persistence deteriorates and the individual gives up the task if he can.

We noted in Chapter 2 that achievement motivation, and with it aspirations for success in tasks, began to emerge at an early age. At four years children may begin to set themselves levels of aspiration; but they do this more readily, and the level to which they aspire is higher, in so far as they are encouraged and given opportunities for self-help, and praised for their success. As they grow older, and consciousness of self and feelings of self-esteem develop, aspirations become more pronounced, and children persist longer in their attempts to attain the goal to which they have aspired. This development depends partly on how well they do in a task; sometimes those who have performed well lower their level of aspiration, while those who have performed badly, raise it.[22] But the level of aspiration is also affected by comparison with the performance of other children, and is equated with what is thought to be characteristic of comparable groups. Thus if children are more backward than the others in their class in school work, they may lose confidence in their ability to perform any task satisfactorily. Sometimes this causes them to set a low level of aspiration and even to cease trying, in order to defend themselves against the pain of failure. But it has also been found that some very anxious and diffident children set themselves an impossibly high level of aspiration, which seems to act as a kind of substitute for the goal they can never achieve.[23] Also, they need not blame themselves if they are unable to make such a good performance. They show no flexibility in adjusting their level of aspiration to their actual performance.

Adults tend to regulate their level of aspiration in accordance with what they think may be expected of them; and if they are highly involved in successful performance—that is to say, they feel that success is important—they may compete with themselves and try continuously to improve.[24] This is most likely to happen if they are somewhat uncertain as to how well they may be able to perform. But also they measure their performance against that of other groups of people.[25] If they are working in a group, they tend to set their level of aspiration in accordance with the performance of the group, especially if it is one with which they are closely affiliated and identified. But they may also respond to what they think to be the performance of other groups with which they have no direct contact. Thus students were told that their scores on a number of tests exceeded, in one case, or fell short of, in another, the scores of one of three groups of people—school children, undergraduate and graduate students.[26] In general, when told they had exceeded, they set their level of aspiration lower; the fall in level of aspiration was greatest when the comparison group consisted of graduates, less with undergraduates, and least with school children. On the other hand, if they were informed that their scores fell short of the other groups, they raised their level of aspiration, and the rise was greatest when the comparison group consisted of school children, less with undergraduates and least with graduates. It would seem that they geared their level of aspiration to the performance of comparable groups.

However, in Western societies there is a general cultural stress on achievement and improvement of efficiency such that people feel that they ought to aspire to higher levels of performance.[27] Thus it is usually found in experiments on level of aspiration that these are set somewhat beyond the limits of actual performance; and there may be a corresponding tendency to feel discontented and inferior when these aspirations are not realized.[28] It would seem that those in favourable economic positions are less likely to set high levels of aspiration than those in less favourable. But if people are informed that their previous performance was about average for the group, their level of aspiration for future performances tends to fall, because they are relieved at having done sufficiently well and no longer feel that they must struggle to do better.[29]

But there are considerable individual differences in the manner in which different people set their levels of aspiration. In the first place, people differ in the extent to which they feel involved in tasks; that is to say, in how much it matters to them whether they succeed or not. If the task is one which appeals to their interests or to their pride in their intelligence and professional skill, their level of aspiration is higher than if it is merely a spare-time activity or an experiment in which they have been asked to participate.[30] Indeed, if they are very fully involved, their level of aspiration may bear little relationship to what they can actually attain.[31] Moreover, performance of such tasks may be less efficient than with a more moderate degree of involvement, and there is a danger of a breakdown in tasks which are very difficult to perform.[32] If a person is concerned with preserving his self-esteem above everything else, he is not likely to do very well. And failure may impair his performance still further, especially if he is anxious as well as ego-involved.[33] In the individual who is only very slightly involved in the task, there is no relationship between level of aspiration and attainment, and naturally the latter tends to be poor.

Levels of aspiration are more realistic in the generally secure, and in those able to tolerate failure well; they may be excessively high in those who are dissatisfied with their social and intellectual status and are striving to improve it.[34] The levels also vary according to the individual's confidence in his ability to perform well. The more self-confident anticipate success, set themselves a high level of aspiration, and work hard to achieve it. Even if they do not reach the level they set themselves, they try hard and hope to do better next time. The less confident are anxious and afraid of failing. But they also respond rapidly to actual success and failure. If their subsequent performance fails because it is impaired by anxiety, they may then lower their level of aspiration greatly.[19] But if they reach the level, confidence may be restored, performance improved and the level raised again. Consequences of further failure may be great disappointment, followed by discouragement, attempts to give up the task and even hostility towards the experimenter. Or sometimes there is the curious behaviour of raising the level of aspiration after failure and lowering it after success.[35] This seems to be associated with the behaviour, also found in children (see p. 119) of making high estimates which become goals in themselves, the performer defending himself against the disagreeable consciousness of failure. Thus students who expected to fail in their courses chose either very easy or very difficult courses; those who expected success chose moderately easy ones.[36] Again, the careers selected by those who expect failure may be much beyond or beneath their ability to succeed in them.[37] In the latter case, there appears to be a withdrawal into a simple occupation in order to avoid the challenge of a more demanding career involving possible failure.

Another reaction to failure may be an attempt to explain it away, attributing it to chance factors or to unfavourable circumstances. This device of 'rationalization' is discussed in Chapter 9. Neurotic patients suffering from anxiety states are particularly prone to over-estimate their level of future performance, for the reasons described above.[38]

It would appear that these differences in level of aspiration may arise from individual differences in motivation of a general nature; and in particular from ingrained differences in achievement motivation. This is one of the motives or needs postulated by Murray (see p. 100); very considerable discussion and experiment have been devoted to it, which will be outlined in the next section.

5. ACHIEVEMENT MOTIVATION

Achievement motivation may be associated with a variety of goals, but in general the behaviour adopted will involve activity which is directed towards the attainment of some standard of excellence.[39] It may include competition with others, in which they are surpassed. But on the other hand, the individual may be chiefly concerned to set himself a high standard of performance or level of aspiration, and to reach this through his own efforts, overcoming any obstacles to his success. Thus ambition is frequently involved. But it is probable, as we have seen, that the standard is based more or less directly on the attainments and achievements of others, or upon general social standards. Though the individual is not necessarily concerned to surpass any particular persons, and indeed this might not satisfy him if he did not feel that he had reached the standard he had set himself, yet it has been found in some studies that there is a high correlation between attempts to achieve an aim for its own sake, and to obtain the esteem of others by so doing.[40] It is argued that certain persons have a strong persistent desire for achievement, especially of long-term goals, in a variety of situations, and not merely an impulse to achieve a few limited short-term aims. Also these persons may attach more importance to excellence than to prestige; and they generally wish to achieve through their own independent actions. Independence and achievement are closely related together. But achievement motivation may also be related specifically to particular spheres of interest, whereas in unrelated activities little achievement may be desired.

But it would appear that there are other persons whose positive desire for achievement is counteracted or even outweighed by their anxiety lest they fail. They may, for instance, be children of parents who are themselves very distinguished, or who may have set them unduly high standards. The chief desire of these people may be the security of avoiding failure by not hoping for too much. In some of the tests of achievement used by Atkinson and McClelland, these individuals appeared to possess a moderate or medium strength of achievement motivation. Those with little achievement motivation were the unambitious, little concerned with success or failure.

The principal method used to investigate achievement motivation has been to require individuals to carry out tasks with instructions aimed at arousing achievement motivation; stating, for instance, that performance of these measures intelligence or leadership abilities. Sometimes additionally it was made to appear that the performers were succeeding or failing in these tasks. They then wrote stories about T.A.T. pictures, mainly depicting scenes related to some form of effort or struggle, which were compared with stories written in relatively relaxed conditions. In general, the latter contained fewer episodes than the former related to success, struggle for achievement, overcoming obstacles. After failure experiences, the number of success stories decreased, and the number of failure stories increased. However, it was also found that children who had done poorly in their school work produced fewer stories about failure in responses to T.A.T. pictures than did children who had done well.[41] Thus it would appear that long-term failure may give rise to the avoidance of such experiences.

It was also possible to distinguish the three adult groups, outlined above, with high, medium and low achievement motivation. It should be noted, however, that this differentiation appears more clearly with pictures related to the specific interests or occupations of those who perform the T.A.T. tests. Moreover, although the situations described above aroused desires for success and leadership in male students, they had no such effect on women students, who responded only in situations in which achievement was related to social acceptability; that is to say, they wished to be successful only in achieving social skill and acceptance.[42]

Performance was also studied in several other tasks related to achievement motivation. In general people with high achievement motivation tended to prefer tasks which required personal initiative and inventiveness, and which presented some difficulty, a challenge rather than the assurance of success. They were willing to postpone immediate reward for the sake of an ultimately greater reward; and to take moderate risks to attain this. During performance, they tended to improve more than others as time went on; for instance in tasks such as the unscrambling of words with letters in random order. They also performed best when achievement was deliberately stimulated, but were relatively unaffected by monetary rewards. Those with moderate achievement motivation might become anxious over possible failure when achievement was emphasized, and perform less well. Those with strong achievement motivation appeared to be stimulated by failure in a task, and to determine more firmly to achieve a goal they had set for themselves; and they tended to over-estimate their probability of succeeding.[43] Those who were anxious about their ability to succeed and under-estimated their chance of success were discouraged by failure, though they sometimes improved if a specific goal was set them by the experimenter.[44] Again, those with moderately high levels of aspiration as to future success showed a considerable fear of failure in T.A.T. stories.[45] But those with high and low rather than with moderate levels of aspiration produced more T.A.T. stories relating to the attainment of positive goals.[46] Thus again a distinction may be drawn between those who are more concerned with desire for success and those anxious over possible failure. Heckhausen has recently prepared two keys for scoring T.A.T. stories, one relating to hope of success, the other to fear of failure, which differentiate these people.[41]

Further studies of these two types of reaction to achievement were carried out by using separate measures of achievement and anxiety. These are described in the Appendix. For the former, the T.A.T. or the French test were employed; for the latter, the Test Anxiety questionnaire. Some people showed relatively high positive achievement motivation and low anxiety; others, a high degree of anxiety and low achievement. The former preferred tasks of moderate difficulty to either very difficult or very easy tasks, presumably because these afforded their best means of demonstrating achievement.[47] The latter preferred either tasks which were very easy, in which they were unlikely to fail; or very difficult tasks. The latter finding is similar to that obtained in experiments on level of aspiration in which some people who performed badly set themselves a very high level of aspiration. Those whose motivation to achieve was stronger than their fear of failing showed greater persistence in an achievement-related task—time spent in working in an examination—and also were more efficient than those whose fear of failure was stronger than their desire for success.[48]

A recent study, however, indicated that although those who demonstrate high achievement motivation in the T.A.T. form a clearly defined group, those who do not do so may not necessarily be potential failures.[49] People who gave relatively few achievement-orientated responses produced either responses related to the performance of tasks, though without much striving for achievement; or responses which were quite different in nature. The former appeared to be individuals who tended to be conservative, to conform socially and to avoid insecurity and risk. But the latter were unconventional, fond of risks, sometimes highly original, and on the whole as able and intelligent in work as those with high achievement motivation. This type of independent behaviour appeared less frequently when achievement motivation was deliberately stimulated by the situation, as in Atkinson's original experiment. But it may well indicate the existence of people who are relatively unwilling to exert themselves and strive hard in response to social pressure, though able to do so along the lines of their own interests.

There has been much investigation of the relation of academic attainment to achievement motivation. Naturally such attainment depends also on ability, and intelligence and achievement are not necessarily related. However, the highest attainment appears in those who possess both good intelligence and strong achievement motivation, especially when there is little anxiety as to possible failure; but strong achievement motivation cannot compensate for low intelligence.[41] The more creatively intelligent individuals tend to high levels of aspiration to attain highly valued and desirable goals through determined and persistent goal-directed activity, as we showed in section 1. In general, achievement motivation is stronger in adults who have received a university education and are in professional occupations, than in others.[50]* However, if fear of academic failure is greater than anticipation of success, there may be an inhibiting effect on attainment and also upon the choice of a career, in students. Those shown by a questionnaire to possess a high degree of anxiety aspired to occupations of lower social status than did the less anxious; and with the former there was a greater gap between what they would like to do and what they expected to do.[51] The relationship to anxiety was more noticeable than the relationship to achievement motivation. However, aspirations for upward mobility of occupation in adolescents and adults are associated with high achievement motivation; and also the inclination to seek an occupation which is interesting and likely to lead to success, rather than one easy to obtain, or promising security.[52] People with such aspirations are relatively independent of their families, and are willing to leave them in order to obtain a good job. Long-term achievement is more valued than immediate satisfaction. Thus Air Force officer candidates high in achievement motivation performed a task better when its importance to their careers was stressed.[53] Those low in achievement motivation performed better when an immediate goal, 'You may leave early', was emphasized.

Clearly another factor which is of great importance in producing

* However, note the association between achievement motivation and 'entrepreneurial' occupations discussed on p. 126.

academic achievement is the type of interest we described in section 1. There may even be a conflict between interest in a subject for its own sake and desire for achievement. One experiment showed that students demonstrated better understanding of a psychological text when their curiosity as to its significance was stimulated than when achievement in learning was stressed.[54] Though those high in achievement motivation are often willing to engage in tasks which are interesting in themselves, for instance the solution of interesting problems, there is also a danger that they may fail to persevere in them if they do not provide the experience of success.[55]

Experiments have also been carried out distinguishing behaviour in performance of tasks of those high in achievement motivation and those with strong affiliation motivation. The former may show little evidence of affiliation motivation, for instance in the desire to comply with the experimenter's wishes; and they tend to be low in social popularity. Indeed, there may even be an inverse relationship between achievement and affiliation motivation. Those high in achievement motivation showed a higher degree of autonomic reactivity, as measured by the GSR, when tested in conditions in which academic attainment was stressed; and they might decrease their efficiency after apparent intellectual failure.[56] Those high in affiliation motivation reacted physiologically when informed that they were being tested for their warmth and friendliness; and their performance might be impaired if they thought they had failed socially. They liked to work together cooperatively in groups, and were stimulated by the information that they were cooperating satisfactorily.[57] Those relatively higher in achievement motivation preferred individual work. If they were asked to choose a partner to help them perform a task, they chose a competent worker even if they didn't like him much. Those high in affiliation motivation chose someone they liked even if he was rather incompetent.

But the appearance and causes of achievement motivation seem to vary considerably as between men and women. Thus marked achievement in women may react with social disapproval, and therefore they may show achievement-oriented behaviour only in friendly social surroundings. On the other hand, there has been evidence that women of high academic ability are more independent and less socially conforming than are men of high academic ability.[58] Again, it has sometimes appeared that maternal warmth in childhood contributes to high achievement motivation in adult women; in other studies, that the latter is facilitated by a critical attitude in the mother.[40] This was particularly noticeable in the better educated families, in which a somewhat aggressive interplay between mother and daughter leads to a masculine type of achievement-orientated behaviour in the latter.

McClelland has made an extensive study of the social consequences of achievement motivation.[59] Such motivation was studied cross-culturally, by investigating the occurrence of achievement ideas and imagery in the T.A.T. stories produced by individuals in a number of civilized and more primitive societies, and also their responses to other tests such as Aronson's (see Appendix). Furthermore, achievement themes were assessed in the folk-tales of primitive societies, and in the popular stories in the reading books of children in literate societies. McClelland reached the conclusion that the economic growth of societies was related to the frequency with which achievement themes appeared in such material; and in particular that a large amount of achievement imagery in children's stories was associated with the onset of a period of economic growth developing about thirty years later—that is to say, when these children became adult. A high degree of achievement motivation led to the expansion of 'entrepreneurial' occupations. Entrepreneurs are the business organizers, managers and salesmen who exercise control over the means of economic production and trade. The characteristics of entre-preneurs, as were demonstrated to a considerable extent by experimental investigations, are: a liking for taking moderate, though not excessive, risks, and confidence in the ability to succeed in such tasks; energetic action directed towards self-advancement; the desire for freedom and individual responsibility; obvious attainment of individual success, usually signalled by the acquisition of wealth. All these characteristics are associated with strong achievement motivation. But the successful entrepreneur must also possess skill in organization, and the capacity for long-term planning. However, it should be noted that not all those high in achievement moti-vation necessarily choose such occupations. If they belong to the upper social classes, they are more likely to attempt careers in exploration or scientific research, success in which appears to them more valuable. Moreover, adolescents in the lower social classes may think that success is just as much a matter of luck as of achievement through their own efforts.[60]

High achievement motivation, as we have seen, is unrelated to affiliation motivation, and indeed may be negatively correlated with it. Neverthe-less, as was pointed out in Chapter 7, successful entrepreneurial activities do, according to McClelland, involve 'other-directedness'—the capa-city to adapt one's behaviour flexibly to the desires and needs of others, and to treat people as individuals, not merely in accordance with tradi-tional attitudes. This supplies a check on excessive personal motivation. Thus these activities are most successful when strong achievement moti-vation is accompanied by 'other-directedness'.

In addition to his studies of existing societies, McClelland also investi-gated the historical rise and decline of earlier civilized societies, with respect particularly to their economic success. He studied the achievement themes to be found in the literature most characteristic of these societies at different eras. Thus the economic growth of Greece, and especially of Athens, as assessed from their trading activities, occurred most obviously during the period 900–475 B.C., to be followed by a climax of success from 475–362 B.C., and a decline from 362–100 B.C. In each era, the rise and fall in frequency of achievement themes in the writings of, for instance, Hesiod, Xenophon and Aristotle, preceded economic growth and decline. A similar study was made of the periods of economic growth in England from the Elizabethan era, followed by a decline in the late seventeenth and early eighteenth centuries, and a further expansion at the time of the Industrial Revolution. These changes were preceded by the presence or absence of achievement themes in the poetry of, for instance, Shakespeare; Milton and Addison; and Wordsworth and Shelley.

McClelland considered that the principal psychological factor involved in the occurrence of high achievement motivation was parental treatment, as we noted in Chapter 2. That is to say, mothers expected their sons to be capable of self-reliant and independent action at an early age. They placed relatively few restrictions on their actions, except that they strongly discouraged childish dependent behaviour. Fathers also did not seek to dominate over their sons; and both parents treated the children warmly. On the other hand, children who regarded their mothers as rejecting tended to be low in achievement motivation, and were particularly responsive to social disapproval, and even to lack of obvious approval, in that they performed less competently in tasks.[61] Over-protected children reacted in a somewhat similar way; they responded particularly readily when they received social approval. According to McClelland, in the third Greek era of economic decline, children were often brought up by slaves who encouraged dependence rather than self-reliance, hence minimizing achievement motivation. But excessive stress on power and dominance in a society was not associated with economic development, but rather with political authoritarianism, as in totalitarian states.

It is of course true that stimulating methods of child-rearing are likely to result from a generally liberal climate of opinion at the time of social expansion, and a dependent and conservative atmosphere at the time of consolidation and decline. We cannot therefore conclude that child-rearing methods are the cause of these changes. They may be the consequence, although they probably have a reinforcing effect. Moreover, it is clear that economic growth and decline are related to a vast complex of political, social and ideological factors which we cannot consider here. It is impossible to say whether they operate in part through the mediation of changes in achievement motivation; or whether the increase in the latter is simply the result of social and economic expansion.

It is clear that McClelland regards achievement as a long-term goal which is of great importance to many individuals. Moreover, he and his colleagues suggest that it is a general type of motivation which may affect the performance of a variety of activities by one and the same person; that is to say, anyone who is strongly achievement-orientated is likely to attempt good performance in more or less everything he does. It seems improbable that this behaviour continues after youth and early adult life. It is more probable that the majority of people as they grow older tend to concentrate their achievement motivation upon one or two main centres, such as their occupation and their principal leisure interest. Moreover, it is not clear that possession of a high degree of achievement is as relevant to superior attainment in all occupations as it appears to be in entrepreneurial occupations. McClelland himself noted that in another type of occupation, that of the 'bureaucrat', a different form of motivated activity may predominate—conscientious hard work without much hope of reward. Again, in occupations such as those described on p. 111, which necessitate a high degree of intrinsic interest, achievement motivation may be of minor importance; the pursuit and furtherance of the interest is its own reward (see, for instance, the findings quoted on pp. 124–5). Indeed, in so far as achievement motivation tends to focus attention on the self and the attainment of self-esteem and the esteem of others, it may impair rather than reinforce performance of interest-centred activities.

Finally, it cannot be assumed that a high degree of achievement motivation necessarily leads to long-term goal-directed activity. It could be satisfied by the successful attainment of a series of minor and quite trivial goals, provided that the individual was involved in these. Thus some business men may experience achievement only when, through intelligence, foresight and perseverance, they have built up a large and powerful concern. But others do so when, without any great foresight or long-term planning, they attain through their own cunning and efforts a continuing series of small successes.

6. WORK

Work in an occupation is usually regarded as the principal long-term activity of human life, at least in civilized societies. However, it can be argued that in many cases people are forced to work by the necessity of gaining a livelihood, and by social pressures to do this, rather than instigated by persistent goal-directed motivation; although the latter may operate when strong interests are involved. Indeed, motivation would seem to vary in goal-directedness all the way from that of the highly talented individuals described in section 1 to that of the casual labourer drifting aimlessly from one job to another. These marked individual differences are partly a function of intelligence and abilities; but also partly of varying forms of motivation and the degree of energy or activation of these. The differences would seem to be due to a considerable extent to differing types of upbringing, including those characteristic of different social classes. Thus several studies have shown that conscious and deliberate intention to enter a particular occupation is more frequent among middle-class adolescents than in working-class adolescents.[62] The latter tend to drift indecisively into the nearest job available. But this is due to lack of opportunity and ability, as well as to absence of purposiveness.

There are also differences related to occupations, and to the characteristics of individuals within occupations. It would seem that persistent goal-directed motivation operates most strongly in the choice and pursuit of professional careers involving special interests of the kind described in section 1, accompanied perhaps by creative and exploratory motivation. When achievement motivation is very strong, any occupation may be chosen in which the individual believes he is likely to succeed; and the energy with which he works will be related to his degree of activation, and to the conditions favouring achievement which we have just considered. However, other types of motivation appear in some occupational choices. Thus one study of such choices showed that those who wished to take up careers in architecture, drama and art possessed strong desires for self-expression and creativeness; those who chose social work, teaching and medicine wanted opportunities to work with and be helpful to other people; and those choosing business occupations were more concerned to attain wealth and prestige.[63] We noted McClelland's association of achievement motivation with entrepreneurial business occupations. The author obtained evidence of somewhat similar variations of motivation in the activities and choices of studies and of occupations in school children, students and employed adults.[64] From discussion with these people of their work and leisure activities and their feelings about these it was possible to infer the influence of the following types of motivation: activity (the employment of energy), security, pleasure and variety, self-reliance and independence, superiority and achievement, dominance or power, social conformity, self-display, altruism.

But it is probable that the most important motivation for work in many people is the attainment of a secure livelihood. Many studies of the factors most conducive to job satisfaction have shown that security is given the greatest importance.[63] Even if the income gained is not high, to obtain a steady job with regular wages and an assured tenure is a very widespread aim, especially among lower paid workers. Their margin of security is less than that of the better paid, and many remember the poverty and unemployment which were general earlier in this century. Indeed, it has been stated that British workers have increased in security mindedness in recent years.[65] Thus many school leavers seek primarily for a safe steady job; and parents may be still more concerned that they should enter one.

But although the primary concern of so many people may be the earning of wages to maintain livelihood, it is clear that motivation other than security may be involved in working. In one American investigation, men were asked if they thought they would go on working if they inherited enough money to live on without working; and 80 per cent said that they would do so.[63] There were more among the younger than the older men, and among professional than unskilled workers. Nevertheless, 58 per cent even of the latter answered 'Yes'. It would seem likely that the social status of a gainful occupation was involved also. It must be recognized that people may be less concerned about the actual amount of wages they earn, at least above a bare sufficiency, than by the comparison between their own wages and those of people in similar occupations. Any apparent inequality and injustice in wage payment gives rise to frustration, even to aggressive reactions, since it appears as an attack on social status by comparison with that of people in comparable jobs.

Again, workers relate their wages to their particular needs, and to those of their dependents. Some are satisfied with moderate comforts and amenities; others desire a high income and even wealth. But the latter provide more than amenities; they are also a mark of achievement which enhances self-esteem and are associated with high social status. We have already noted that such motivation is of great importance to those who take up occupations in business. But there are other occupations which attract by their prestige and the social status they confer on those who enter them. Such occupations are sought especially by those whose fathers are in high status professions. Occupations have a hierarchy of social status closely related to class stratification. Managerial and professional occupations are at the summit; then business and clerical; skilled manual; semi-skilled; and unskilled. Within these categories there are also differing status levels, some of which are remarkably uniform. Thus a recent enquiry showed that among professional occupations in both Britain and the United States, doctors were the most highly valued, and after them, lawyers.[66] Physicists and engineers were also well thought of; but politicians, poets and musicians were not highly regarded. However, in industrial occupations, certain trades may vary in status from one locality to another; for instance, employment in textile mills may be esteemed more highly than in factories in one town, but less highly in another. But almost any kind of occupation creates some degree of status. Thus it was found that one of the greatest hardships endured by those suffering from long-term unemployment in the 1930's was the belief that they had lost status; they no longer had the place in society afforded by a useful occupation. Relief work was carried on apathetically, because this lacked such status.

Again, people may strive to attain status within their occupations, by promotion to a better-paid job with greater social status. It is interesting to note that a conflict may arise here between behaviour directed towards social conformity and towards improvement of status. Though members of a group may respect someone who attains authority over them, they may also envy him. Thus it has sometimes been found that men—and still more women—may refuse promotion to foreman or charge-hand because they want to continue belonging to a group as an equal member, and because they are afraid to lose the support of their fellows and incur their resentment. Yet failure to obtain hoped-for promotion may also produce resentment against an unjust denial of status. Perhaps the so-called 'white-collar' or middle-class worker attaches greater value to improved status than does the manual worker. Many 'status symbols' may be employed to maintain or improve status: a monthly salary rather than a weekly wage; an office or a telephone to oneself; a carpet and a larger desk; even a title, such as 'rodent operator' rather than 'rat catcher'.

High status is often associated with the opportunity to dominate and exercise power over others, and this may constitute an attraction especially to those with strong power motivation. Indeed, such motivation may over-ride all others, and may operate in careers, such as the political, in which wealth is of minor importance. So also the promise of promotion may attract by the increase of power it affords. Again, resentment is caused by the lack of freedom and power to determine their own activities accorded to employees who feel that they are at the mercy of employers who do not consider their interests, and may discharge them arbitrarily and without explanation. The work of Elton Mayo demonstrated that groups of workers who felt themselves to be valued by management might improve their output enormously by contrast with those who were resentful against and suspicious of management.[67] If they feared that management would cut piece-work rates, they tended to restrict and limit their output.

But other forms of social motivation are involved in aims which seem independent of economic and status considerations. Many people may find in their employment a satisfaction for affiliation motivation, through the social companionship of other workers and the membership of small work-groups or large institutional occupational groups such as trades unions. An important type of motivation stimulating women to return to work after marriage seems to be the social companionship it affords. Again, women workers have stated that congenial social intercourse is a factor of great importance in their choice and retention of a job.[68] Moreover, Elton Mayo showed that the membership of small groups of workmates exercised great influence on the manner in which they worked. Clearly there was a high degree of social conformity to the work norms of the group. Such conformity also appears in the willingness to obey trades union regulations, or the demands of unofficial strike leaders, which often surprises outsiders. But the feeling of belongingness and the desire for social approval are reinforced by the appeal of security supplied by trades union protection. Social conformity may also appear in those who choose an occupation because it is fashionable; because their parents or teachers persuade them to enter it; or because their friends are working in it.

Another form of motivation which affects the choice and exercise of a career is the 'altruistic'—the desire to help and protect the weak, and the oppressed. We considered this on p. 114. There are also those who are influenced by the complementary form of motivation, towards dependence on and protection by others. Although this does not lead very obviously to any particular type of career, it does cause people to enter and retain jobs in which their work is directed and ordered by others, and requires no individual initiative. This type of motivation is said to be characteristic of the so-called 'authoritarian' personality, which prefers dependence on strongly directive leadership, though it may be accompanied by domineeringness over subordinates.[63] Again, it may be related to dependence on the 'approval motive' (see p. 104), producing excessive acquiescence to the demands of social groups of which the individual is a member; and which may be distinguished from the social conformity of more normal people.

But others may choose an occupation which will give them a reasonable degree of independence—the freedom to decide just how they think their work should be carried out. An important factor making for job satisfaction, especially in the independent type of person, is the opportunity for responsibility and for making decisions.[63] Inability to control the pace at which work is carried out, as in much automated work, is disliked rather generally. The more intelligent and self-reliant person is dissatisfied with highly repetitive work; and he wishes to engage in an occupation which appears to have some aim or purpose, and in which he can utilize to the full those abilities which he believes he possesses. In some cases such occupations may involve the employment of physical activity and strength, and in others of self-expression and self-display. These include physical sports, acting and dancing.

Long-term goals can hardly arise in connection with motivation to obtain pleasure, except when it is involved in the pursuit of wealth. Variety also would seem to be a somewhat superficial motive if it is related mainly to the desire for passive experience of novelty which we considered on p. 90. It may cause people to change their jobs frequently; and to avoid monotonous repetitive work, or to become easily bored with this and do it badly.[69] However, it is likely that many people find an opportunity for experiencing novelty and variety in their leisure activities. The more active and energetic search for the new and unfamiliar, on the other hand, may as we noted appear in adventure, exploration, discovery and creative work.

This discussion of long-term motivational goals as demonstrated in the choice of a career or occupation is highly speculative. There is little reliable experimental evidence to establish the relationships which have been suggested as existing between certain types of motivation, and occupations and the manner in which people work in these. Evidence is particularly difficult to obtain, since almost certainly the motivation operating differs considerably in different people; and as we have noted people are often not fully aware as to their real motivation in choosing and entering an occupation. Much of the information on job satisfaction is based on answers to questionnaires asking what factors make people satisfied or dissatisfied with particular occupations. It is unlikely that these answers reflect all the real reasons. Thus people who in reality choose a job in order to obtain power and status may believe that they are motivated by other considerations, especially if these seem to be more socially desirable.

Many people who are unable to exercise the pursuit of their interests in their occupations may do so in their leisure activities, which demand all degrees of talent, skill and knowledge. Thus the persistent consciously goal-directed activity which characterizes the pursuit of an interest may find satisfaction here, though perhaps with less reinforcement of status feelings and ego-enhancement than when it is the main occupation of life. On the other hand, an occupation which has little appeal to interest may nevertheless lead to persevering action, success and satisfaction if it provides a sense of achievement and an adequate social status.

9

FRUSTRATION AND CONFLICT

1. THE CONSEQUENCES OF FAILURE

It has become clear that motivated behaviour frequently does not achieve its object without interruption. Physical or social obstacles intervene, and cause delay or even complete failure, though attainment is sometimes reached as the result of further efforts. In such circumstances, individuals tend to experience frustration through the thwarting of motivation; and the situation is sometimes said to create 'psychological stress'.* Moreover, thwarting may also occur when there is a conflict of motivation; when two or more incompatible types of motivated behaviour exist which cannot be pursued simultaneously. Thus frustration may be due to two causes:

(1) An inhibitory tendency in opposition to a positively motivating tendency;

(2) The simultaneous action of two competing tendencies.[2]

One of the most frequent instances of frustration and thwarting is some kind of approach behaviour based on achievement and the desire for success, in conflict with avoidance behaviour resulting from fear of failure or social opposition. There are certain forms of activity in which both these types of motivation may be integrated and function together; but more commonly this is impossible, and one or other must be temporarily or permanently suppressed. In this case, the frustration caused by thwarting results from conflict between achievement motivation and fear of social opposition; and there are many other instances of similar conflict and frustration. Mere failure and lack of satisfaction caused by some type of obstacle inherent in environmental circumstances over which we have little or no control tends to produce further striving until it is seen to be useless; after which all attempts are abandoned. Disappointment, resignation, grief, may be experienced, but not frustration; and the after effects of frustration which we shall consider in this chapter do not appear. These tend to occur when the cause of failure is perceived as some kind of social opposition and thwarting, and particularly if personal failure is experienced with a threat to self-esteem.

* 'Psychological stress' must be distinguished from the physiological stress discussed by Selye, which occurs in situations in which there is difficulty in maintaining homeostasis, and an 'adaptation syndrome' takes place, involving various internal physiological changes.[1]

134

Some obstacles may result in further and more effective striving, particularly obstruction to the attainment of the long-term goals described in the previous chapter. These may stimulate perseverance and increased effort in attempts of the kind already made, especially if there is some expectation of success. But they may also lead to the appearance of adventurousness and ingenuity in thinking out a new and more successful course of action. This is particularly likely to happen when there is some incongruity or dissonance between what was expected to occur and what actually happens. Indeed, it is possible that all learning to adapt oneself more appropriately to environmental circumstances, especially when intelligently directed, is produced by the blockage of habitual actions and of the achievement of motivational satisfaction. New and 'functionally autonomous' motivated behaviour may develop.* Thus if a career in which one is interested proves impossible, another may be chosen instead. However, if no strong genuine personal motivation is involved, the activity may be abandoned. Or the individual may form a conscious intention to persevere and succeed which is unlikely to be very effective as regards action. Indeed, it may function as a goal in itself, as we noted in cases in which inadequate performers satisfied themselves by setting impossibly high levels of aspiration. It has been demonstrated that in adolescents general ideals of conduct may be inversely related to socially desirable behaviour and good social adjustment.[4]

In general, older and more mature people are better able to tolerate obstruction and failure and adjust to it successfully than are younger, less mature and less stable personalities. The former are more able to postpone immediate satisfaction of their desires, and to persevere and mobilize their energies to overcome obstacles. They are more ingenious in discovering ways of circumventing these. And if they finally fail, they can meet the situation with fortitude, and even dismiss it from mind. This will happen especially if they perceive the obstruction as an inevitable consequence of some external situation. Such a 'task-induced' stress may, for instance, be produced by distraction or interruption, and it leads to 'need-persistent' rather than to defensive action.[5] Many people may have become accustomed to interference, and are therefore less affected by it. Indeed, those who had become practised and adapted in certain tasks actually improved their performance in the stress of distraction; whereas if they had not, performance was impaired.[6] But if individuals believe that failure can be attributed to some inadequacy in themselves, or that it

* The concept of 'functional autonomy of motives' was introduced by G. W. Allport to cover motivation, peculiar to particular individuals, which developed originally from universal basic motivation, but had become independent of it.[3] This may occur through emergence of complex social motivation, of interests and of sentiments. But the concept may also be applied appropriately to motivated substitute activities.

threatens their security or prestige, they are more likely to experience personal frustration and to resort to some form of more or less maladaptive behaviour, such as the defensive reactions described in section 4.[7] This is likely to occur in those low in achievement motivation, with low self-esteem and a strong fear of failure. But this does not always happen; they may strive harder to attain similar goals, and thus restore their self-esteem.[8] Those high in self-esteem are more aware than those with low self-esteem of the discrepancy between the actual and the ideal self, and are better able to tolerate it.[9] But they are also more likely to evaluate their performance in terms of their own efforts; whereas those low in self-esteem pay more regard to what they think others expect of them.

Younger and less mature people tend more readily to react to failure maladaptively. They are less able to think out an appropriate course of action, and indeed to tolerate any delay of immediate action to achieve success, or any state of uncertainty. They may try to avoid a situation in which failure is probable. This naturally occurs especially in children. Thus it was found that when children were asked which of two jig-saw puzzles they would like to repeat, those who chose one which they had previously failed to solve had a mental age four years above those who chose one which they had succeeded in solving.[10] Achievement motivation may also be involved. Children low in achievement motivation chose a puzzle similar to one which they had succeeded in solving; those high in achievement motivation chose a different type.[11] But complete failure may not only produce avoidance of that particular situation, but also impair performance in subsequent activities. After failure in a puzzle game, intelligence test performance in children may deteriorate, especially in the more difficult items involving some thought. Speeded items are done more quickly and inaccurately, and there may be a general decline in willingness, cooperativeness, cheerfulness, self-confidence, alertness and persistence.[12] As children grow older, their reactions to failure become more effective. In a group aged 3–6 years, the younger ones, after failing in a socially competitive situation, tended to conceal or gloss over their failure; to interrupt the task, shift to another one or withdraw; or to behave aggressively to the experimenter.[13] These responses decreased in frequency with increasing age, and there was a greater effort to overcome failure by persistent effort. However, children who were trained constructively, and rewarded for constructive efforts in problem solving, subsequently behaved more constructively after frustration; whereas those trained to behave aggressively and rewarded for their aggression reacted aggressively to frustration.[14] Again, experience of partial failure may be more effective in producing adaptive behaviour than is complete success. A group of children was initially given adult approval for their work which was subsequently withdrawn.[15] Afterwards they learnt a simple task more effectively than did another group which had received approval throughout.

There are individual differences in these responses even in young children. Some are more concerned to achieve success, others to avoid failure. Self-defensive actions occur more often in the less intelligent and self-critical. Maladjusted children are particularly likely to be affected by difficulty and failure. Thus their performance on the Terman-Merrill test of intelligence may deteriorate appreciably if they are given some of the more difficult items before the easier ones.

Adults who suffer from a high degree of anxiety may also have difficulty in adapting to failure. Some instances of this were quoted in the last chapter. Whereas those with a low degree of anxiety were stimulated to perform better when told they had done badly in previous tasks, those with a high degree of anxiety performed less well, for instance in the Wechsler Digit-Symbol test.[16] The latter performed better when given encouragement, but less well when discouraged; the former did the opposite. Those with a high degree of anxiety tended to blame themselves for their failures rather than other people, or the environmental situation.[17] If failure is deliberately made to reflect on a person's capacities—if for instance he is told that it suggests that he is in some way maladjusted—then his behaviour may become more rigid and less adaptable in consequence.[18]

But people may compare their circumstances with those of others in like situations, and experience frustration when they believe themselves more hardly treated. A man may accept difficulties when those around him are similarly affected, but resent them if other people such as himself do not share them. Instances of this were shown in answers to a questionnaire administered to men in the American Army during the 1939 war.[19] Whether or not men felt they had been badly treated or had grievances depended upon whether they thought that other men of the same status or in the same unit had been treated better or in the same way. Older married men who had been skilled tradesmen tended to feel aggrieved when drafted into the Army, because many men similar to themselves were not drafted. Negroes, on the other hand, were often glad to be drafted, because it promised them an improvement of status. Again, men in units in which promotion was frequent were more resentful of lack of promotion than were those in units in which promotion was infrequent.

2. LEWIN'S THEORY AS TO THE NATURE AND CONSEQUENCES OF MOTIVATIONAL CONFLICT

The most systematic treatment of motivational conflict, its occurrence and the behaviour to which it leads, has been given by K. Lewin and his colleagues.[20] It is desirable to consider first Lewin's theory as to the dynamics of motivation. He states that there is a continuing interaction between forces in the environment which impinge on the individual, and motivational forces within him. The latter are conceived of as tensions set up by internal needs; and they are organized in more or less permanent systems. There is a hierarchy of needs from the temporary and superficial to the long-lived and closely personal. Single needs or combinations of need may set up 'quasi-needs', voluntary intentions to action which sometimes become functionally autonomous, but sometimes die away if the forces behind them are not strong enough, for instance, when interests change. Tension systems may also interact with each other more or less harmoniously, as when different types of motivation facilitate or counter-act each other. Or they may be segregated from each other by firm boundaries, as in individuals with different and unrelated interests. In different persons, the degree of differentiation may be greater or less; children, for instance, possess simple and rather crude systems, while adults, especially intelligent adults, may have highly complex systems, greatly modified by learning. In some people, such as the old, systems have become rigid through ageing. In mental defectives, systems are both rigid and relatively undifferentiated, so that there is little variety or adaptation of action. But neurotics have excessively fluid systems, such that general uncontrolled action tends to occur readily.

Finally, the contents of systems, that is to say, the needs to which they relate, differ in different persons, apart from those related to the basic needs; the differences resulting from variations in experience.

These systems tend to discharge their tensions in action whenever this is possible; but frequently they cannot do so because there are barriers or obstacles to action. Objects and events in the external environment, when perceived as related to needs, possess valences, which are positive or negative according to whether they are likely to satisfy or frustrate needs. When these are perceived, the individual is stimulated by vectors or drives to action which will tend to discharge tension. But particular actions are related, not to single need tension systems, but to many related systems in so far as they are not segregated from each other. Systems may however be held within firm boundaries which are either external obstacles or internal restraints. No immediate overt action may then be possible, but energy may be discharged in other ways, and particularly in substitute actions.

Whether or not direct action takes place depends partly on the amount of energy possessed by the need tension systems, which is related to the total energy which the individual can mobilize—his activation level in fact. Thus some people always have a low energy supply, and seldom resort to strong action. Others tend to employ all their energy too readily and have little in reserve; thus they 'go off at half-cock'. Still others can regulate the employment of energy in action which is appropriate to the situation—its importance and stressfulness. But the emergence of direct action depends also on the strength of a particular need, on the corresponding object valences, and on the existence of barriers to action. Rapid impulsive action is most likely to occur in children, whose needs are immediate and imperative, whose tension systems are relatively unsegregated from each other, and who do not realize the existence of barriers, nor the consequences of their actions. These are increasingly understood as the children develop. Moreover, they acquire the capacity for restraint by forming their own internal barriers or controls. Thus they become able to mobilize the appropriate degree of energy, and direct it at the right moment into effective courses of action. Control barriers are provided in the first place by parental commands and prohibitions, and by the example of parents' behaviour; later, through the observance of social regulations, and through the internalizing of these in forethought and prudence, and the voice of conscience. Thus deliberate voluntary actions occur, and impulsive behaviour appears only when valence and need are so strong that all barriers are overridden.

Conflicts of valences often occur, related to different need tension systems, especially when the latter are of approximately equal strength. In the first place, there may be a conflict between positive valences, when two equally desirable objects or activities are perceived. The individual will then try to obtain or participate in both. But if this is impossible at the same moment, he may then vacillate between the two. However, sooner or later he usually feels one to be more desirable than the other, and hence approaches the former and relinquishes the latter. But this is more difficult when it must be totally abandoned. Thus prolonged vacillation was shown by children asked to choose between a 'sweet' and a toy soldier; and by adolescent girls who had to choose between two parties.

There may be a conflict between a positive and a negative valence, as when an object is approached and then found to be surrounded by a barrier, and therefore not readily attainable. The barrier may appear increasingly formidable as it is approached, and the object may then lose its attractiveness and be abandoned. This is particularly likely to happen with children. Thus it was found that children thought that a toy which they were allowed to win as a prize for a game was highly attractive.[21] But when they were not allowed to win it, they considered it to be less attractive. However, the mere temporary removal of a toy made it more desirable.[22] Again, this 'sour grapes' attitude is less common in older children and adults, who may value an object more highly if it is difficult to obtain. The older child will say that a toy behind bars is nicer than the toys he has, and will continue to try to get it.[23] A game may appear more attractive if it is difficult to play.

Another type of conflict between a positive and a negative valence occurs when the achievement of an attractive object, or following a desired course of action, may at the same time lead to undesirable consequences, for instance, punishment or social disapproval. Such a conflict may result in vacillation. A child may begin trying to obtain sweets which he has been forbidden to take on threat of punishment, and then withdraw in fear; and continue to repeat this behaviour. Sometimes the threat of punishment, like a barrier, may increase the desirability of an object. But actual punishment and repeated failure to obtain it are likely to decrease its attractiveness to such an extent that the child finally gives up trying. He may 'go out of the field', as Lewin terms it, and depart to do something else. But before this he is likely to attempt 'detour behaviour', in order to 'get round' the prohibition; he may plead to be allowed to have it, or attempt to persuade his parents to give it to him. This type of conflict is exemplified in the situation described in Chapter 2 in which the child seeks to exercise his independence, yet fears punishment or loss of love from his parents in consequence. And it recurs in adults who seek some type of achievement, yet fear social disapprobation.

Thirdly, there may be a conflict between two negative valences, as when an individual cannot decide which of two evils to avoid. For instance, a child is told to do something he dislikes, or be punished for not doing it. Vacillation may occur, or a complete blockage of action. But more commonly he will try to 'go out of the field'; that is to say, escape from the situation, unless he is surrounded by insurmountable barriers. For instance, he may be shut up and told to do his homework in a room from which he cannot escape. Restless behaviour is then likely to occur. But in older children and adults, the barriers may be those of social commands and prohibitions, which may be internalized in the conscience. Even then the individual may strive to escape from the situation by withdrawal into himself, or through emotional outbursts.

Conflicts involving negative valences are usually more painful and difficult to solve than are those between positive valences. In an experiment, pairs of personality characteristics were selected and presented to people who were asked to choose between them; for instance: 'Which would you rather be? More attractive than you are, or more intelligent than you are?'[24] Here there were conflicts between positive valences. Conflicts between negative valences were presented by substituting the word 'less' for the word 'more'. The choice was harder to make in the second case. Sometimes there were blockages, and choice was impossible to make. Or people attempted to withdraw from the field by giving up the task.

One type of experience involving a conflict between a positive and a negative valence is that of 'satiation'. An individual is compelled or feels bound to go on performing a task which gives him no experience of interest or success because it is so boring and trivial, and no goal is achieved. It may involve the continual repetition of some minor action, as in many machine operations in industry; or the sustained attention to a series of signals which have no natural interest. Many inspection tasks in industry are of this kind; and so were the vigilance tasks described on p. 89. Energy becomes dammed up, and there is no release of tension through the attainment of a goal. However, if the self is involved—if the individual feels that he is demonstrating his power and competence in carrying out the task—he will not become satiated. Satiation tends to produce irregular, careless and inaccurate work; and fatigue of the kind which disappears immediately the activity is changed. Indeed, even a small variation in the manner of working or the nature of the task may dispel satiation. But if it is indefinitely prolonged, there may be emotional breakdown, with anger and disgust. Satiation may even spread to related occupations, which then seem equally tedious. Normally the incentive for continuing industrial tasks is the earning of wages, and this may act as a goal to be achieved. Even to see the articles one has made pile up before one may serve this purpose, and prevent the satiation which occurs if they are removed as soon as they are finished. In one experiment, people were asked to draw pencil strokes on paper over and over again, until some of them were unable to continue.[25] But one or two took this task as a demonstration of their persistence, and were able to continue much longer.

Often when there is a conflict or a barrier to direct action, there will be a resort to some kind of substitute action, that is to say, some different kind of activity which to a greater or lesser extent affords a means of discharging tension. Substitute actions provide a satisfactory compensation for frustration in so far as they have some connection or similarity with the initial course of action which has been blocked. They must also possess some equivalence in the degree of aspiration involved.[26] The more highly specific and relevant the substitute activity, the greater the discharge of tension. Thus a student who is unable to follow a particular career may satisfactorily substitute another career if it is similar in nature and equally valued. Again, someone who has experienced a loss of self-esteem through business failure may seek some compensatory form of gain.[27] A conflict caused by the disapproval of others may be relieved by demonstrating one's value to the group in other ways. If one performs activities which lead to loss of approval of oneself, one may attempt some form of expiation, for instance, through renunciation of material gain.

It is often more difficult for children than for adults to find satisfying substitute actions because their lives are more confined, and they have less forethought and knowledge in discovering satisfactory alternatives. But it is often possible for adults to suggest substitutes, for instance an alternative form of play instead of a forbidden one. However, children are more willing than are adults to utilize substitute activities on what Lewin has termed the 'level of unreality', for instance, symbolic 'make-believe' play, or talk (sometimes taking the form of boasting or lying), or mere day-dreaming. Such substitutes will not be acceptable in cases of real need; a hungry child will not be satisfied by 'make-believe' food, though he may play with it when he is not hungry.[28] Experiments have been carried out to assess the degree of satisfaction provided by various substitute activities by giving the latter to children who have been interrupted in performing an initial activity. The more satisfying the substitute activity, the greater the discharge of tension and the less likely is the child to resume the initial activity if he is given the chance. Again if the desire for the 'real' activity is strong, substitute activities are unsatisfying. A child who wants to cut out with scissors will not accept cardboard scissors as a substitute; but he will do so in 'make-believe' play with dolls. In cases of genuine need, where the action required is fairly obvious, the child has no difficulty in distinguishing between the 'real' and 'unreal'; but he may require training and experience in making this distinction in other situations, for instance in differentiating between actually doing a job and merely talking about it.

The Freudian concept of 'sublimation' resembles in many ways that of substitute action. Although it is included by the Freudians among the 'mechanisms of defence' (see section 5), it is nevertheless more positive and ego-enhancing than merely defensive. It is supposed that the child is guided by ego processes to direct the desires of the 'id', the open expression of which is punished or prevented, into socially approved activities. These result in a reduction of tension, and in freedom from anxiety. Thus it is suggested that anal erotic desires to play with faeces and dirt may be redirected into painting and sculpture, and even cooking; oral erotic desire to suck the breast into smoking or playing a wind instrument. These explanations may seem somewhat far-fetched; but the activities symbolize the originally repressed behaviour and the individual is quite unconscious of the connection. More comprehensible is the sublimation of adult sexuality into love, and even religion. Aggressive impulses may also be sublimated and appear in forms acceptable to the conscience, such as moral indignation; and into efforts for achievement generally.

Thus sublimation may afford substitute activity which is not only socially approved but is also accepted by the ego—that is to say, it operates on the level of reality. In adults, the differentiation between reality and unreality is firmer than in children, and they are seldom satisfied by unreal substitutes although they may resort to them at times; for instance in talking about what they want or grumbling about their dislikes. On the whole, actual speech is a more satisfying substitute than is uncommunicated thought. Nevertheless, adults may formulate imaginary ideal goals when real ones are unattainable. Or they may simply day-dream and build castles in the air. The latter are particularly common in adolescents, who are prevented by their immaturity and dependence from attaining their real goals. We have seen also that those who perform a task badly may sometimes console themselves by setting an impossibly high level of aspiration. The more an individual is inhibited from performing overt actions, the more likely he is to resort to substitute action with some degree of unreality. However, in general he possesses more opportunities than do children for real substitute activities. He has more freedom of action and more capacity for thinking of alternatives. Moreover, his time perspective is greater. He can postpone immediate satisfaction in the anticipation of future satisfaction; this is difficult if not impossible for children.

The more frequent and painful the blockage or failure of an activity, the less easy it is to find a satisfying substitute activity. This is also the case if the activity has been severely punished, or if failure is felt to be due to personal inadequacy or inferiority. However, for the child the mother's sympathy and consolation may lessen the pain of failure, or may even enable him to surmount environmental barriers. She may encourage him to persevere in performing a difficult task, or show him how it may lead to a desirable end—for instance, the achievement of skill in a difficult game. She may suggest to him ways of getting round obstacles. Or when an activity is totally forbidden, she may be able to convince him that it possesses an impersonal danger or unhealthiness; or that it is contrary to general social regulations and would bring him widespread social disapproval. As the child grows older, he is able to envisage such considerations for himself, and regulate his activities accordingly. But even the adult continues to be stimulated to prolong action to overcome difficulties by the encouragement of others, especially those he loves; and to be consoled by their sympathy when he fails.

There is one type of substitute on the level of unreality which is employed by both children and adults, namely dreaming. In children's dreams there may be little disguise of unfulfilled wishes and unavoided fears; their expression may appear fairly obviously. The contents of adult dreams sometimes represent directly events which have just occurred; for instance, violent dreams after excessive emotional stress, such as the battle dreams of soldiers.[29] Sexual dreams, leading to erection and orgasm, are common especially in the sexually deprived. But often the dream contents are unreal and chaotic. Freud hypothesized that they symbolized conflicts arising in infant life which the adult was unable to resolve and eliminate, and of which he might be completely unconscious in waking life. The symbolic expression resulted partly from the inability of the unconscious mind to express itself in terms of reality; and partly to protect the sleeper from the unpleasant effects of a conscious realization of his conflicts. There has been considerable disagreement as to whether, as Freud supposed, symbolism has universal meanings, usually sexual; or whether it should be interpreted differently in different people. Moreover, it is denied that dreams necessarily express infantile conflicts; they may also represent recent ones. But new evidence has been obtained which demonstrates the general importance of dreaming in maintaining psychological stability.

It was found that soon after falling asleep, and at intervals subsequently, there occurred periods of light sleep during which, in spite of bodily relaxation, EEG records indicated a degree of brain activity similar to that of waking life.[30] Moreover, it was possible to demonstrate the occurrence of rapid eye movements during these periods from changes in the electrical potential of the retinas, although in deep sleep eye movements almost ceased. If the sleeper was awoken at these times, he almost always reported that he had been dreaming. The greater the brain activity shown in the EEG, the more active the dream. Moreover, physiological symptoms often indicated that intense emotion was being experienced. Periods of dreaming alternated with deeper sleep, and amounted to about $1\frac{1}{2}$–2 hours each night. If people were woken each time that dreaming began, and were prevented from dreaming for some nights in succession, they became fatigued, irritable, forgetful and unable to concentrate in waking life. On the first night they were allowed to dream freely, they spent much longer in dreaming than was normal. But the interruption of deep sleep did not produce these effects. Thus it would appear that dreaming plays an important part in life; and it seems that its function may be to enable the sleeper to express and live through, either directly or symbolically, emotional experiences which cannot be expressed in the waking state, including motivational conflict and frustration.

3. ANXIETY

It is not possible in every case for the individual to discover some satisfying form of substitute action, when his initial activity has been frustrated; and it is particularly difficult for the less intelligent and mature. Again, if someone is very strongly motivated towards a given aim, he is unlikely to accept any substitute. When this occurs, a variety of forms of frustration behaviour may arise which do perform some adaptive function in producing a discharge of tension, but which are seldom completely satisfying since they do not lead to the attainment of motivational goals. These types of behaviour have been classed as extrapunitive, intropunitive and impunitive.[31] In the first, punishing action is directed outwards towards some person who is believed to be the cause of the frustration. In the second, such action is directed inwards towards the self, in anxiety and guilt. In the third, reactions to frustration are denied or avoided, for instance by employing one of the mechanisms of defence (see next section).

We discussed at some length in Chapter 4 the circumstances in which the extrapunitive behaviour of aggression and displaced aggression arose. But we concluded that these were not caused by frustration in itself, but by some form of obstruction or interference with motivated activity which appeared as a personal attack or humiliation producing an impairment of self-esteem. When no such obstruction occurs, but frustration is the result of failure or internal conflict, it is likely that the consequence will be some form of intropunitive or impunitive behaviour. One of the most frequently occurring types of intropunitiveness is anxiety.

We mentioned that anxiety is sometimes said to arise in situations in which individuals anticipate danger or pain which they seek to avoid. But it was suggested that it might be preferable to term this experience 'fear'. Anxiety is typically felt in association with failure and frustration in attempts to reach a goal, and with motivational conflict. Freud supposed anxiety to be caused by frustration of the sexual desires of the 'id', through parental, ego and super-ego control and inhibition. But other psychologists have considered that anxiety arises in the first case in the conflict between the child's desires for self-gratification and independence on the one hand, and on the other his fears that he may lose affection and support as a punishment for the expression of these desires. Such an expression is often contrary to social custom; thus anxiety is related to socialization. In later life, fear of social disapproval is one of the main factors which precipitates anxiety; but self-disapproval for failure and consequent impairment of self-esteem may be even more important. Thus individuals fear to perform activities aimed at self-gratification which may meet with social disapproval; but also to encounter situations in which their incompetence or failure reflects their personal inadequacy and inferiority.

Anxiety over social disapproval is widespread, and indeed it acts as one of the most important means of social control. But as people grow up, they usually acquire the capacity to deal with such anxiety in a realistic manner, through control of anti-social impulses and the substitution of socially approved means of obtaining satisfaction. Anxiety over personal inferiority, caused by threats to self-esteem, appears much more frequently in some people than in others. Thus in one study in which students were told that their test performances had been poor, and that they must take an intelligence test to assess their academic ability, 39 per cent of the students were undisturbed by this threat, and performed better than the other students who had not been threatened.[32] The remainder did experience anxiety, and performed less well. However, in many of these anxiety may have been merely transient, a result of particular circumstances. But in some cases, anxiety may have been more frequent and pervasive. Such people have a personality, often immature and unstable, which is disposed to feel anxiety in a wide variety of situations. This disposition may to some extent originate in temperamental disposition. But in all probability it has been enhanced by inadequate parental treatment in childhood, and particularly by rejection or lack of affection. These people may feel anxious even in situations which present no obvious threat, but which may be associated in their minds with threatening incidents. They are particularly likely to suffer anxiety in situations of stress, when they are strongly ego-involved, but fear that they may appear incompetent or inferior. They may attempt to avoid such situations if they can, but this may be impossible, or may give rise to additional social disapproval. We noted that there were people, low in self-confidence and self-esteem, who seemed to be more affected by the fear of failure than by a positive desire for achievement. They usually preferred easy to more difficult tasks, involving only a moderate degree of risk. Other experiments have indicated that they tend to be rigid, to adhere to familiar methods and techniques even when these are no longer really appropriate, especially if some risk is involved in trying a new method.[33]

We noted in Chapter 4 another situation in which people may fear social disapproval, and indeed inferiority also, namely that in which aggression is aroused. Aggressive action may be repressed and directed inwards towards the self, arousing anxiety and guilt. Though guilt and anxiety frequently accompany each other, the former seems to be related to behaviour which might give rise to moral condemnation by the conscience; and to occur more frequently in those of rather forceful personality, with strong achievement motivation. But anxiety is associated with prevailing timidity, low self-esteem and feelings of inferiority.

In people prone to feel anxiety, the arousal of anxiety by stress or threat is liable to affect on-going activities.[34] It is true that a moderate degree of anxiety may even improve performance of simple tasks, by stimulating greater attention and care; though they may be done more slowly. But any difficult task, of learning, problem-solving, and so on, is liable to deteriorate. Discrimination is impaired, and the anxious individual may respond only to a small selection of the stimuli presented to him. Responses may become uncoordinated and variable. They are sometimes quite effective, at others wholly erroneous; and these may alternate with each other in almost blind trial-and-error.

4. THE MECHANISMS OF DEFENCE

There is a variety of procedures to which resort may be made in states of conflict and stress, which enable the individual to avoid painful anxiety and its disruptive effects, and to protect the self from admitting inferiority. These operate involuntarily and unconsciously; and they were termed by Freud the 'dynamisms' or 'mechanisms of defence'. Though Freud supposed that they came into action mainly when the libido was thwarted, it would appear that in fact they may be utilized when any form of motivated behaviour in which the individual is greatly involved is frustrated for a prolonged period. They enable the individual to avoid any consciousness of anxiety or guilt over actions which might incur social disapproval or the condemnation of conscience; and also they preserve self-esteem through the avoidance of conscious failure. The self is supported and protected, but at the cost of self-deception: the failure to admit to consciousness thoughts or actions which could impair it. Thus some degree of dissociation within the personality is involved.

The mechanisms of defence take one or other of two main forms: in the first unacceptable thoughts are concealed or disguised, and in the second they are denied or repressed. One of the most frequently employed forms of disguise is 'rationalization'.[35] This may appear in a sensible, logical or morally acceptable explanation of behaviour which is not approved by the individual or by society; thus motivational conflict is avoided. Aggressive attacks on, or even persecution of, followers of some religion other than one's own may be justified by moral disapprobation of that religion. War against another country may be excused as defence against its war-like intentions; Hitler's invasion of Czechoslovakia was of this nature. Prejudiced individuals frequently rationalize their prejudices by attributing undesirable behaviour to those against whom they are prejudiced, as we noted on p. 67. But also rationalization may be employed in connection with failure in activity or inability to continue it. Either the 'sour grapes' explanation is used; an unattainable object or a difficult course of action is not worth the effort. Or the individual may explain his failure by saying that he was unwell, or that others were cheating him or obstructing him unfairly.

Another method of disguising the full consequences of actions which are socially undesirable or morally reprehensible and of avoiding a conflict between self-gratification and social disapproval, is called 'compartmentalization'. The individual may exhibit different types of motivated behaviour within different 'compartments' of his life which are dissociated from each other. In his business he may be aggressive and greedy, but outside the office he may also be a tender and considerate husband and father, and even a good churchman. Or an individual may exhibit 'public attitudes' of tolerance, cooperativeness and egalitarianism which differ widely from his 'private attitudes' of hostility and prejudice, to which he would be afraid or ashamed to admit publicly.

In 'projection', a person attributes his socially undesirable motivation to others. He may conceal from himself that he possesses this motivation, and attribute it to the anti-social behaviour of others. Thus his aggression is said to be caused by the attacks of others, which may be wholly fancied. Ethnic prejudice may be attributed, for example, to the threat of coloured people to white people's own livelihood. Such prejudices clearly involve rationalization, as we noted above. They can rarely be removed by logical argument; but they can in some cases be lessened by giving people an insight into their defensive tendencies, for instance by discussing with them the nature of ego-defence and its expression in projection, followed by the description of actual cases.[36] However, people with a strong tendency towards projection may be very resistant, especially against direct attempts to change their ethnic prejudices. It has been found that a highly prejudiced individual has often been restricted and frustrated in childhood by an authoritarian father, and may fear to direct aggression towards him or towards other authoritarian figures.[37] These may be treated with adulation and exaggerated deference, while aggression is displaced on to inferior and relatively harmless subordinates, or on to a minority group. With the latter, the aggression is justified by attributing socially undesirable behaviour to this group.

Another method of avoiding the implications of undesirable and anti-social motivation is through 'reaction formation'; behaving in a manner directly opposed to that resulting from socially unacceptable motivation. Thus aggression may be concealed by a show of submissiveness, by promulgating tolerance and peacefulness, by protesting a willingness to help others. Over-sensitivity to pain and suffering in others may result from unconscious cruelty. Over-protectiveness in parents is sometimes produced by concealed tendencies to rejection. Excessively puritanical and prudish individuals may be concealing unconscious sexual desires. It may even be that adolescent delinquents break the law in order to overcome their anxieties and demonstrate their bravado to their friends and associates. But it should be noted that behaviour in reaction formation is frequently exaggerated and unnatural, involving excessive condemnation of the motivational tendencies concealed in themselves.

These forms of defence are to some extent extrapunitive in that unacceptable motivational tendencies are not only disguised but also in part directed outwards, away from the self. In other cases they may be treated impunitively and denied entry to consciousness; or the individual altogether withdraws from them. These procedures have the advantage that they not only protect the self from damaging social disapproval and feelings of anxiety, but also they make interaction with others easier and more agreeable; whereas people who tend to resort to projection may experience disagreement and counter-aggression.

In one method of preventing or limiting awareness of internal conflict which has been called 'denial', perception of objects or events likely to arouse undesirable motivational tendencies is retarded or completely suppressed. A large number of experiments has been carried out in which 'taboo' words—words with sexual meanings not usually spoken in polite society—are presented for brief intervals of time.[38] It is then found that some individuals, though not all, take longer to perceive these than words with no such meaning. The supposition is that because the reading of these words would set up a conflict between sexual motivation and fear of social disapproval, there is a blockage against perceiving them. However, there is evidence to suggest that frequently the observer does in fact perceive them, but is hesitant to utter them. Nevertheless, with some people a similar blockage seems to occur for words associated with painful experiences. Thus denial may operate also in anticipation of pain, as we noted in the case of pre-operation fears (see p. 54).

One very common method of avoiding awareness of socially undesirable motivation, of conflicts and of the anxiety they may arouse, is through 'repression'. According to Freudian theory, painful emotional experiences and motivation unacceptable to the conscious ego may be repressed, more or less completely, into the unconscious mind. So also may infantile ideas originating in the id which are too archaic, chaotic and unrealistic to be consciously acceptable. Ideas and impulses which are morally undesirable may be repressed by the super-ego. But perhaps the most important form of repression is of painful and insoluble conflicts occurring in early childhood, which would continue to give rise to excessive anxiety and guilt were they not repressed. However, repression is not always complete, in the sense that the effects of repressed conflicts are not altogether eliminated. They may give rise to morbid anxiety, the cause of which is unknown to the individual experiencing it, and to a variety of neurotic symptoms. Again, partially repressed ideas and wishes may direct people's behaviour, causing them to choose courses of action the reasons for which they cannot explain.

However, not all repression is deep-seated. Repression of painful memories may also occur in adult life. Apparently unaccountable lapses of memory may take place which are associated with past actions of a socially unacceptable nature, or situations involving a painful failure. Thus we may forget the names of people who were connected with such situations. Freud cites the case of a man, A, jilted by his fiancée who subsequently married another man, B.[39] Although A knew B well, he was frequently thereafter unable to remember his name. Again we may fail to remember intentions to perform actions which might cause us inconvenience or displeasure, for instance, to congratulate a colleague on the occasion of his promotion to a higher rank which we regard as undeserved. Sometimes instead of forgetting there is a 'slip of the tongue' which inadvertently reveals one's true opinions instead of concealing them. Thus Freud wrote to a patient intending to advise him to 'consult Professor X'; but instead he wrote 'insult' not 'consult'!

A considerable number of experiments has been carried out to discover if repression of unpleasant or painful experiences can be demonstrated even in laboratory experiments. The technique most frequently employed is to present people with a series of small tasks, and to interrupt the performance of some of these before they are completed.[40] Subsequently they are asked to recall what tasks they were given; and the normal tendency is for them to remember more of the incompleted than of the completed tasks. The explanation given is that tensions set up by the purpose of performing the tasks effectively are discharged when they are completed; but the undischarged tensions associated with the interrupted tasks caused them to be retained in memory. However, if completion of a task is regarded as success and incompletion as failure, it may be found that completed tasks are remembered better than interrupted tasks.[31] This occurred if the tasks were presented as an intelligence test, but not if they were thought to be purely informal.[41] Again, those who attributed incompletion of the task to some failure or shortcoming in themselves were particularly likely to forget interrupted tasks.[42] This happened with people who had a low tolerance for failure or a low need for achievement. Others with a high tolerance for failure or a high need for achievement regarded failure to complete a task as a challenge to persevere; and they preferred the interrupted tasks and remembered them better than the completed ones.[43] However, people high in self-esteem recalled fewer incompleted tasks than did those low in self-esteem.[44] But it seemed that repression of memories of interrupted tasks was relatively temporary. If the individuals who forgot them were reassured, and any threat to the self or suggestion of inferiority removed, they were then remembered.

But the assumption that these experiments demonstrate the effects of repression has been criticized on the grounds that it is uncertain which of the tasks was learnt best in the first place. Indeed, even in experiments using other techniques, for instance the differential remembering of emotional and neutral words presented in a free association test, there may be selective original learning.[7] A form of denial may prevent the assimilation of words likely to be associated with emotional conflict. But this is not always the case. Those who in experiments such as the above tended to remember tasks in which they succeeded and forget those in which they failed also forgot nonsense syllables accompanied by electric shocks, in a list they had learned.[45] But they showed no difference in the initial learning of these from people who tended to remember failed tasks and nonsense syllables accompanied by shocks. Thus it would appear that some people consistently tend to repress the memory of failures and unpleasant experiences, even when they were fully conscious of them at the time. However, this repression must be distinguished from the normal tendency to forget unpleasant experiences by contrast with pleasant ones. Such forgetting is gradual; whereas denial and repression occur during or immediately after the disagreeable experience.[34]

Finally, Freudian theory has postulated another rather surprising mechanism of defence termed 'regression'. It is supposed that when an individual is excessively frustrated, especially during childhood, he may retreat or regress to an earlier stage of development, especially if he was 'fixated' at this earlier stage. In 'fixation' there is a failure to develop, or to develop satisfactorily beyond a particular stage and to relinquish completely the sexual gratifications proper to that stage. And when full development is retarded the individual may then regress to that stage. Thus a child who experiences frustration of his dependence on his mother through the birth of a younger brother or sister may regress to infantile behaviour and become enuretic. Similar regression may appear when he first goes to school and is removed from his mother's protection; and in addition there may occur thumb-sucking, crying, temper tantrums and baby talk appropriate to early childhood.

Regression is a type of defence more frequent in children than in adults. Temporary regression has been studied experimentally in children. A group of children aged about four years was given two sets of toys to play with, one more and the other less attractive.[46] After a short time a grid was lowered between them and the more attractive toys, which they could still see; and they were left with the less attractive. Their activities were observed, including the manner in which they played with the less attractive toys, their attempts to get at the toys behind the grid, and to escape from the situation. All play activities were rated for constructiveness; and it was found that these ratings were lower after the withdrawal of the more attractive toys. Attempts to escape and crying also appeared. Thus it was concluded that even temporary frustration can give rise to regressive actions, and the appearance of less mature and more infantile behaviour. Another experiment on children of 10–11 years gave similar results. These children were given tasks on successive days which became gradually harder and finally impossible because, unknown to the learner, the material presented for learning changed from trial to trial.[47] At this point cooperativeness in many cases decreased; the children became less attentive and more childish in their behaviour, and some of them tried to withdraw from the situation.

Adults under severe psychological stress may also regress to childish behaviour, for instance to excessive clinging and dependence on others. But it cannot be assumed that this form of behaviour is necessarily mal-adaptive, nor that it imitates exactly the behaviour of early childhood. There may be a temporary disorganization of mature behaviour under stress, involving a reasonable degree of dependence. Normal persons abandon such behaviour immediately the stress is past; and it is only its prolongation which may be regarded as infantile and maladaptive.

The evidence for the existence of the mechanisms of defence depends largely on clinical studies; and it is apparent that controlled investigation of these mechanisms is not extensive. It is doubtful whether, except per-haps in children, they can be set in action by artificial causes such as those available in laboratory experiments. The mechanisms are based on deep-rooted causes of which the individual is seldom conscious. Nevertheless, without accepting entirely the Freudian theory of the unconscious mind and its instinctive processes, it is possible to recognize the frequent occur-rence of types of behaviour such as we have discussed in many people, not necessarily neurotic, in their ordinary everyday lives. The concept of the mechanisms affords a valuable insight into some of the more obvious forms of irrational behaviour, and would repay further and more detailed study, even if this was confined to systematic observations of everyday life operation of the mechanisms, the kinds of situation in which they appear and the type of personality in whom they occur.

It is probably true that the majority of the defence mechanisms operate only in situations of considerable stress and frustration, although most people resort to them from time to time. Maintenance of these defences itself involves tension which not everyone can tolerate beyond a point. Indeed, if defence becomes intolerable, there may be complete breakdown and disorganization of behaviour. Neurosis may occur; or there may be a state of withdrawal into the self marked by resignation and apathy, when the individual gives up the struggle to solve his problems and overcome his difficulties. Such behaviour was observed in some prisoners of war; and also in those who suffered long periods of unemployment in the 1930's, who, as we noted on p. 130, became unable to make the effort to perform the relief work offered to them.

However, between these states and the much more satisfactory sub-stitute activities there lies a variety of behaviour which has been attributed to so-called 'coping mechanisms'.[34] These types of behaviour seem to afford a relief of tension in states of frustration and conflict involving the damming up of energy which cannot be employed in direct or substitute action. They may thus do little to ameliorate the conflict or circumvent the source of frustration. But they afford a temporary relief, and perhaps enable an individual to make a fresh and more intelligent start on the solution of his problems. They include various types of displaced activity, some of it similar to that described in animals by the ethologists; for instance, eating, drinking and sleeping; taking alcohol and drugs; verbal behaviour such as cursing, irrelevant exclamations, jokes, explanations and apologies; laughing and crying. Physical activity is frequent, including both the more directed forms and also a variety of random erratic behaviour, or the curiously stereotyped repetition of inappropriate actions. Random erratic movement was first demonstrated by the Russian psychologist, Luria.[48] In his experiments, individuals were required to react to a series of words, some of them with highly emotional meanings, by speaking the first word that came into their minds. At the same time, they were to press a rubber bulb held in the right hand; and involuntary movements of the left hand were recorded by means of a 'tambour', a stretched rubber sheet on which the hand rested. It was found that individuals disturbed by emotional conflicts, including examination candidates, neurotics and criminals, when aroused by the emotional words, could not control the movements made in pressing the rubber bulb, and made a series of irregular pressures rather than a single one. Moreover, an irregular coarse tremor was recorded in the left hand. It would appear that in these states activation was excessive; and Luria suggested that there was a decrease in cortical control of the voluntary movements of the right hand and even more of the involuntary movements of the left hand.

Similar effects have been demonstrated to occur as the result of tasks producing frustration and conflict; for instance, performing a difficult discrimination task during distraction, and responding to ambiguous stimuli, with administration of electric shock for wrong responses.[49] The individuals in this experiment lay on a pneumatic mattress which transmitted their movements to a recording apparatus. Involuntary restless movement was greater when their increased GSR response indicated that they were emotionally disturbed. However, this movement appeared to have some useful function in that those in whom it was greater recovered their internal equilibrium, as assessed by the GSR, more quickly than did those who fidgeted less.

The second type of behavioural impairment which may occur as a consequence of frustration or failure is a stereotyping or rigidifying of response. Sometimes a form of activity which was at one time appropriate is rigidly maintained when circumstances alter. Thus those whose failure in performing a task seemed to constitute a threat to their self-esteem continued to employ a rather lengthy procedure to solve a problem when a shorter and simpler one would have been possible.[18] In other cases, a response may be repeated although it has been found to be incorrect and unsuccessful. This type of behaviour was found to occur with monkeys in a state of motivational conflict when a fear-arousing toy snake was put into their feeding box which they could reach after pressing the correct lever.[50] They sometimes depressed the wrong lever as many as a hundred times. Similar behaviour was observed in several human experiments. In one case, individuals were enclosed in a small room with four doors, only one of which was unlocked, and were required to get out as soon as possible.[51] The correct door varied on successive trials; and if the individual chose an incorrect door, he received an electric shock or a shower of cold water. Instead of working systematically from one door to another, many individuals tried them at random, and even attempted several times to open the same incorrect door. In another experiment with a choice discrimination task, individuals were shocked at random for incorrect responses, so that it was impossible for them to learn the correct one.[52] Again there was a tendency to make the same incorrect response, alternating with aggressive behaviour, regression in weeping and attempts to give up the task. Those who made stereotyped responses were on the whole lacking in self-confidence; the more self-confident persevered in the task. When a soluble task followed an insoluble one—trying to find out the pattern of a maze—there was a greater number of repetitions of the wrong response in the soluble problem when the insoluble problem had been presented a large number of times.[33] However, again some individuals persevered and learnt the soluble problem more quickly than did others.

Rigidity in behaviour may appear as a general defensive characteristic in certain people, notably those possessing the strongly prejudiced 'authoritarian personality'.[53, 37] They do not adapt readily to unfamiliar or stressful situations, especially those involving some degree of ambiguity or conflict, but defend themselves against the demands or threats of these by clinging to accustomed modes of behaviour and thought. Often their parents have been strict, rigid, and fussy, demanding their complete submission.

In some cases, however, the reaction to stress may be increased impulsiveness rather than rigidity. Thus it was found that people low in self-esteem, when informed that they were not highly regarded by other members of their group, made impulsive and ill-considered judgments.[54] In particular, when asked to write a character sketch of someone from his ratings on a variety of personality characteristics, they selected only the more obvious ones and disregarded minor and conflicting characteristics.

5. THE CAUSES OF VARIATION IN FRUSTRATION BEHAVIOUR

We have on several occasions noted that different persons react in different ways to frustration and conflict; and indeed that the same individuals vary their reactions from time to time. The latter variations are associated with the severity and duration of frustration. Thus there is a tendency for active attempts at overcoming difficulties to occur first, perhaps alternating with substitute activities. If these are unavailable or ineffective, the 'coping mechanisms' may then come into action. But as frustration increases, and particularly when it is accompanied by attack or insult, aggressive behaviour of progressive violence may occur. However, it would seem that these forms of behaviour do not follow any coordinated sequence; and many people adopt a variety of responses.[55] In prolonged states of frustration, there may be a resort to one or more of the mechanisms of defence, especially in those who have experienced much frustration and conflict in childhood. Finally, there may be an emotional breakdown in some, and withdrawal into resignation and apathy in others. Again, when there is prolonged conflict, stemming from childhood, neurosis may develop.

Nevertheless it is clear that there are individual differences in the extent to which different types of response are employed. We noted the investigation in which children of 10–11 years were given learning tasks which became more difficult on successive days, and on the fourth day were impossible.[47] Some children maintained their poise, attentiveness and agreeable social manner throughout, though occasionally becoming slightly aggressive on the fourth day. Another group, inferior in personality and intelligence, became inattentive and apathetic, and no longer tried to learn; or showed the regressive behaviour of crying. Others exhibited anxiety and a variety of neurotic symptoms such as thumb-sucking, nail-biting, etc.

In adults, as we have seen, those with strong achievement motivation struggle longer to succeed in difficult tasks. The more tolerant of failure, who are often more mature and stable in personality, continue the activity even if it is hard to overcome difficulties. Those who are less confident and more fearful of failure do not persist so long, and endeavour to conceal their abandonment of the task by adopting one of the 'coping' mechanisms, or even a mechanism of defence such as rationalization. The more intelligent and adventurous may seek the soonest for satisfying substitute activities. The extrapunitive individual, especially if of irascible temperament, quickly resorts to aggression, though often with displacement to some object other than the true cause of frustration. The more timid and intropunitive individual rapidly becomes anxious, and may attempt to withdraw from the situation. The impunitive try to condone or conceal their failure. It should be noted, however, that Rosenzweig, who devised this classification, was by no means certain that individuals were consistent in their responses; indeed, it appeared in his study that there might be a considerable variation of behaviour in different situations of frustration and failure.[31] However, he concluded that the most consistently and obviously extrapunitive individuals tended to be dominant and aggressive, and low in affiliation motivation.

It is also a matter of some interest to determine whether certain mechanisms of defence are more readily adopted by certain personalities than by others. It might be supposed that those with extrapunitive tendencies would resort predominantly to projection; the intropunitives to some form of displacement not involving projection, possibly to regression; and the impunitives to denial or repression. However, these associations are largely speculative, and there is no reliable evidence for their existence. Another hypothesis for which there appears to be some evidence is that individuals who possess a high degree of self-esteem tend to exclude threats from consciousness, for instance by denial; while those low in self-esteem distort them, perhaps by projection.[44] Levitt has suggested, on the basis of clinical observations, that the employment of certain mechanisms of defence may be linked to particular personality traits.[34] Thus those who show denial tend to be stubborn, self-assertive and unimaginative; those who employ projection are critical, hostile and intolerant. Regression is associated with dependence, demandingness and irresponsibility; and repression occurs in those who are inhibited, withdrawn and guarded.

However, it is probable that the mechanisms of defence which are habitually adopted are determined in part through social interaction. Thus it has been shown that denial of failure is most frequent in children who have seldom been rewarded by their parents, but have been harshly treated, forced to be obedient in an arbitrary manner, and severely punished.[56] It is also more frequent among working-class boys of poor intelligence. Repression of failure, apparently a more mature form of defence, occurs more often in children whose parents use psychological discipline, with reasonable requests for obedience. These tend to be middle-class children. They also readily become anxious about any tendency to aggression and then inhibit it; but working-class boys do not.

10

INDIVIDUAL DIFFERENCES IN MOTIVATED BEHAVIOUR

We have suggested that human motivation may be classified into certain broad areas, which have been discussed in the preceding chapters. Nevertheless, it has become clear that such a classification is based on inferences as to the internal tendencies within the individual which supposedly determine his behaviour in certain consistent and observable ways in particular situations. But it is also obvious that a number of different behaviour patterns, varying in different persons, may be associated with one and the same basic motivation. Because of the uncertainty as to the existence and nature of the particular motivation involved, G. W. Allport has preferred as units of observable motivated behaviour 'personality traits', defined as recognizable and consistently appearing patterns of behaviour, but without any assumptions as to their origin.[1] We gave some instances of these in the last chapter—self-esteem, hostility, dependence, and so on. Clearly these are motivational in nature, but there are many others. There is also a large number of emotional traits, such as cheerfulness, depression, fearfulness, etc.; and there are also the interests and sentiments we discussed in Chapter 8. All these interact within the personality, and it is often difficult to delimit them from purely motivational traits. Again, the latter may occur very generally; for instance, ascendance and submission, the incidence of which Allport assessed in large numbers of people by means of a questionnaire.[2] Other traits are less widely distributed. Moreover, the behaviour denoted by a trait name is not necessarily identical in everyone in whom it appears; it may vary considerably through its associations with other traits. Thus in an investigation by Asch it was found that the traits of a person characterized as 'skillful—industrious—warm—determined—practical—cautious' were regarded as quite different from those in someone in whom 'cold' was substituted for 'warm'.[3] Again, some traits are deeply rooted and develop early in life; others appear later and become functionally autonomous, that is to say, independent of any earlier appearing trait.

The analysis of motivation in terms of traits has certain advantages in that it describes the motivated behaviour of each individual in terms of unitary patterns which are peculiar to him. Thus it is valuable in making studies, for instance in clinical psychology, in which one is concerned principally with single individuals; and indeed in our everyday judgments of people we generally use trait names. But because the number of possible traits is very large, and because they vary from person to person, they must be classified into broader categories if we are to consider human motivation generally. Moreover, there is some danger that too close an adherence to readily recognizable traits may encourage superficiality in the understanding of the whole motivational endowment of the individual. We have seen that certain forms of behaviour are more comprehensible and meaningful if they are attributed to motivation which is not immediately observable, and of which the individual himself may be unconscious.

It would therefore appear preferable in a study of this kind to consider the broad classes of motivation which have already been described, always bearing in mind that each one may appear in a variety of behaviour patterns which differ in different individuals. Moreover, the more complex and highly developed the motivation, such as the functioning in the goal-directed behaviour described in Chapter 8, the greater the individual variability. Nevertheless, it is possible to trace certain consistent associations between the types of motivated behaviour appearing in certain individuals, and to contrast them with the types of motivated behaviour which occur in others.

Before we proceed to discuss types of individual variation, it is desirable to note that individual differences in motivation are sometimes confused with and even concealed by differences in emotional arousal and expression. The latter differences underlie the introversion–extraversion dichotomy, and similar types of temperament and personality classification. It seems that, quite independently of strength and type of motivation, some people, the out-going and extraverted, are very ready to express their desires and emotions openly. They may also easily be aroused to emotions of jollity and aggression. Others keep their feelings to themselves and inhibit their open expression; and such people may frequently be timid or depressed. Still others would appear to be passive and phlegmatic, with little tendency to feel emotion, and therefore little expression of it.

Now it may be that there is a parallel, though not necessarily a related, distinction between those who have been characterized as motivated towards approach, and those who tend to show avoidance. Thus the former may be high in self-esteem, eager to achieve, confident in their ability to succeed, perhaps liable to behave aggressively if they are attacked or thwarted. In some cases they may seek to dominate over others; but also they may be independent and prefer to go their own way, relying on their own resources. The latter, often submissive, dependent and low in self-esteem, seek to avoid challenge and difficulty; they are prone to expect failure and to fear pain and danger, and perhaps even more social disapproval, and experience frequent anxiety. But they may resort to the mechanisms of defence to escape these experiences.

This is undoubtedly a very broad classification, which includes many individual variations in strength and type of motivation. There are also exploration and competence; these would seem to be forms of approach motivation, closely associated with strong interests but independent of dominance and achievement. Again, social motivation would appear to vary differently. Though affiliation may be somewhat higher in those who show predominantly approach motivation, it is low in people with very high achievement, dominance and independence motivation, as also in those who avoid through withdrawal. 'Nurturant' or altruistic motivation would seem to vary in somewhat the same way, though it is not necessarily allied to affiliation as shown in social conformity.

Some of the varied interactions between these types of motivation are illustrated by studies of motivation in research chemists and Peace Corps volunteers.[4]* The majority of the 116 research chemists studied were high in achievement motivation; but nevertheless they varied considerably in other types of motivation. In the first group, who were the most creatively active, high achievement was associated with affiliation and play; they were cooperative with but not dependent on their associates. The second group was ambitious and aggressive, and the third highly independent though not aggressive; neither were very cooperative. The fourth group appeared to be of the 'bureaucratic' type described by McClelland (see p. 128); they were driven by conscientiousness to perform hard and meticulously careful work. Finally, there were those who were of relatively poor ability, lacking in creative activity, in whom affiliation was greater than achievement; they tended to be anxious, insecure and dependent on others. Thus they resembled the 'failure oriented', described on p. 122. Not all the chemists fell exactly into one or other of these groups; there were also intermediate cases.

The other study, carried out in a similar manner, of 80 young men accepted for training for the Peace Corps, showed that although all were highly desirous of helping and supporting those in need, they possessed varying degrees of achievement and dominance motivation, of conformity or independence and dislike of restriction. There seemed to be no very

* It should be noted that the assessment of motivation in this enquiry was based on self-ratings on descriptions of Murray's needs, and may therefore not be altogether reliable. It would appear that the achievement motivation described related chiefly to the performance of their work. It should be noted that the picture presented by these chemists is somewhat different from that of the physical scientists described on p. 111. The latter most nearly resemble the third group of chemists. It seems possible that the attainment of real scientific distinction occurs mainly when there is this type of motivation, detached from social participation, but accompanied by a high degree of activation.

close relationship between these types of motivation and the men's success during training and in their work subsequently.

One very important characteristic of motivational variation lies in the absolute and relative strengths of the various types of motivation. We noted that Lewin stressed the effects of the total amount of energy available, and of the manner in which it was deployed in motivated behaviour. The former would seem to depend on degree of activation; and the latter on cortical control over activation, in directing it appropriately. Such direction must be closely associated with the interaction between different types of motivation. Thus some persons possess a single strong form of motivation which overrides all others, or is reinforced by those which are relevant. The very ambitious man is motivated mainly by achievement, but in conjunction with dominance, independence and aggression. Again, in the physical scientists (described on p. 111), interest and exploration in scientific discovery were the predominant motivation, though independence and some degree of aggression were associated with them. In both, social motivation was at a discount. The strength of their motivation was due probably both to high activation, and also to the single-mindedness with which it was directed towards a particular goal.

On the other hand, when there is a conflict of motivation, such as we have discussed extensively, little energy may be available for action, since the activation of the conflicting motivation is cancelled out. However, certain people are able to reconcile conflicts in such a way that different types of motivation reinforce rather than counteract each other, the result being great energy and persistence in goal-directed behaviour. We instanced the social reformers whose achievement and aggressive motivation was harnessed to altruistic sentiments and actions. It seems possible that in these persons there is a considerable degree of self-actualization.

Finally, there are those in whom the total energy supply is small and the activation of motivation low. Some of these persons are of a relatively placid nature, who demand little of life and seem content to take it as it comes, even if it is rather monotonous and unexciting, provided that it affords the basic essentials of existence. There are others whose behaviour is not persistently directed towards the attainment of long-term goals; but who flutter or drift from one activity to another, in search of novelty, variety and amusement. One might say that they are trying to increase their deficient arousal through environmental variation.

As regards the origins of these variations in motivation: certain of them may have an innate basis, for instance differences in activation, and possibly in aggression and timidity. There is some evidence that autonomic patterns accompanying arousal and activation show characteristic long-term individual differences; and that tendencies towards persistence in behaviour are comparatively stable from childhood upwards.[5] But it has become quite clear that many forms of motivation are reinforced or modified by a variety of social pressures, notably those exerted on the child by his parents. Others, such as achievement and some forms of social motivation, may be largely created by interaction with the parents. Thus it might be suggested that those in whom the 'approach' type of motivation predominates have been stimulated and encouraged by their parents towards achievement and independence. But the parents have not been too accepting; they have been critical, and demanded high standards of behaviour, and in some cases of intellectual interest and achievement. The attainment of these standards has been rewarded by praise; but possibly there has been some threat of the loss of approval and love when effort has been inadequate and too readily abandoned. Such children should develop a strong conscience, but a rewarding rather than a punitive one, when the parents have been affectionate and themselves admirable. If intellectual abilities and talents are superior, 'self-actualization' may also be attained.

But in those in whom approach behaviour is less confident and more dominating or aggressive, there may have been too little parental encouragement and reward; demands have been too severe, physical punishment or threats of punishment too frequent. Or the child may have gained the impression from his parents' behaviour that domineeringness and aggression are the types of behaviour most successful in the attainment of ends.

There are a number of forms of parental treatment which tend to give rise to avoidance and anxiety. First there may be actual rejection or complete indifference, such that the child is perpetually anxious through lack of security, affection and approval. Or there may have been excessive severity and harshness, and the child has come to fear that nothing he can do will meet with encouragement or reward. Even over-protectiveness, which as we saw might be a type of reaction-formation, tends to create anxiety; the child and the adult cling to anyone who might protect and support them, and doubt their capacity to achieve through their own efforts.

Clearly parental treatment in childhood has a great effect in developing social motivation, and especially affiliation. Children who have experienced normal warm and affectionate relations with their parents usually show a good capacity to make social relations, with a reasonable degree of social conformity, lacking aloofness or excessive dependence. However, it is possible that when the parents have encouraged the strong independent interests of their children, the latter may be relatively detached from social relationships. Those who have suffered deprivation, and especially maternal deprivation in early childhood, may grow up unable to make and sustain normal social relations. They may show 'affect hunger'— continual demand for affection, support and social acceptance without any corresponding affection or cooperation on their part. Outright rejection by parents may also give rise to incapacity for making social relations, and in addition an apparent lack of any desire for these or for normal social acceptance; the psychopath is the extreme example of this. But overprotectiveness and over-affection may produce a clinging dependence, an excessive desire for social approval and an inability to take any responsibility or give support to others. Finally, placid and variety-seeking individuals may have had easy-going or unencouraging and rather indifferent parents.

But the associations between innate disposition, parental treatment and adult motivation remain far from clear. It is also a matter of doubt which forms of motivation lead to persistent goal-directed behaviour in which the individual feels himself highly involved; and which to temporary and fluctuating patterns of activity. It would seem that the former is more likely to arise from strong interests and sentiments, and in those who have reached the stage of self-actualization. But much further and more intensive study of human behaviour is necessary to elucidate these questions.

ASSESSMENT OF MOTIVATION

It is difficult to assess the nature and strength of motivation, since verbal reports, although used extensively, do not necessarily reveal these accurately, especially when motivation is partly unconscious in origin. Therefore Atkinson and McClelland have suggested that a better measure is some form of 'projection test' which indicates motivation indirectly, without the individual tested being aware of this. They have utilized in particular the Thematic Apperception Test (T.A.T.).[1] This consists of a series of pictures, some of which are taken from the series originally selected by H. A. Murray,[2] which relate more or less directly to a particular type of motivation. In general, this has previously been aroused by some appropriate environmental situation; for instance, hunger motivation by food deprivation, sexual desire by sexual arousal. Individuals are asked to write a story about each picture describing what is happening in it; what past events have led up to it; and what is likely to happen in future. The stories are then assessed for the number of images and ideas they contain which are related to the particular motivational state. These indicate the amount of phantasy engendered, which is organized into the story production. Atkinson and McClelland consider that their claim as to the assessment of degree of motivation from the number of relevant T.A.T. responses is vindicated in the study which showed the increase, with increasing food deprivation, of responses related to food getting.[3] So also achievement responses increased when instructions stimulated achievement motivation (see p. 122). The test has been used most extensively for assessing individual differences in achievement and social motivation. In these cases some motivational arousal may be employed, but it must not be too intense, for if it is, individual differences may not appear.

It is claimed that this type of test is superior to more direct measures of motivation, such as descriptions and self-ratings of experienced motivation, since the individual may not be fully conscious of his actual motivation; or he may fear to express it openly, as for instance with aggression. But inner motivation is said to be 'tapped' by the T.A.T. However, it was apparent in the studies of sexual arousal that expression of sexual desire was sometimes inhibited even in T.A.T. responses. Moreover, it may be important to assess the 'reality-oriented' preferences made in self-ratings, since these may be more closely related to overt motivated behaviour. Again, in the T.A.T. merely temporary and rather uncharacteristic motivational states may be exhibited. Consistent and recurring tendencies towards certain types of motivated behaviour are not necessarily indicated unless the T.A.T. is administered repeatedly. Such tendencies may also be assessed by means of observations such as those made in clinical interviews. Although these may not afford sensitive measures of current motivation, they probably give more valid evidence of long-term and enduring motivation. But the results often do not correlate highly with those of the T.A.T. The validity of T.A.T. findings has been criticized fairly extensively; P. E. Vernon has given a full discussion of this.[4]

One disadvantage of the T.A.T. is the difficulty of assessing which parts of the stories are relevant to a particular motivational state, in what manner and to what degree. Some training in scoring the test is essential, though there is usually a good agreement between trained judges. (Correlation between the assessments of different judges is as high as 0·9.) Other tests, easier to score, have been designed; for instance the Iowa Picture Interpretation Test, in which a set of pictures is accompanied in each case by four statements about it, one relating to achievement, one to anxiety, one to hostility and one to 'blandness' (indifference).[5] Individuals are required to rank the statements in order of their apparent relevance to the picture. It is supposed that the rank order is determined by the individual's prevailing motivation. In the French Test of Insight, a series of short sentences describing various types of motivated behaviour is presented, and individuals are asked to 'explain' or comment on these.[6] For instance, with the sentence, 'Tom always lets other fellows win', they have to explain why Tom does this; and the explanations indicate the predominant motivation of those who give them. In a 'graphic' or non-verbal test designed by Aronson, a slide is exposed briefly on which is a number of abstract designs or scribbles, and individuals are then asked to reproduce these.[7] Their reproductions are claimed to show significant differences of form corresponding to differences in amount of achievement motivation (see p. 126). Those high in achievement motivation make relatively few, distinct and clear lines.

In addition to the tests designed by Atkinson, McClelland and their colleagues, there is a great variety of questionnaires consisting of statements about motivated behaviour; those to whom these are administered are asked to state whether or not they behave in these ways. These are used particularly often in the assessment of anxiety. Anxiety as a general characteristic of personality is frequently assessed by means of the Taylor Manifest Anxiety Scale, containing questions about chronic anxiety reactions.[8] It is less effective in assessing anxiety aroused by a particular situation than is the Test Anxiety Questionnaire.[9] Again it has been found that in situations arousing achievement motivation, anxiety is sometimes facilitating and sometimes debilitating; the Achievement Anxiety Test distinguishes these two effects.[10] These tests differ considerably in their findings.[11] Moreover, they are to a greater or lesser extent open to the criticism of Atkinson and McClelland that they involve awareness of motivational states or tendencies, and conscious selection of appropriate responses. They lack the advantage claimed for the T.A.T. of spontaneous production of responses not under conscious control, the significance of which is unknown to those who make them. But the T.A.T. responses depend to a considerable extent on verbal facility, and can be made adequately only by comparatively well-educated persons who are able to invent and organize satisfactory stories. Tests such as the Rorschach Ink-Blot Test are less open to this criticism; but the Rorschach does not measure specific motivation at all clearly.

NOTES AND REFERENCES

CHAPTER 1: *The nature of motivation*

1 L. T. Troland, *The Fundamentals of Human Motivation*. Princeton, N.J.: Van Nostrand. 1928.
2 P. T. Young, *Motivation and Emotion*. New York: Wiley. 1961.
3 W. McDougall, *An Introduction to Social Psychology*. London: Methuen. 1908.
4 W. McDougall, *The Energies of Men*. London: Methuen. 1932.
5 R. Fletcher, *Instinct in Man*. London: Allen & Unwin. 1957.
6 The ethological studies of Tinbergen and Lorenz are discussed in: N. Tinbergen, *A Study of Instinct*, Oxford University Press. 1951; and in W. H. Thorpe, *Learning and Instinct in Animals*, London: Methuen. 1956.
7 J. B. Watson, *Behavior: an Introduction to Comparative Psychology*. New York: Holt. 1914.
8 I. P. Pavlov, *Conditioned Reflexes*. Oxford University Press. 1927.
9 J. B. Watson and R. Rayner, Conditioned emotional reactions. *J. Exper. Psychol.* 1920, **3**, 1.
10 E. L. Thorndike, *The Psychology of Learning*. New York: Teachers' College. 1913.
11 C. L. Hull, *Principles of Behavior*. New York: Appleton-Century-Crofts. 1943.
12 W. H. Thorpe, *Learning and Instinct in Animals*. London: Methuen. 1956.
13 R. S. Woodworth, *Dynamics of Behavior*. London: Methuen. 1958.
   D. O. Hebb, Drives and the conceptual nervous system. *Psychol. Rev.* 1955, **62**, 243.
   J. S. Brown, *The Motivation of Behavior*. New York: McGraw-Hill. 1961.

CHAPTER 2: *Emergence and development of motivation in children*

1 L. Carmichael, The onset and development of behavior. In L. Carmichael (ed.), *Manual of Child Psychology*. New York: Wiley. 1954.
2 K. C. Pratt, The neonate. *Ibid.*
3 H. L. Rheingold and G. C. Keene, Transport of the human young. In B. M. Foss (ed.), *Determinants of Infant Behaviour*, III. London: Methuen. 1965.
4 M. Wertheimer, Psychomotor coordination of auditory and visual space at birth. *Science*. 1961, **134**, 1692.
5 N. M. Munn, Learning in children. In L. Carmichael (ed.), *Manual of Child Psychology*. New York: Wiley. 1954.
6 D. P. Marquis, Can conditioned reflexes be established in the newborn infant? *J. Genet. Psychol.* 1931, **39**, 479.
7 D. P. Wickens and C. Wickens, A study of conditioning in the neonate. *J. Exper. Psychol.* 1940, **26**, 94.

8 A. T. Jersild, Emotional development. In L. Carmichael (ed.), *Manual of Child Psychology*. New York: Wiley. 1954.

9 B. Malinowski, Prenuptial intercourse between the sexes in the Trobriand Islands, N.W. Melanesia. *Psychoanal. Rev.* 1927, 14, 20.

10 K. W. Hattendorf, A study of the questions of young children concerning sex. *J. Soc. Psychol.* 1932, 3, 37.

11 R. R. Sears, E. E. Maccoby and H. Levin, *Patterns of Child Rearing*. Evanston, Ill.: Row, Patterson. 1957.

12 H. F. Jones and M. Jones, A study of fear. *Child. Educ.* 1928, 5, 136.

13 H. R. Schaffer, The onset of fear of strangers and the incongruity hypothesis. *J. Child Psychol. Psychiat.* 1966, 7, 95.

14 D. O. Hebb, *A Textbook of Psychology*. Philadelphia: Saunders. 1958.

15 A. T. Jersild and F. B. Holmes, Some factors in the development of children's fears. *J. Exper. Educ.* 1935, 4, 133.

16 A. O. England, Non-structured approach to the study of children's fears. *J. Clin. Psychol.* 1940, 2, 364.

17 R. R. Hagman, A study of fears of children of pre-school age. *J. Exper. Educ.* 1932, 1, 110.

18 H. F. Harlow and R. R. Zimmerman, Affectional responses in the infant monkey. *Science.* 1959, 130, 421.

19 K. M. B. Bridges, *The Social and Emotional Development of the Pre-School Child*. London: Kegan Paul. 1931.

20 F. L. Goodenough, Anger in young children. *University of Minnesota Institute of Child Welfare Monog. Ser.* No. 9. 1931.

21 J. R. Davitz, The effects of previous training on post-frustration behavior. *J. Ab. Soc. Psychol.* 1952, 47, 309.

22 A. Bandura, Social learning through imitation. In M. R. Jones (ed.), *Nebraska Symposium on Motivation*, 1962. University of Nebraska Press.

23 C. Bühler, *From Birth to Maturity*. London: Kegan Paul. 1935.

24 R. L. Fantz, Pattern vision in young infants. *Psychol. Rec.* 1958, 8, 43.

25 H. M. Halverson, An experimental study of prehension in infants. *Genet. Psychol. Monog.* 1931, 10, 107.
    A. Gesell and F. L. Ilg, *Infant and Child in the Culture of Today*. New York: Harper. 1943.

26 D. H. Stott, An empirical approach to motivation based on the behaviour of a young child. *J. Child Psychol. Psychiat.* 1961, 2, 97.

27 W. R. Charlesworth, Persistence of orienting and attending behavior in infants. *Child Devel.* 1966, 37, 473.

28 N. L. Pielstick and A. B. Woodruff, Exploratory behavior and curiosity in two age and ability groups of children. *Psychol. Rep.* 1964, 14, 831.

29 M. K. Rosenthal, Effects of a novel situation and of anxiety on two groups of dependency behaviours. *Brit. J. Psychol.* 1967, 58, 357.

30 H. R. Schaffer, Objective observations of personality development in early infancy. *Brit. J. Med. Psychol.* 1958, 31, 174.

31 W. Goldfarb, Emotional and intellectual consequences of psychological deprivation in infancy. In P. Hoch and J. Zubin (eds), *Psychopathy of Childhood*. New York: Grune & Stratton. 1955.

32   P. C. Green and M. Gordon, Maternal deprivation: its effects on exploration in infant monkeys. *Science*. 1964, **145**, 292.
33   R. A. Butler and H. F. Harlow, Persistence of visual exploration in monkeys. *J. Comp. Physiol. Psychol*. 1954, **47**, 258.
34   R. A. Butler, Incentive conditions which influence visual exploration. *J. Exper. Psychol*. 1954, **48**, 19.
35   H. F. Harlow *et al*. Learning motivated by a manipulative drive. *J. Exper. Psychol*. 1950, **40**, 228.
36   J. Piaget, *Play, Dreams and Imitation in Children*. London: Heinemann. 1951.
37   C. Hutt, Exploration and play in children. In P. A. Jewel and C. Loizos (eds), *Play, Exploration and Territory in Mammals*. London: Academic Press. 1966.
38   C. Loizos, Play in mammals. *Ibid*.
39   K. de Hirsch *et al*. *Predicting Reading Failure*. New York: Harper & Row. 1966.
40   H. Heckhausen, *The Anatomy of Achievement Motivation*. New York: Academic Press. 1967.
41   D. C. McClelland, Risk taking in children with high and low need for achievement. In J. W. Atkinson (ed.), *Motives in Fantasy, Action and Society*. Princeton: Van Nostrand. 1958.
42   E. E. Maccoby, Role-taking in childhood and its consequences for social learning. *Child Devel*. 1959, **30**, 239.
43   R. Griffiths, *A Study of Imagination in Early Childhood*. London: Kegan Paul. 1935.
      M. Lowenfeld, *Play in Childhood*. London: Gollancz. 1935.
44   J. A. Ambrose, The development of the smiling response in early infancy. In B. M. Foss (ed.), *Determinants of Infant Behaviour*, II. London: Methuen, 1961.
45   D. G. Freedman, Smiling in blind infants and the issue of innate *v*. acquired. *J. Child Psychol. Psychiat*. 1964, **5**, 171.
46   H. L. Rheingold *et al*. Social conditioning of vocalizations in the infant. *J. Comp. Physiol. Psychol*. 1959, **52**, 68.
47   J. Bowlby, Separation anxiety. *J. Child Psychol. Psychiat*. 1960, **1**, 251.
48   J. M. Arsenian, Young children in an insecure situation. *J. Ab. Soc. Psychol*. 1943, **38**, 225.
49   C. M. Heinicke, Some effects of separating two-year-old children from their parents. *Hum. Rel*. 1956, **9**, 105.
50   M. Roudinesco *et al*. Responses of young children to separation from their mothers. *Courrier*. 1952, **2**, 66.
51   B. Seay *et al*. Mother-infant separation in monkeys. *J. Child Psychol. Psychiat*. 1962, **3**, 123.
52   Y. Spencer-Booth and R. A. Hinde, The effects of separating rhesus monkey infants from their mothers for six days. *J. Child Psychol. Psychiat*. 1966, **7**, 179.
53   J. Bowlby, *Child Care and the Growth of Love*. London: Penguin Books. 1953.
54   H. L. Rheingold, The modification of social responsiveness in institutional babies. *Monog. Soc. Res. Child Devel*. 1956, **21**, no. 2.

55 R. R. Sears, Relation of early socialization experiences to aggression in middle childhood. *J. Ab. Soc. Psychol.* 1961, **63**, 466.

56 Berkowitz, L. *The Development of Motives and Values in the Child.* New York: Basic Books. 1964.

57 R. R. Sears, Dependency motivation. In M. R. Jones (ed.), *Nebraska Symposium on Motivation*, 1963. University of Nebraska Press.

58 R. R. Sears *et al. Identification and Child Rearing.* London: Tavistock. 1965.

59 E. M. Hetherington and G. Frankie, Effects of parental dominance, warmth and conflict on imitation in children. *J. Pers. Soc. Psychol.* 1967, **6**, 119.

60 G. Watson, Some personality differences in children related to strict or permissive parental discipline. In G. R. Medinnus (ed.), *Readings in the Psychology of Parent-Child Relations.* New York: Wiley, 1967.

61 M. Winterbottom, The relation of childhood training in independence to achievement motivation. Quoted in D. C. McClelland *et al., The Achievement Motive.* New York: Appleton-Century-Crofts. 1953.

62 H. A. Moss and J. Kagan, Stability of achievement and recognition seeking behaviors from early childhood through adulthood. *J. Ab. Soc. Psychol.* 1961, **62**, 504.

63 B. C. Rosen, Race, ethnicity and achievement syndrome. *Amer. Sociol. Rev.* 1959, **24**, 47.

64 D. Baumrind and A. E. Black, Socialization practices associated with dimensions of competence in preschool boys and girls. *Child Devel.* 1967, **38**, 291.

65 B. C. Rosen and B. C. D'Andrade, The psychological origins of achievement motivation. *Sociometry.* 1959, **22**, 185.

66 E. Fraser, *Home Environment and the School.* University of London Press. 1959.

67 J. Newson and E. Newson, *Infant Care in an Urban Community.* London: Allen & Unwin. 1963.

68 H. T. Himmelweit, Socio-economic background and personality. In E. P. Hollander and R. G. Hunt (eds), *Current Perspectives in Social Psychology.* Oxford University Press. 1963.

69 U. Bronfenbenner, Towards a theoretical model for the analysis of parent-child relationships in a social context. *Ibid.*

70 E. Douvan, Social status and success strivings. *J. Ab. Soc. Psychol.* 1956, **52**, 219.

71 D. R. Miller and G. E. Swanson, *Inner Conflict and Defense.* New York: Holt. 1960.

72 M. B. Parten, Social participation among preschool children. *J. Ab. Soc. Psychol.* 1932, **27**, 243.

73 L. B. Murphy, *Social Behavior and Child Personality.* New York: Columbia University Press. 1937.

74 H. R. Marshall and B. R. McCandless, Relationship between dependence on adults and social acceptance by peers. *Child Devel.* 1957, **28**, 413.

75 J. Piaget, *The Moral Judgment of the Child.* London: Kegan Paul. 1932.

76 T. H. Wolf, *The Effect of Praise and Competition on Persisting Behavior of Kindergarten Children.* University of Minnesota Press. 1938.

77 H. Levin and A. L. Baldwin, Pride and shame in children. In M. R. Jones (ed.), *Nebraska Symposium on Motivation*, 1959. University of Nebraska Press.

78 L. B. Ames, The sense of self of nursery school children as manifested by their verbal behavior. *J. Genet. Psychol.* 1952, **81**, 193.

79 J. Piaget, *The Language and Thought of the Child*. London: Kegan Paul, 1932.

80 W. McDougall, *An Introduction to Social Psychology*. London: Methuen. 1908.

81 W. Mischel, Preference for delayed reinforcements. *J. Ab. Soc. Psychol.* 1958, **56**, 57.

82 M. Rosenberg, *Society and the Adolescent Self-Image*. Princeton University Press. 1965.

CHAPTER 3: *The satisfaction of the biological needs*

1 M. Sherif, *An Outline of Social Psychology*. New York: Harper. 1948.

2 R. Levine *et al.* The relation of intensity of a need to the amount of perceptual distortion. *J. Psychol.* 1942, **13**, 283.

3 J. W. Atkinson and D. C. McClelland, The projective expression of needs, II. The effect of different intensities of hunger drive on thematic apperception. *J. Exper. Psychol.* 1948, **38**, 643.

4 S. Epstein, The measurement of drive and conflict in humans. In M. R. Jones (ed.), *Nebraska Symposium on Motivation*, 1962. University of Nebraska Press.

5 G. S. Gates, An observational study of anger. *J. Exper. Psychol.* 1926, **9**, 325.

6 P. T. Young and J. P. Chaplin. Studies of food preference, appetite and dietary habit, III. Palatability and appetite in relation to bodily need. *Comp. Psychol. Monog.* 1945, **18**, 1.

7 W. A. Mason and H. F. Harlow, Initial responses of infant rhesus monkeys to solid foods. *Psychol. Rep.* 1959, **5**, 193.

8 R. Harper. Some attitudes to vegetables and their implications. *Nature.* 1963, **200**, No. 4901, 14.

9 M. Mead, *Cultural Patterns and Technical Change*. Paris: UNESCO. 1954.

10 K. Lewin, Group decision and social change. In T. Newcomb and E. C. Hartley (eds), *Readings in Social Psychology*. New York: Holt. 1947.

11 Much of the discussion in this section is taken from: C. S. Ford and F. A. Beach, *Patterns of Sexual Behaviour*. London: Eyre & Spottiswoode. 1952. An extensive discussion of relations between the sexes is given in: M. Mead, *Male and Female*. London: Gollancz. 1950.

12 H. F. Harlow, The heterosexual affectional system in monkeys. *Amer. J. Psychol.* 1962, **17**, 1.

13 R. A. Clark and M. R. Sensibar, The relationship between symbolic and manifest projections of sexuality with some incidental correlates. *J. Ab. Soc. Psychol.* 1955, **50**, 327.

14 P. H. Mussen and A. Scodel, The effects of sexual stimulation under varying conditions on T.A.T. sexual responsiveness. *J. Consult. Psychol.* 1955, **19**, 90.

15 D. Byrne and J. Sheffield, Response to sexually arousing stimuli as a function of repressing and sensitizing defenses. *J. Ab. Soc. Psychol.* 1965, **70**, 114.

16 B. Malinowski, *Sex and Repression in Savage Society.* London: Kegan Paul. 1927.

17 K. Horney, *The Neurotic Personality of Our Time.* London: Kegan Paul. 1947.

18 K. Lorenz, *On Aggression.* London: Methuen. 1967.

19 H. L. Rheingold (ed.), *Maternal Behaviour in Mammals.* New York: Wiley. 1963.

    I. DeVore, *Primate Behavior.* New York: Holt, Rinehart & Winston. 1965.

20 J. Newson and E. Newson, *Infant Care in an Urban Community.* London: Allen & Unwin. 1963.

21 M. Mead, *Sex and Temperament.* London: Routledge. 1935.

22 G. Bateson and M. Mead, *Balinese Character.* New York Acad. Sci. Spec. Pub. 1942.

23 E. Waters and V. J. Crandall, Social class and observed maternal behavior from 1940 to 1960. *Child Devel.* 1964, **35**, 1021.

24 V. J. Crandall and A. Preston, Verbally expressed needs and overt maternal behaviors. *Child Devel.* 1961, **32**, 261.

25 G. R. Medinnus and F. J. Curtis, The relation between maternal self-acceptance and child acceptance. *J. Consult. Psychol.* 1963, **27**, 542.

CHAPTER 4: *Motivated behaviour in the emergency reactions*

1 E. Mira, *Psychiatry in War.* London: Chapman & Hall. 1944.

2 J. S. Tyhurst, Individual reactions to community disaster. *Amer. J. Psychiat.* 1951, **107**, 764.

3 L. F. Shaffer, Fear and courage in aerial combat. *J. Consult. Psychol.* 1947, **11**, 137.

4 A. M. Meerloo, *Total War and the Human Mind.* London: Allen & Unwin. 1944.

5 P. E. Vernon, Psychological effects of air-raids. *J. Ab. Soc. Psychol.* 1941, **36**, 457.

6 R. D. Gillespie, *Psychological Effects of War on Civilian and Soldier.* London: Chapman & Hall. 1942.

7 P. E. Vernon, A study of war attitudes. *Brit. J. Med. Psychol.* 1942, **19**, 271.

8 S. Epstein and W. D. Ferry, Theory and experiment in the measurement of approach-avoidance conflict. *J. Ab. Soc. Psychol.* 1962, **64**, 97.

9 E. L. Walker *et al.* The expression of fear-related motivation in thematic apperception as a function of proximity to an atomic explosion. In J. W. Atkinson (ed.), *Motives in Fantasy, Action and Society.* Princeton: Van Nostrand. 1958.

10 W. A. Scott, The avoidance of threatening material in imaginative behavior. *J. Ab. Soc. Psychol.* 1956, **52**, 338.

11 K. R. L. Hall and E. Stride, The varying response to pain in psychiatric disorders. *Brit. J. Med. Psychol.* 1954, **27**, 48.

12 P. G. Zimbardo *et al.* Control of pain motivation by cognitive dissonance. *Science.* 1966, **151**, 217.

13 R. Melzack and T. H. Scott, The effects of early experience on the response to pain. *J. Comp. Physiol. Psychol.* 1957, **50**, 155.

14 H. W. Nissen *et al.* Effects of restricted opportunity for tactual, kinaesthetic and manipulative experience on the behavior of a chimpanzee. *Amer. J. Psychol.* 1951, **64**, 485.

15 K. R. L. Hall, Studies of cutaneous pain. *Brit. J. Psychol.* 1953, **44**, 279.

16 E. M. Opton and R. S. Lazarus, Personality determinants of psychophysiological response to stress. *J. Pers. Soc. Psychol.* 1967, **6**, 291.

17 L. C. Kolb, *Med. Clin. N. Amer.* 1950, **34**, 1029.

18 R. D. Hare, Denial of threat and emotional response to impending painful stimulation. *J. Consult. Psychol.* 1966, **30**, 359.

19 I. L. Janis, Motivational factors in the resolution of decisional conflicts. In M. R. Jones (ed.), *Nebraska Symposium on Motivation*, 1959. University of Nebraska Press.

20 S. Milgram, Behavioral study of obedience. *J. Ab. Soc. Psychol.* 1963, **67**, 371.

21 I. Sarnoff and P. G. Zimbardo, Anxiety, fear and social affiliation. *J. Ab. Soc. Psychol.* 1961, **62**, 356.

22 R. L. Helmreich and B. E. Collins, Situational determinants of affiliative preference under stress. *J. Pers. Soc. Psychol.* 1967, **6**, 79.

23 J. H. Geer and A. Turteltaub, Fear reduction following observation of a model. *J. Pers. Soc. Psychol.* 1967, **6**, 327.

24 K. Lorenz, *On Aggression.* London: Methuen. 1967.

25 K. R. L. Hall, Aggression in monkey and ape societies. In J. D. Carthy and F. J. Ebling (eds), *The Natural History of Aggression.* London: Academic Press. 1964. Other essays in this book contribute a valuable discussion on human and animal aggression.

26 I. DeVore, *Primate Behavior.* New York: Holt, Rinehart & Winston. 1965.

27 M. Mead, *Sex and Temperament.* London: Routledge. 1935.

28 C. I. Hovland and R. R. Sears. Minor studies of aggression, VI. Correlation of lynchings with economic indices. *J. Psychol.* 1940, **9**, 301.

29 J. Dollard *et al. Frustration and Aggression.* New Haven: Yale University Press. 1939.

30 N. E. Miller *et al.* The frustration-aggression hypothesis. *Psychol. Rev.* 1941, **48**, 337.

31 N. Pastore, The role of arbitrariness in the frustration-aggression hypothesis. *J. Ab. Soc. Psychol.* 1952, **47**, 728.

32 For a discussion of the nature of aggression from these two different points of view, see: L. Berkowitz, *Aggression*, New York: McGraw-Hill. 1962;

and A. Buss, *The Psychology of Aggression*. New York; Wiley. 1961. The following also contains an apposite discussion: A. B. Yates, *Frustration and Conflict*. London: Methuen, 1962.

33 The experiment by A. Buss (Instrumentality of aggression, feedback and frustration as determinants of physical aggression. *J. Pers. Soc. Psychol.* 1966, 3, 153) is somewhat difficult to follow; hence this claim cannot be regarded as completely substantiated.

34 H. Kaufmann, Definitions and methodology in the study of aggression. *Psychol. Bull.* 1965, 64, 351.

35 G. S. Gates, An observational study of anger. *J. Exper. Psychol.* 1926, 9, 325.

36 D. C. McClelland and F. S. Apicella, A functional classification of verbal reactions to experimentally induced failure. *J. Ab. Soc. Psychol.* 1945, 40, 376.

37 L. Berkowitz, Some factors affecting the reduction of overt hostility. *J. Ab. Soc. Psychol.* 1960, 60, 14.

38 L. Berkowitz, Repeated frustrations and expectations in hostility arousal. *J. Ab. Soc. Psychol.* 1960, 60, 422.

39 N. B. Otis and B. McCandless, Responses to repeated frustration of young children differentiated according to need area. *J. Ab. Soc. Psychol.* 1955, 50, 349.

40 A. Bandura *et al.* Transmission of aggression through imitation of aggressive models. *J. Ab. Soc. Psychol.* 1961, 63, 575.

41 L. Wheeler and S. Smith, Censure of the model in the contagion of aggression. *J. Pers. Soc. Psychol.* 1967, 6, 93.

42 E. Stotland, Peer groups and reactions to power figures. In D. Cartwright (ed.), *Studies in Social Power*. Ann Arbor: Inst. for Soc. Res. 1959.

43 A. Pepitone and G. Reichling, Group cohesiveness and the expression of hostility. *Hum. Rel.* 1955, 8, 327.

44 L. E. Hewitt and R. L. Jenkins, *Fundamental Patterns of Maladjustment: The Dynamics of their Origin*. Springfield, Ill.: Green. 1946.

45 J. Kagan and H. A. Moss, *Birth to Maturity*. New York: Wiley. 1962.

46 J. W. Thibaut and J. Coules, The role of communication in the reduction of interpersonal hostility. *J. Ab. Soc. Psychol.* 1952, 47, 770.

47 M. Rosenbaum and R. DeCharms, Direct and vicarious reduction of hostility. *J. Ab. Soc. Psychol.* 1960, 60, 105.

48 J. E. Hokanson *et al.* Effects of displaced aggression on systolic blood pressure. *J. Ab. Soc. Psychol.* 1963, 67, 214.

49 D. S. Holmes, Effects of overt aggression on level of physiological arousal. *J. Pers. Soc. Psychol.* 1966, 4, 189.

50 M. Horwitz *et al.* Effects of two methods of changing a frustrating agent on reduction of hostility. *O.N.R. Technical Rep.* 1954.

51 P. Worchel, Catharsis and the relief of hostility. *J. Ab. Soc. Psychol.* 1957, 55, 238.

52 J. E. Gordon and F. Cohn, The effects of affiliation drive arousal on aggression in doll interviewing. Unpublished thesis quoted in L. Berkowitz, *op. cit.* (see 32).

53 A. Bandura and R. H. Walters, *Adolescent Aggression*. New York: Ronald. 1959.

54 N. E. Miller and R. Bugelski, Minor studies in aggression, II. The influence of frustrations imposed by the in-group on attitudes expressed toward out-groups. *J. Psychol.* 1948, **25**, 437.

55 A. Buss, *op. cit.* (see 32).

56 I. Sarnoff, *Personality Dynamics and Development*. New York: Wiley. 1962.

57 G. R. Bach, Young children's play fantasies. *Psychol. Monog.* 1945, **59**, no. 2.

58 P. H. Mussen and H. K. Naylor, The relationship between overt and fantasy aggression. *J. Ab. Soc. Psychol.* 1954, **49**, 235.

59 G. S. Lesser, The relationship between overt and fantasy aggression as a function of maternal response to aggression. *J. Ab. Soc. Psychol.* 1957, **55**, 218.

60 S. Feshbach, The drive-reducing function of fantasy behavior. *J. Ab. Soc. Psychol.* 1955, **50**, 3.

61 A. R. Pytkowicz *et al.* An experimental study of the reduction of hostility through fantasy. *J. Pers. Soc. Psychol.* 1967, **5**, 295.

62 L. Festinger *et al.* Some consequences of de-individuation in a group. *J. Ab. Soc. Psychol.* 1952, **47**, 382.

CHAPTER 5: *The emotions*

1 W. McDougall, *An Introduction to Social Psychology*. London: Methuen. 1908.

2 For a detailed discussion of the various theories of emotion, see: J. Hillman, *Emotion*. London: Routledge & Kegan Paul, 1960.

3 M. B. Arnold, *Emotion and Personality*, vol. 1. London: Cassell. 1961.
D. Bindra, *Motivation: a Systematic Reinterpretation*. New York: Ronald. 1959.

4 J. Dewey, The theory of emotion, II. The significance of emotions. *Psychol. Rev.* 1895, **2**, 13.

5 H. D. Meyer, A perceptual-motivational theory of the occurrence and intensity of emotion. *J. Gen. Psychol.* 1950, **43**, 105.

6 J. McV. Hunt *et al.* Situational cues distinguishing anger, fear and sorrow. *Amer. J. Psychol.* 1958, **71**, 136.

7 P. T. Young, *Motivation and Emotion*. New York: Wiley. 1961.

8 Earlier work on self-stimulation is described in: J. Olds and P. Milner, Positive reinforcement produced by electrical stimulation of the septal area and other regions of the brain, *J. Comp. Physiol. Psychol.* 1954, **47**, 419. A summary of this and more recent work is given in: J. Olds, Emotional centres in the brain. *Science Journal*, 1967, **3**, 87.

9 McClelland's theory is not easy to follow. It is discussed fully in: D. C. McClelland *et al. The Achievement Motive*. New York: Appleton-Century-Crofts. 1953.

10 R. G. Heath (ed.). *The Role of Pleasure in Behavior*. New York: Harper & Row. 1964.

11 J. A. Easterbrook, The effect of emotion on cue utilization and the organization of behavior. *Psychol. Rev.* 1959, **66**, 183.

12 C. Darwin, *The Expression of the Emotions in Man and Animals*. London: Murray. 1872.

13 H. Schlosberg, The description of facial expressions in terms of two dimensions. *J. Exper. Psychol.* 1952, **44**, 229.

14 J. Thompson, Development of facial expression of emotion in blind and seeing children. *Arch. Psychol.* 1941, No. 264.

15 C. Lange and W. James. *The Emotions*. Baltimore: Williams & Wilkins. 1922.

16 W. B. Cannon, *Bodily Changes in Pain, Hunger, Fear and Rage*. New York: Appleton-Century-Crofts. 1929.

17 Much of the following discussion is taken from: E. Gellhorn and G. N. Loufbourrow, *Emotions and Emotional Disorders*. New York: Harper & Row. 1963.

18 E. E. Levitt, *The Psychology of Anxiety*. Indianapolis: Bobbs-Merrill. 1967.

19 S. I. Cohen and A. J. Silverman, Psychophysiological investigation of vascular response variability. *J. Psychosom. Res.* 1959, **3**, 185.

20 E. Gellhorn and G. N. Loufbourrow, *op. cit.* (see 17).

21 J. I. Lacey *et al.* Autonomic response specificity. *Psychosom. Med.* 1953, **15**, 8.

22 J. I. Lacey and B. C. Lacey, Verification and extension of the principle of autonomic response-stereotypy. *Amer. J. Psychol.* 1958, **71**, 50.

23 H. A. Murray, Studies of stressful interpersonal disputations. *Amer. Psychol.* 1963, **18**, 28.

24 H. C. Klüver and P. C. Bucy, Preliminary analysis of functions of the temporal lobes in monkeys. *Arch. Neurol. Psychiat.* 1939, **42**, 979.

25 S. Schachter and J. E. Singer, Cognitive, social and physiological determinants of emotional state. *Psychol. Rev.* 1962, **69**, 379.

26 C. L. Burt, The factorial analysis of emotional traits, *Char. & Pers.* 1939, **7**, 238 and 285.

27 E. Kretschmer, *Physique and Character*. New York: Harcourt. 1925.

28 W. H. Sheldon, *The Varieties of Temperament*. New York: Harper. 1942.

CHAPTER 6: *Activation, arousal, exploration and competence*

1 E. Duffy, *Activation and Behavior*. New York: Wiley. 1962.

2 H. Heckhausen. *The Anatomy of Achievement Motivation*. New York: Academic Press. 1967.

3 D. Bindra, Organization in emotional and motivated behaviour. *Canad. J. Psychol.* 1955, **9**, 161.

4 H. A. Murray, Studies of stressful interpersonal disputations. *Amer. Psychol.* 1963, **18**, 28.

5 J. I. Lacey *et al.* The visceral level: situational determinants and behavioural correlates of autonomic response patterns. In P. Knapp (ed.), *Expression of the Emotions*. New York: International Universities Press. 1963.

6 A. T. Welford, Stress and achievement. *Austral. J. Psychol.* 1965, **17**, 1.

7   R. C. Travis and J. L. Kennedy, Prediction and automatic control of aware-
    ness, II. Calibration of the alertness indicator and further results. *J. Comp.
    Physiol. Psychol.* 1949, **42**, 45.
8   J. R. Brobeck, Regulation of energy exchange. *Ann. Rev. Physiol.* 1948,
    10, 315.
9   D. O. Hebb, *The Organization of Behavior.* New York: Wiley. 1949.
10 S. R. Maddi, Unexpectedness, affective tone and behavior. In D. W. Fiske
    and S. R. Maddi (eds), *Functions of Varied Experience.* Homewood,
    Ill.: Dorsey. 1961.
11 W. I. Welker, Some determinants of play and exploration in chimpanzees.
    J. Comp. Physiol. Psychol. 1956, **49**, 84.
12 For a discussion of this and other 'vigilance' tasks, see: D. E. Broadbent,
    Perception and Communication. London: Pergamon. 1958.
13 R. S. Daniel, Alpha and theta EEG in vigilance. *Percept. Motor Skills.* 1967.
    25, 697.
14 This work is described and discussed extensively in: D. P. Schultz,
    Sensory Restriction: Effects on Behavior. New York: Academic Press.
    1965.
15 R. H. Wendt *et al.* Self-maintained visual stimulation in monkeys after
    long-term visual deprivation. *Science.* 1963, **139**, 336.
16 S. R. Maddi *et al.* Effects of monotony and novelty on imaginative pro-
    ductions. *J. Pers.* 1962, **30**, 513.
17 S. R. Maddi *et al.* Three expressions of the need for variety. *J. Pers.* 1965,
    33, 82.
18 D. E. Berlyne, Conflict and information-theory variables as determinants
    of human perceptual curiosity. *J. Exper. Psychol.* 1957, **53**, 399. The
    influence of complexity and novelty in visual figures on orienting
    responses. *J. Exper. Psychol.* 1958, **55**, 289.
19 R. S. Woodworth, *Dynamics of Behavior.* London: Methuen. 1958.
20 R. W. White, Motivation reconsidered: the concept of competence.
    Psychol. Rev. 1959, **66**, 297.

CHAPTER 7: *Social motivation*

1   I. DeVore, *Primate Behavior.* New York: Holt, Rinehart & Winston.
    1965.
2   M. Phillips, *Small Social Groups in England.* London: Methuen. 1965.
3   M. Mead, *Sex and Temperament.* London: Routledge. 1935.
4   M. Mead, *Coming of Age in Samoa.* New York: Blue Ribbon Books. 1934.
5   M. Kerr, *The People of Ship Street.* London: Routledge & Kegan Paul. 1958.
6   E. Mayo, *The Human Problems of an Industrial Civilization.* New York:
    Macmillan. 1933.
7   H. A. Murray, *Explorations in Personality.* Oxford University Press. 1938.
8   E. Frenkel-Brunswik, Motivation and behavior. *Genet. Psychol. Monog.*
    1942, **26**, 121.
9   M. Argyle, *The Psychology of Interpersonal Behaviour.* London: Penguin
    Books. 1967.

10 J. W. Atkinson *et al.* The effect of experimental arousal of the affiliation motive on thematic apperception. *J. Ab. Soc. Psychol.* 1954, **49**, 405.

11 T. E. Shipley and J. Veroff, A projective measure of need for affiliation. *J. Exper. Psychol.* 1952, **43**, 349.

12 D. Byrne, Anxiety and the experimental arousal of affiliation need. *J. Ab. Soc. Psychol.* 1961, **63**, 660.

13 E. P. Hollander and R. A. Willis, Some current issues in the psychology of conformity and non-conformity. *Psychol. Bull.* 1967, **68**, 62.

14 M. Jahoda, Conformity and independence. *Hum. Rel.* 1959, **12**, 99.

15 D. P. Crowne and D. Marlow, *The Approval Motive.* New York: Wiley. 1964.

16 D. Riesman, *The Lonely Crowd.* New Haven: Yale University Press. 1950.
    D. Riesman, *Faces in the Crowd.* New Haven: Yale University Press. 1952.

17 W. H. Whyte, *The Organization Man.* New York: Simon & Schuster. 1956.

18 D. R. Miller and G. E. Swanson, *Inner Conflict and Defense.* New York: Holt. 1960.

19 F. Zweig, *The Worker in an Affluent Society.* London: Heinemann. 1961.

20 L. Boehm, The development of independence. *Child Devel.* 1957, **28**, 84.
    H. J. Butcher *et al.* Personality factors and school achievement. *Brit. J. Educ. Psychol.* 1963, **33**, 276.

21 D. C. McClelland, *The Achieving Society.* Princeton: Van Nostrand. 1961.

22 V. O. Packard, *The Status Seekers.* London: Longmans. 1960.

23 J. Veroff, Development and validation of a projective measure of power motivation. *J. Ab. Soc. Psychol.* 1957, **54**, 1.

24 A. H. Maslow, Dominance-feeling, behavior and status. *Psychol. Rev.* 1937, **44**, 404.

25 A. H. Maslow, Self-esteem (dominance-feeling) and sexuality in women. *J. Soc. Psychol.* 1942, **16**, 259.

CHAPTER 8: *Goal-directed behaviour*

1 S. Koch, Behavior as 'intrinsically' regulated. In M. R. Jones (ed.), *Nebraska Symposium on Motivation*, 1956. Nebraska University Press.

2 J. P. Guilford *et al.* A factor analysis study of human interests. *Psychol. Monog.* 1954, **68**, No. 4.

3 E. L. Thorndike, The interests of adults. *J. Educ. Psychol.* 1935, **26**, 497.

4 E. Spranger, *Types of Men.* Halle: Niemeyer. 1928.

5 G. W. Allport, P. E. Vernon and G. Lindzey, *Study of Values.* Boston: Houghton Mifflin. 1951.

6 E. Duffy, A critical review of investigations employing the Allport-Vernon *Study of Values* and other tests of evaluative attitude. *Psychol. Bull.* 1940, **37**, 597.
    E. Duffy and W. J. E. Crissy, Evaluative attitudes as related to vocational interests and academic achievement. *J. Ab. Soc. Psychol.* 1940, **35**, 226.

7   K. S. Yum, Student preferences in divisional studies and their preferential activities. *J. Psychol.* 1942, **13**, 193.

8   L. Hudson, *Contrary Imaginations*. London: Methuen. 1966.

9   J. P. Guilford, The structure of intellect. *Psychol. Bull.* 1956, **53**, 267.

10 A. J. Cropley, Divergent thinking and science specialists. *Nature*. 1967, **215**, 671.
    A. J. Cropley and T. W. Field, Intellectual style and High School science. *Nature*. 1968, **217**, 1211.

11 A. Roe, A psychological study of eminent psychologists and anthropologists, and a comparison with biological and physical scientists. *Psychol. Monog.* 1953, **67**, No. 2.
    D. C. McClelland, On the psychodynamics of creative physical scientists. In H. E. Gruber *et al.* (eds), *Contemporary Approaches to Creative Thinking*. New York: Atherton. 1962.

12 M. Smith, Some studies in the laundry trade. *Indust. Fat. Res. Board Rep.* No. 22. 1922.

13 E. K. Strong, *Change of Interests with Age*. Stanford University Press. 1931.

14 W. McDougall, *The Energies of Men*. London: Methuen. 1932.

15 H. A. Murray and C. D. Morgan, A clinical study of sentiments. *Genet. Psychol. Monog.* 1945, **32**, 3.
    V. V. French, The structure of sentiments. *J. Pers.* 1947, **15**, 247.

16 A. H. Maslow, *Motivation and Personality*. New York: Harper. 1954.
    A. H. Maslow, Some basic propositions of a growth and self-actualization psychology. In G. Lindzey and C. S. Hall (eds), *Theories of Personality*. New York: Wiley. 1965.

17 G. C. Helmstatter and D. S. Ellis, Rate of manipulative learning as a function of goal-setting techniques. *J. Exper. Psychol.* 1952, **43**, 125.

18 M. Jucknat, Leistung, Anspruchsniveau und Selbstbewusstsein. *Psychol. Forsch.* 1937, **22**, 89.

19 N. T. Feather, Level of aspiration and performance variability. *J. Pers. Soc. Psychol.* 1967, **6**, 37.

20 L. Worell, The effect of goal-value upon expectancy. *J. Ab. Soc. Psychol.* 1956, **53**, 48.

21 M. E. Gebhard, Changes in the attractiveness of activities. *J. Exper. Psychol.* 1949, **39**, 404.

22 H. H. Anderson and H. F. Brandt, Study of motivation involving self-announced goals of fifth grade children and the concept of level of aspiration. *J. Soc. Psychol.* 1939, **10**, 209.

23 P. S. Sears, Levels of aspiration in academically successful and unsuccessful children. *J. Ab. Soc. Psychol.* 1940, **35**, 498.

24 J. D. Frank, Some psychological determinants of the level of aspiration. *Amer. J. Psychol.* 1935, **47**, 285.

25 D. W. Chapman and J. Volkmann, A social determinant of the level of aspiration. *J. Ab. Soc. Psychol.* 1939, **34**, 225.

26 L. Festinger, Wish, expectation and group standards as factors influencing level of aspiration. *J. Ab. Soc. Psychol.* 1942, **37**, 184.

27 H. A. Murray and C. Kluckholn, Outline of a conception of personality. In C. Kluckholn and H. A. Murray (eds), *Personality in Nature, Society and Culture*. New York: Knopf. 1949.

28 R. Gould, An experimental analysis of 'level of aspiration'. *Genet. Psychol. Monog.* 1939, **21**, No. 1.

29 M. Hertzman and L. Festinger, Shifts in explicit goals in a level of aspiration experiment. *J. Exper. Psychol.* 1940, **27**, 439.

30 J. A. Bayton, Interrelations between levels of aspiration, performance and estimates of past performance. *J. Exper. Psychol.* 1943, **33**, 1.

31 R. R. Holt. Level of aspiration: ambition or defense? *Psychiatry.* 1945, **8**, 299.

32 M. A. Iverson and M. E. Reader, Ego involvement as an experimental variable. *Psychol. Rep.* 1956, **2**, 147.

33 S. B. Sarason *et al.* The effect of differential instructions on anxiety and learning. *J. Ab. Soc. Psychol.* 1952, **47**, 561.

34 J. W. Gardner, The relation of certain personality variables to level of aspiration. *J. Psychol.* 1940, **9**, 191.

35 R. W. Moulton, Effects of success and failure on level of aspiration as related to achievement motives. *J. Pers. Soc. Psychol.* 1965, **1**, 399.

36 R. L. Isaacson, Relation between *n* achievement, test anxiety and curricular choices. *J. Ab. Soc. Psychol.* 1964, **68**, 447.

37 C. H. Mahone, Fear of failure and unrealistic vocational aspiration. *J. Ab. Soc. Psychol.* 1960, **60**, 253.

38 H. T. Himmelweit, A comparative study of the level of aspiration of normal and neurotic persons. *Brit. J. Psychol.* 1947, **37**, 41.

39 Much of the earlier work described here on achievement motivation is taken from: D. C. McClelland *et al. The Achievement Motive.* New York: Appleton-Century-Crofts. 1953; and J. W. Atkinson (ed.), *Motives in Fantasy, Action and Society*. Princeton: Van Nostrand. 1958.

40 J. Kagan and H. A. Moss, *Birth to Maturity*. New York: Wiley. 1962.

41 H. Heckhausen, *The Anatomy of Achievement Motivation*. New York: Academic Press. 1967.

42 E. G. French and G. S. Lesser, Some characteristics of the achievement motive in women. *J. Ab. Soc. Psychol.* 1964, **68**, 119.

43 J. E. Williams, Mode of failure, interference tendencies and achievement imagery. *J. Ab. Soc. Psychol.* 1955, **51**, 573.

44 J. F. Bryan and E. A. Locke, Goal setting as a means of increasing motivation. *J. Appl. Psychol.* 1967, **51**, 274.

45 D. C. McClelland *et al. op cit.* (see 39).

46 R. A. Clark *et al.* Hope of success and fear of failure as aspects of need for achievement. *J. Ab. Soc. Psychol.* 1956, **53**, 182.

47 J. W. Atkinson *et al.* The achievement motive, goal setting and probability preferences. *J. Ab. Soc. Psychol.* 1960, **60**, 27.

48 J. W. Atkinson and G. H. Litwin, Achievement motive and test anxiety conceived as motive to approach success and motive to avoid failure. *J. Ab. Soc. Psychol.* 1960, **60**, 52.

49 K. Shrable and L. H. Stewart, Personality correlates of achievement imagery. *Percept. Motor Skills.* 1967, **24**, 1087.

50 J. Veroff *et al.* The use of the thematic apperception test to assess motivation in a nationwide interview study. *Psychol. Monog.* 1960, **74**, No. 12.

51 E. Burstein, Fear of failure, achievement motivation and aspiring to prestigeful occupations. *J. Ab. Soc. Psychol.* 1963, **67**, 189.

52 E. Douvan and J. Adelson, The psychodynamics of social mobility in adolescent boys. *J. Ab. Soc. Psychol.* 1958, **56**, 31.

53 E. G. French, Some characteristics of achievement motivation. *J. Exper. Psychol.* 1955, **50**, 232.

54 A. J. Caron, Curiosity, achievement and avoidant motivation as determinants of epistemic behavior. *J. Ab. Soc. Psychol.* 1963, **67**, 535.

55 M. Henle, On activity in the goal region. *Psychol. Rev.* 1956, **63**, 299.

56 W. Vogel *et al.* Intrinsic motivation and psychological stress. *J. Ab. Soc. Psychol.* 1959, **58**, 225.

57 E. G. French, Motivation as a variable in work partner selection. *J. Ab. Soc. Psychol.* 1956, **53**, 96.

58 R. S. Wyer, Behavioral correlates of academic achievement. *J. Pers. Soc. Psychol.* 1967, **6**, 255.

59 D. C. McClelland, *The Achieving Society.* Princeton: Van Nostrand. 1961.

60 F. M. Katz, The meaning of success: some differences in value systems of social classes. *J. Soc. Psychol.* 1964, **62**, 141.

61 A. B. Heilbrun *et al.* Perceived maternal child-rearing patterns and the effects of social nonreactions upon achievement motivation. *Child Devel.* 1967, **38**, 267.

62 M. E. Hebron, *Motivated Learning.* London: Methuen. 1966.

63 V. H. Vroom, *Work and Motivation.* New York; Wiley. 1964.

64 M. D. Vernon, The drives which determine the choice of a career. *Brit. J. Educ. Psychol.* 1937, **7**, 302; 1938, **8**, 1. Characteristic motivation in the activities of school-girls. *Brit. J. Psychol.* 1938, **29**, 121; 1939, **29**, 232. The relationship of occupation to personality. *Brit. J. Psychol.* 1941, **31**, 294.

65 F. Zweig, *The Worker in an Affluent Society.* London: Heinemann. 1961.

66 D. E. Broadbent, Aspects of human decision-making. *Advancement Sci.* 1967, **24**, 53.

67 E. Mayo, *The Human Problems of an Industrial Civilization.* New York: Macmillan. 1933.

68 S. Wyatt and J. N. Langdon, Fatigue and boredom in repetitive work. *Indust. Health Res. Board Rep.* No. 77, 1937.

69 See for instance, S. Wyatt and J. N. Langdon, *op. cit.*

CHAPTER 9: *Frustration and conflict*

1 H. Selye, *The Stress of Life.* London: Longmans Green. 1957.

2 J. S. Brown and I. E. Farber, Emotions conceptualized as intervening variables—with suggestions towards a theory of frustration. *Psychol. Bull.* 1951, **48**, 465.

3 G. W. Allport, *Personality*. New York: Holt. 1937.
4 E. Frenkel-Brunswik, Motivation and behavior. *Genet. Psychol. Monog.* 1942, **26**, 121.
5 R. S. Lazarus *et al.* The effects of psychological stress upon performance. *Psychol. Bull.* 1952, **49**, 293.
6 D. M. Broverman and R. S. Lazarus, Individual differences in task performance under conditions of cognitive interference. *J. Pers.* 1958, **26**, 94.
7 P. C. Goldin, Experimental investigation of selective memory and the concept of repression and defense. *J. Ab. Soc. Psychol.* 1964, **69**, 365.
8 I. L. Child and J. W. M. Whiting, Determinants of level of aspiration. *J. Ab. Soc. Psychol.* 1949, **44**, 303.
9 J. G. Martire, Relationships between the self-concept and differences in the strength and generality of achievement motivation. *J. Pers.* 1956, **24**, 364.
10 S. Rosenzweig, Further comparative data on repetition-choice after success and failure as related to frustration tolerance. *J. Genet. Psychol.* 1945, **66**, 75.
11 H. B. Gewirtz, Generalization of children's preferences as a function of reinforcement and task similarity. *J. Ab. Soc. Psychol.* 1959, **58**, 111.
12 B. Lantz, Some dynamic aspects of success and failure. *Psychol. Monog.* 1945, **59**, No. 271.
13 H. Heckhausen, *The Anatomy of Achievement Motivation.* New York: Academic Press. 1967.
14 J. R. Davitz, The effects of previous training on post-frustration behavior. *J. Ab. Soc. Psychol.* 1952, **47**, 309.
15 W. W. Hartup, Nurturance and nurturance withdrawal in relation to the dependency behavior of preschool children. *Child Devel.* 1958, **29**, 191.
16 R. S. Lazarus and C. W. Eriksen, Effects of failure stress upon skilled performance. *J. Exper. Psychol.* 1952, **43**, 100.
17 J. Doris and S. Sarason, Test anxiety and blame assignment in a failure situation. *J. Ab. Soc. Psychol.* 1955, **50**, 335.
18 E. L. Cowen, The influence of varying degrees of psychological stress on problem-solving rigidity. *J. Ab. Soc. Psychol.* 1952, **47**, 512.
19 R. K. Merton and A. S. Kitt, Contributions to the theory of reference group behavior. In R. K. Merton and P. F. Lazarsfeld (eds), *Contributions to Social Research.* 1950.
20 K. Lewin, *A Dynamic Theory of Personality.* New York: McGraw-Hill. 1935.
   K. Lewin, Behavior and development as a function of the total situation. In L. Carmichael (ed.), *Manual of Child Psychology.* New York: Wiley. 1954.
21 R. J. Filer, Frustration, satisfaction and other factors affecting the attractiveness of goal objects. *J. Ab. Soc. Psychol.* 1952, **47**, 203.
22 E. A. Turner and J. C. Wright, Effects of severity of threat and perceived availability on the attractiveness of objects. *J. Pers. Soc. Psychol.* 1965, **2**, 128.

23 H. F. Wright, The effect of barriers upon strength of motivation. In R. G. Barker (ed.), *Child Behavior and Development*. New York: McGraw-Hill. 1943.

24 A. Arkov, Resolution of approach-avoidance and avoidance-avoidance conflict. *J. Ab. Soc. Psychol.* 1957, **55**, 402.

25 A. Karsten, Psychische Sättigung. *Psychol. Forsch.* 1928, **10**, 142.

26 K. Lissner, Die Entspannung von Bedürfnissen durch Ersatzhandlungen. *Psychol. Forsch.* 1933, **18**, 218.

27 I. L. Janis, Motivational factors in the resolution of decisional conflicts. In M. R. Jones (ed.), *Nebraska Symposium on Motivation*, 1959. University of Nebraska Press.

28 S. Sliosberg, Zur Dynamik des Ersatzes in Spiel- und Ernstsituationen. *Psychol. Forsch.* 1934, **19**, 122.

29 I. Oswald, *Sleeping and Waking*, Amsterdam: Elsevier. 1962.

30 M. Jouvet, The sleeping brain. *Science J.* 1967, **3**, 105.
G. Luce and J. Segal, *Sleep*. London: Heinemann. 1967.

31 S. Rosenzweig, The experimental measurement of types of reaction to frustration. In H. A. Murray, *Explorations in Personality*. Oxford University Press. 1938.

32 R. E. Walker and J. T. Spence, Relationship between digit span and anxiety. *J. Consult. Psychol.* 1964, **28**, 220.

33 L. C. T. Jones, Frustration and stereotyped behaviour in human subjects. *Quart. J. Exper. Psychol.* 1954, **6**, 12.

34 E. E. Levitt, *The Psychology of Anxiety*. Indianapolis: Bobbs-Merrill. 1967.

35 Much of the following discussion is taken from: I. Sarnoff, *Personality Dynamics and Development*. New York: Wiley. 1962.

36 D. Katz et al. Ego defence and attitude change. *Hum. Rel.* 1956, **9**, 27.

37 T. W. Adorno et al. *The Authoritarian Personality*. New York: Harper. 1950.

38 For discussion of these experiments, see: M. D. Vernon, *The Psychology of Perception*, Chapter 11. London: Penguin Books. 1962.

39 S. Freud, *The Psychopathology of Everyday Life*. London: Fisher Unwin. 1920.

40 B. Zeigarnik, Das Behalten erledigter und unerledigter Handlungen. *Psychol. Forsch.* 1927, **9**, 1.

41 C. W. Eriksen, Defense against ego-threat in memory and perception. *J. Ab. Soc. Psychol.* 1952, **47**, 230.

42 T. G. Alper, The interrupted task method in studies of selective recall. *Psychol. Rev.* 1952, **59**, 71.

43 J. W. Atkinson, The achievement motive and recall of interrupted and completed tasks. *J. Exper. Psychol.* 1953, **46**, 381.

44 I. Silverman, Self-esteem and differential responsiveness to success and failure. *J. Ab. Soc. Psychol.* 1964, **69**, 115.

45 R. S. Lazarus and N. Longo, The consistency of psychological defenses against threat. *J. Ab. Soc. Psychol.* 1953, **48**, 495.

46 R. Barker, T. Dembo and K. Lewin, Frustration and regression. *Univ. Iowa Stud. Child Welfare.* 1941, **18**, No. 1.

47 A. F. Zandler, A study of experimental frustration. *Psychol. Monog.* 1944, **56**, No. 3.

48 A. R. Luria, *The Nature of Human Conflicts*. New York: Liveright. 1932.

49 G. L. Freeman and J. H. Pathman, The relation of overt muscular discharge to physiological recovery from experimentally induced displacement. *J. Exper. Psychol.* 1942, **30**, 161.

50 J. H. Masserman and C. Pechtel, Conflict-engendered neurotic and psychotic behavior in monkeys. *J. Nerv. Ment. Dis.* 1953, **118**, 408.

51 J. R. Patrick, Studies in rational behavior and emotional excitement. *J. Comp. Psychol.* 1934, **18**, 153.

52 D. I. Marquart, The pattern of punishment and its relation to abnormal fixation in adult human subjects. *J. Gen. Psychol.* 1948, **39**, 107.

53 E. Frenkel-Brunswik, Tolerance towards ambiguity as a personality variable. *Amer. Psychol.* 1948, **3**, 268.

54 J. E. Dittes, Effects of changes in self-esteem upon impulsiveness and deliberation in making judgments. *J. Ab. Soc. Psychol.* 1959, **58**, 348.

55 D. C. McClelland and F. S. Apicella, A functional classification of verbal reactions to experimentally induced failure. *J. Ab. Soc. Psychol.* 1945, **40**, 376.

56 D. R. Miller and G. E. Swanson, *Inner Conflict and Defense*. New York: Holt. 1960.

CHAPTER 10: *Individual differences in motivated behaviour*

1 G. W. Allport, *Personality*. New York: Holt. 1937.

2 G. W. Allport, A test for ascendance-submission. *J. Ab. Soc. Psychol.* 1928, **23**, 118.

3 S. E. Asch, *Social Psychology*. New York: Prentice-Hall. 1952.

4 M. L. Stein, Explorations in typology. In G. Lindsey and C. S. Hall (eds), *Theories of Personality*. New York: Wiley. 1965.

5 M. E. Hebron, *Motivated Learning*. London: Methuen. 1966.

APPENDIX

1 D. C. McClelland, Methods of measuring human motivation. In J. W. Atkinson (ed.), *Motives in Fantasy, Action and Society*. Princeton: Van Nostrand. 1958. The detailed application of the T.A.T. is discussed in other articles in this book.

2 H. A. Murray, *Explorations in Personality*. Oxford University Press. 1938.

3 J. W. Atkinson and D. C. McClelland, The projective expression of needs, II. The effect of different intensities of hunger drive on thematic apperception. *J. Exper. Psychol.* 1948, **38**, 643.

4 P. E. Vernon, *Personality Assessment*. London: Methuen. 1964.

5 J. R. Hurley, The Iowa Picture Interpretation Test. *J. Consult. Psychol.* 1955, **19**, 372.

6 E. G. French, Development of a measure of complex motivation. In J. W. Atkinson (ed.), *Motives in Fantasy, Action and Society*. Princeton: Van Nostrand. 1958.

7   E. Aronson, The need for achievement as measured by graphic expression. *Ibid.*
8   J. A. Taylor, A personality scale of manifest anxiety. *J. Ab. Soc. Psychol.* 1953, **48**, 285.
9   G. Mandler and S. B. Sarason, A study of anxiety and learning. *J. Ab. Soc. Psychol.* 1952, **47**, 166.
10 R. Alpert and R. N. Haber, Anxiety in academic achievement situations. *J. Ab. Soc. Psychol.* 1960, **61**, 207.
11 See discussion of anxiety tests in: E. E. Levitt, *The Psychology of Anxiety.* Indianapolis: Bobbs-Merrill. 1967.

The following are selected from the preceding references as being particularly worth study:

CHAPTER 1

N. Tinbergen, *A Study of Instinct.* Oxford University Press. 1951.
W. H. Thorpe, *Learning and Instinct in Animals.* London:Methuen. 1956.
R. S. Woodworth, *Dynamics of Behavior.* London: Methuen. 1958.

CHAPTER 2:

J. Bowlby, *Child Care and the Growth of Love.* London: Penguin Books. 1953.
L. Carmichael (ed.), *Handbook of Child Psychology.* New York: Wiley. 1954.
R. R. Sears, E. E. Maccoby and H. Levin, *Patterns of Child Rearing.* Evanston, Ill.: Row Patterson. 1957.

CHAPTER 3

C. S. Ford and F. A. Beach, *Patterns of Sexual Behavior.* London: Eyre & Spottiswoode. 1952.
I. DeVore, *Primate Behavior.* New York: Holt, Rinehart & Winston. 1965.

CHAPTER 4

L. Berkowitz, *Aggression.* New York: McGraw-Hill. 1962.
A. Buss, *The Psychology of Aggression.* New York: Wiley. 1961.
K. Lorenz, *On Aggression.* London: Methuen. 1967.

CHAPTER 5

M. B. Arnold, *Emotion and Personality.* London: Cassell. 1961.
E. Gellhorn and G. N. Loufbourrow, *Emotions and Emotional Disorders.* New York: Harper & Row. 1963.

CHAPTER 6

E. Duffy, *Activation and Behavior.* New York: Wiley. 1962.
D. W. Fiske and S. R. Maddi (eds). *Functions of Varied Experience.* Homewood, Ill: Dorsey. 1961.

CHAPTER 7

H. A. Murray, *Explorations in Personality.* Oxford University Press. 1938.

CHAPTER 8

J. W. Atkinson (ed.), *Motives in Fantasy, Action and Society*. Princeton: Van Nostrand. 1958.

H. Heckhausen, *The Anatomy of Achievement Motivation*. New York: Academic Press. 1967.

CHAPTER 9

K. Lewin, *A Dynamic Theory of Personality*. New York: McGraw-Hill. 1935.

INDEX OF AUTHORS

Allport, G. W., 135, 137
Arnold, M. B., 71, 72
Atkinson, J. W., 37, 102, 106, 122, 124, 163, 164, 165

Bindra, D., 71, 86
Bowlby, J., 26
Bridges, K. M. B., 19
Brown, J. S., 11
Bucy, P. C., 80
Bühler, C., 20, 22

Cannon, W. B., 77, 78, 80

Darwin, C., 76
Dewey, J., 72
Dollard, J., 62
Duffy, E., 86

Fletcher, R., 5, 6
Frenkel-Brunswik, E., 101
Freud, S., 45, 46, 56, 143, 144, 145, 147, 149, 150

Gates, G. S., 38, 63
Goldfarb, W., 26
Goodenough, F. L., 19
Guilford, J. P., 109, 110

Harlow, H. F., 18, 25, 26
Hebb, D. O., 11, 17
Hebron, M. E., viii
Heckhausen, H., 123
Himmelweit, H. T., 31
Horney, K., 46
Hudson, L., 110
Hull, C. L., 10
Hutt, C., 22

James, W., 77

Klüver, H. C., 80
Kretschmer, E., 84

Lacey, B. C., 79
Lacey, J. I., 79
Lange, C., 77
Levin, H., 28
Levitt, E. E., 156

Lewin, K., 10, 137, 140, 142, 160
Lorenz, K., 6, 7, 8, 46, 57, 58
Luria, A. R., 153

McClelland, D. C., 37, 74, 102, 105, 106, 122, 126, 127, 128, 129, 159, 163, 164, 165
McDougall, W., 4, 5, 8, 35, 46, 56, 71, 112, 115
Mackworth, N. H., 89
Maccoby, E. E., 28
Maslow, A. H., 107, 116, 117
Mayo, E., 99, 131
Mead, M., 47, 59, 97
Miller, N. E., 62
Mira, E., 51
Murray, H. A., 99, 100, 101, 116, 121, 159, 163

Newson, E., 31, 47
Newson, J., 31, 47

Olds, J., 73

Packard, V., 106
Pavlov, I. P., 9
Piaget, J., 22, 32

Riesman, D., 104, 105
Rosenzweig, S., 155

Schacter, S., 80, 81
Sears, R. R., 28
Selye, H., 134
Sheldon, W. H., 84
Spranger, E., 109

Thorndike, E. L., 10, 109
Thorpe, W. H., 8, 10
Tinbergen, N., 6, 7, 8
Troland, L. T., 4

Vernon, P. E., 164

Watson, J. B., 8, 9
White, R. W., 92
Whyte, W. H., 105
Woodworth, R. S., 11, 92

Young, P. T., 4, 73, 75

Zimmerman, R. R., 18, 25, 26

INDEX OF SUBJECTS

achievement motivation, 43, 61, 86, 121, 130, 134, 136, 146, 150, 155, 159, 160, 161, 163–4, 165
  academic, 124–5
  cross cultural studies of, 126–7
  in children, 23, 30, 31, 118, 127
  in entrepreneurial activities, 124, 126
  in men and women, 125
activation, 11, 85–8, 90, 91, 129, 138, 160
affiliation, 102–6, 125, 131, 159
aggression, 56–70, 79, 80, 84, 87, 102, 103, 113, 115, 145, 146, 147, 154, 155
  in apes and monkeys, 58–9
  in other animals, 57–8
  in children, 19–20, 24, 26, 27, 29, 32, 62–4, 68, 156
  individual differences in, 64–5
anger, 38, 62–6, 71–6, 78, 81, 87
  in children, 19, 27, 77
anxiety, 43, 44, 45, 55–6, 69, 70, 72, 79, 83, 104, 122, 123, 137, 144–6, 164, 165
  in children, 19, 24, 25, 28, 29, 161
appetitive behaviour, 6, 8, 74
approach, 74, 134, 158, 159, 161
arousal, 11, 13, 81, 86, 88–90
  over-, 75, 88
aspiration, level of, 117–21, 123, 141
  in children, 31, 35, 118
  individual differences in, 120
attention, 75, 85, 87, 88
authoritarian personality, 132, 154
avoidance, 74, 158, 161

child rearing practices, 28, 47–8, 127
  in primitive societies, 47, 97
compartmentalization, 147–8
competence, 92, 159
  in children, 23, 30
conflict, 43, 55, 117, 134–56, 160
  in children, 27–8, 45
  Lewin's theory of, 137–44
conscience, 82, 115
  in children, 27, 29, 45, 161
construction, constructive activity, 92, 112
  in children, 22–3
convergent and divergent thinkers, 110, 111
coping mechanisms, 152, 155
creative ability, 110, 111, 159

curiosity, 90, 111, 125
  in apes and monkeys, 21
  in children, 21, 92
  sexual, 16

danger, avoidance of, 49, 51, 95
denial, 149, 150, 151, 156
dependence, 113, 152, 156
  in children, 28, 29, 127
deprivation, sensory, 89, 90
displacement activity, 7, 8, 67–8, 153, 155, 156
dominance, 106–7, 160
  in animals, 57, 58–9
  in children, 32, 33
  in parents, 30, 32, 97, 161
dreams, dreaming, 143–4
drive, 6, 8–13

electroencephalogram (EEG), 86, 89, 90, 144
ego defence, mechanisms of, 44, 45, 116, 142, 147–54, 155, 156
ego-ideal, 116
  in children, 34, 45, 82
ego-involvement, 108, 120
emergency reactions, 49–70
emotion, emotions, 5, 49, 71–84, 86, 87, 88, 90, 114, 115, 158
  complex, 81–4
  expression of, 75–7, 158
  physiological processes in, 49, 77–81, 83, 88, 144
  individual differences in physiological processes, 79–80
energy, 7, 11–12, 85, 86, 128, 129, 138–9, 141, 160
  action specific, 6–7
ethology, ethologists, 6–8
exploring, exploration, 90, 91–3, 117, 129, 159, 160
  in children, 20–2, 30, 91, 92
extrapunitive behaviour, 144, 145, 148, 155, 156
extraversion, 54, 83, 100, 158

fear, 49–56, 72, 74–80, 83, 88, 95
  conditioned, 9, 18
  in apes and monkeys, 17, 18
  in children, 17–19, 24, 27

fear (*cont.*)
of failure, 120, 122, 123, 124, 134, 146, 155
of rejection, 102, 104
of strangeness, 17, 19, 21
fight, 7, 56–61, 78
fixed action patterns, 6, 7
flight, 7, 49, 50, 51, 78
food,
deprivation, 10, 37–40
habits, 39
preferences, 38–40
seeking, 7, 12, 16, 36–40
Freudian concepts, Freudian theory, 44–5, 82,
142, 149, 151, 152
frustration, 62, 63, 69, 72, 80, 86, 130, 134–56
in children, 19, 20, 24, 27, 45
functional autonomy, 135, 138

G.S.R. (skin resistance), 52, 87, 125
goal-directed behaviour, 1–3, 4, 11, 13, 108–
133, 158, 160
in children, 22, 108
guilt, guilt feelings, 43, 45, 69–70, 82–3, 145,
146, 147
in children, 29

hatred, 113, 115
hedonism, hedonic theory, 3–4, 73, 74
homosexuality, 41, 42
homeostasis, homeostatic motivation, 5, 10,
36–40
hormic theory, 4, 8
hunger, 16, 37–8, 116, 163
hypothalamus, 38, 40, 73, 80, 85

identification, 68, 115
by children with parents, 24, 28, 29, 30, 82
immobility reaction, in infants, 17, 26
impunitive behaviour, 145, 148, 155
independence, 103, 111, 117, 121, 125, 132,
159, 160
in children, 27, 28, 30, 140, 145, 161
innate releasing mechanisms, 6, 8
instincts
in animals, 4, 6–8, 46, 57, 59
in man, 3–6, 40, 57, 59
love and death, 44
maternal, 46
interests, 108–12, 128, 129, 133
age changes in, 112
classification of, 109–10
cultural, 110
occupational, 108–12

scientific, 111
social-political, 114
introjection, 45, 82
intropunitive behaviour, 144, 145, 155
introversion, 83, 100, 158

jealousy, 26, 81–2
joy, 72, 73, 76, 79

leadership, 106–7
in children, 33
limbic area, 73, 80, 85
love, 43, 113–15, 116, 142
loss of, 27, 28, 82, 145

marriage, 42–3
masturbation, 16, 42, 43
maternal behaviour, 46–8
in animals, 46–7

need
biological, 10, 36–48, 100
psychological (Maslow), 116–17
psychological (Murray), 100, 101, 159, 163
tension systems, 138, 139
novelty, 85, 88, 90, 132, 160
in children, 18, 21, 88, 91

orienting response, 21, 88
other-directedness, 104, 105, 126
over-protection, 27, 29, 48, 91, 127, 148, 161

pain, 49, 53–5, 74–5, 79, 86, 149
avoidance of, 3, 53, 78
in animals, 54
withdrawal from, 9, 14, 15, 49
panic, 49, 50, 51, 78
play, 91
in children, 22–4, 32, 68, 91
pleasure, pleasure seeking, 3, 72, 73–5, 132
power, power seeking, 43, 106–7, 127, 131
prejudice, 60–1, 67–8, 113, 147, 148
projection, 148, 149, 156
punishment, 27, 28, 29, 31, 140, 161

rationalization, 121, 147, 148, 155
reaction formation, 148
reflexes, reflex responses, 4, 9, 14–15
conditioned, 9, 15
Moro, 15, 17
regression, 151–2, 155, 156
repression, 52, 149–51, 156
reticular formation, 11, 80, 85

rigidity, 146, 153–4
 in parents, 28, 154
rituals, ritualization, 59, 60
 in animals, 8, 57

satiation, 140–1
security and insecurity, 55–6, 95, 129–30, 132, 161
self-acceptance, 104, 117
 -actualization, 115–17, 160, 161
 -awareness, 34–5
 -esteem, 35, 62, 66, 103, 104, 107, 115–16, 118, 120, 128, 136, 146, 147, 150, 154, 156, 158
 -stimulation, 73, 74
sentiment, sentiments, 112–15
 altruistic, 132, 160
 development of, 113
 religious, 114
 self-regarding, 35, 115–17
 social-political, 114
separation, from mother,
 in human infants, 25, 26
 in monkeys, 26
sex, sexual behaviour and desire, 10, 40–6, 79, 83, 107, 113, 142, 143, 144, 145, 148, 149, 151, 163
 in apes and monkeys, 41, 42, 43, 80
 in children, 16, 31, 44–5
 in other animals, 7, 40–1
 in primitive societies, 41–3, 46
shame, 82, 83
sign stimuli, 6, 7, 8
sleep, 85, 86, 144
smiling response, 25
social approval, 94, 104, 132, 145
 in children, 27, 33, 127
social behaviour and motivation, 2, 48, 51–2, 94–107, 159, 160, 161, 162, 163
 in children, 25–8, 31–3
 in monkeys, 95, 98
social class,
 and aggression, 65
 and school, 98
 and occupation, 129, 130
 and treatment of children, 31, 48
social conformity, 61, 99, 102–6, 131, 132

in children, 32
social groups, 56, 59, 61, 94–9, 131
 family, 96–7
 in apes and monkeys, 58, 95, 96, 98
 in other animals, 57
 informal, 99
 peers, 98
 unorganized, 94
social status, 105–6, 107, 130–1
startle response, 15, 17
stress, 134, 135, 146, 147, 152
sublimation, 142
substitution, substitute activities, 61, 67, 68, 138, 141–3, 144, 155
 in children, 141–2
 on level of unreality, 142–3
super-ego, 45, 82, 145
sympathetic nervous system, 78–9, 81
sympathy, 72, 82

temperament, temperamental disposition, 83–4, 146, 158
 and physique, 83–4
territory, territories, 57, 60
tests,
 Achievement Anxiety, 165
 Anxiety Questionnaire, 123, 164
 Aronson's, 126, 164
 French, 123, 164
 Iowa Picture Interpretation, 164
 Rorschach, 101, 165
 Taylor Manifest Anxiety, 164
 Thematic Apperception (T.A.T.), 37, 43, 44, 52, 69, 90, 101, 102, 106, 122, 123, 126, 163–5
thirst, 10, 16, 37
traits, personality, 157–8

valences, 138, 139
 conflict of, 139–40
variation, in stimulation, 88, 89, 90, 91, 93, 132, 160
vigilance, 89

war, 59–61, 147
work, 128–33